Hemingway's Brain

Hemingway's
Brain

With a New Preface

Andrew Farah

THE UNIVERSITY OF
SOUTH CAROLINA PRESS

© 2017 University of South Carolina
Preface © 2025 University of South Carolina

Hardcover and ebook original editions published 2017
Paperback and ebook editions published 2025
by the University of South Carolina Press
Columbia, South Carolina 29208

uscpress.com

Printed in the United States of America

Library of Congress Cataloging-in-Publication Data
can be found at http://catalog.loc.gov/

ISBN: 978-1-64336-591-6 (paperback)
ISBN: 978-1-64336-596-1 (ebook)

For Priscilla Farah

It is perfectly true, as the philosophers say, that life must be understood backwards. But they forget the other proposition, that it must be lived forwards.

Søren Kierkegaard, *Journals* (1843)

This may be wrong and I would be glad to have anyone disprove the theory as what we want is knowledge, not the pride of proving something to be true.

Ernest Hemingway, "Out in the Stream: A Cuban Letter" (1934)

Contents

List of Illustrations

Preface

It is difficult to imagine another American author achieving Hemingway's stature. And it is still expanding. Since the publication in 2017 of this neuropsychiatric examination of Hemingway's last years, more biographies, micro-biographies, and volumes of the Hemingway Letters series have been published. *The Hemingway Review* and *One True Podcast* continue to expand their audiences. The Hemingway Society remains robust, and Hemingway's life and work were the subject of a three-part, six-hour documentary produced by Lynn Novick and Ken Burns in 2021.

There is synergy in the unique combination of accessible and enjoyable literature from an author whose own life adventures and plot-twists rival any fiction. Hemingway had the good fortune of groundbreaking talent at the time a limited print media was the only choice and a period in which novels were the entertainment various screen-times now occupy. He had a youthful period of Hollywood looks, and an unfolding biography that highlighted him as a participant in every major historical event of the twentieth century until his death: WWI, the Spanish Civil War, WWII, and the Cuban revolution. And he is easily the writer most associated with the Lost Generation. There were plenty of side shows: big-game hunting, bullfighting, deep-sea fishing, dalliances in every decade, divorces, disputes, magazine articles that kept him in the public eye, and triumphs and tragedies, both large and small. And his tragic last act was worldwide news.

Hemingway also possessed that intangible attribute that fuels celebrity: he had presence. It is still compelling and exudes seemingly from every photograph. Society projected the Hemingway persona onto him, and it fit. At some point, the mask always melds into the face. To live the persona, to act out the expectations of others can only be corrosive, and he discarded true friends and true love many times. But the art, the gift of his transcendent talent, somehow survived it all, continuing to commune with millions of us.

His art was the last holdout against his demise, and some argue it never succumbed to illnesses, whether psychological or neurological. *Hemingway's Brain* brings clarity to the conditions that led to the death of this unique American genius, with attention to how his evolving vulnerabilities affected his work, which served as his lifelong therapy. It hopefully will finally and completely dispel the myth of a "bipolar" Ernest Hemingway.

Although the emphasis of this book is the multiple traumatic brain injuries (TBIs) that Hemingway sustained and the resultant neurological and psychiatric consequences, other factors included alcoholism, chronic medical issues, genetics, and his psychological and spiritual attitudes.

Since the initial hardcover publication, there has been increasing attention to the prevention and treatment of TBI. There have been countless advances, and the chapter "Modern Times," or "what we would do for Hemingway today," has been updated to elaborate the state of the science, and what I currently prescribe as of 2025.

The treatment of concussive injury is often only in the acute phase, or absent altogether. Strategies for the ongoing protection of the brain that may prevent long-term consequences, such as chronic traumatic encephalopathy, are also detailed. Even if a TBI occurred years prior, it may still be possible to lower the risk of dementia.

A life so chronicled will inevitably recount the unpleasantness, cruelties, and flaws of the man. In retelling many unflattering episodes here, the intention is to advance the understanding of the causes rather than continue a voyeuristic pattern.

Two years after Yousuf Karsh photographed Hemingway in Cuba, he recalled that he expected to meet a man who had just stepped out of one of his novels. Instead, in 1957, he found a shy, gentle man, whom life itself had "cruelly battered." That battering was the principal cause of his illness, more obvious after his African plane crashes. Like many Karsh photos, he captured vulnerability as well as greatness.

Another theme of this book is that Hemingway's very act of writing was therapeutic. D. H. Lawrence once wrote to a friend, "One sheds one's sicknesses in books - repeats and presents again one's emotions, to be master of them."[1] (Lawrence, who spent a lifetime in the Oedipal phase, was referring to *Son's and Lovers*.) Hemingway was beyond a cure by self-analysis and simply unable to shed his last illness. The very tools (neurons and connections) he needed to do so were damaged. He was, in his own words, "out of business."

Beyond the neuropsychiatric analysis, a final piece to the puzzle of Hemingway's suicide is his middle-age rejection of Platonism. His concussion during WWI resulted in an out-of-body experience, and he accepted it as proof of his soul's existence. Yet at a portable desk in the African night with the copy of Dante's *Divine Comedy* that he travelled with nearby, and days before his two plane crashes, Hemingway rejected the Platonism of his Protestant youth and current Catholicism:

> Once I had thought my own soul had been blown out of me when I was a boy. And then that it had come back in again . . . I had heard so much talk about the soul and read so much about it that I had assumed that I had one. Then I began to think if Miss Mary or GC or Ngui or Charo or I had been killed by the lion, would our souls have flown off somewhere? I could not believe it and I thought that we would all just have been dead, deader than the lion perhaps, and no one was worrying about his soul.[2]

His soul's exit and reentry were just as he described metaphorically in *A Farwell to Arms,* an illusion, a silk handkerchief manipulated by the magician. His last argument against self-destruction was gone. He ended his life fearing no consequences.

Hemingway's last act should not define his life, and remarkable life should not be viewed only through a prism of illness. It is time to show all facets of modernism's roughest diamond.

Notes

1. D. H. Lawrence, in *The Letters of D. H. Lawrence, Volume 2. June 1913–October 1916,* ed. George J. Zytaruk and James T. Boulton (Cambridge, UK: Cambridge University Press, 1981), 15.

2. Ernest Hemingway, *True at First Light* (New York: Scribner, 1999), 172–73.

Acknowledgments

My thanks go to Cambridge University Press for permission to reprint passages from Rose Marie Burwell's *Hemingway: The Postwar Years and the Posthumous Novels* (Cambridge University Press, 1996); to Simon and Schuster and Penguin Random House UK for permission to reprint passages from *A Movable Feast* (Scribner's, 1964), *Across the River and into the Trees* (Scribner's, 1950), *The Complete Short Stories of Ernest Hemingway* (Scribner's, 1987), *In Our Time* (Scribner's, 1930), Carlos Baker's *Ernest Hemingway: Selected Letters, 1917–1961* (Scribner's 1981), and Carlos Baker's *Ernest Hemingway: A Life Story* (Scribner's, 1969); to Dover Publications for permission to reprint from Wassily Kandinsky's *Concerning the Spiritual in Art* (Dover, 1977); to W. W. Norton for permission to reprint from Bernice Kert's *The Hemingway Women* (W. W. Norton, 1983); to the Hemingway Society for permission to use excerpts from an unpublished letter; to Roxann Livingston for permission to use a photograph by Earl Theisen; and to the dedicated and kind staff of the John F. Kennedy Presidential Library and Museum for access to letters, documents, and images in the Ernest Hemingway Collection; to Martha Williams and Mary Tyson of The Community Library of Ketchum; to scholars and friends Verna Kale, Suzanne del Gizzo, Robert K. Elder, Hilary Justice, Susan F. Beegel, Mark Cirino, Linda Patterson Miller, and Michael Von Cannon; to acquisitions editor Jim Denton who always believed in this project, editor Aurora Bell for her kindness and thoughtful excellence, and the production staff of the University of South Carolina Press.

Introduction

On July 2, 1961, Ernest Miller Hemingway rose quietly so as not to disturb his wife. He put on his bathrobe and slippers, walked down to the basement of his Idaho home, and unlocked his gun case. He climbed the steps to his foyer, placed the barrel of his favorite shotgun to his forehead and pressed the trigger.

Many of those who have never read a Hemingway novel or biography still know the details of this tragedy. His suicide may even be the most famous in American history, competing with those of Marilyn Monroe and Robin Williams for this tragic distinction. He shot himself only six days after his discharge from the Mayo Clinic, where he had been hospitalized twice. The primary goal of his treatment at Mayo for severe depression and psychosis was to prevent this exact scenario. Yet his death was the result not of medical mismanagement but of medical misunderstanding. Hemingway received state-of-the-art psychiatric treatment in 1960 and 1961, but for the wrong illness.

This book is the first comprehensive and accurate accounting of the psychiatric diagnoses that led to the demise of Ernest Miller Hemingway. Thus, *Hemingway's Brain* is a forensic psychiatric examination of his very brain cells—the stressors, traumas, chemical insults, and biological changes—that killed a world-famous literary genius. The method of the forensic psychiatrist is to carefully review all medical records, study any other relevant information available (usually in the form of depositions), and, if possible, interview the subject himself. Even though the subject is America's quintessential writer, the medical chart is still closed and confidential. When his Mayo psychiatrist, Dr. Howard Rome, was approached at professional meetings by colleagues who asked, "Weren't you Hemingway's doctor?," Dr. Rome was known to always lift an index finger to his lips, indicating that they were forever sealed. He was an ethical clinician who maintained patient confidentiality for the rest of his life

Fortunately for this study, there is no shortage of collateral information. We have numerous biographies, Hemingway's extensive catalogue of personal letters, the memoirs of friends and family, and even an FBI file on our patient. With all of this data, it is possible to piece together a narrative of neurological and psychiatric illnesses that were progressing for years. This specific analysis has been missing from the scholarship for too long. Indeed, no scholarship can be complete without integrating these insights, as Hemingway's illnesses informed his relationships, his day-to-day life, and the last two decades of his fiction output. One theme that will become apparent as the reader progresses through *Hemingway's Brain* is that marvelous literature was still possible despite Hemingway's cognitive decline, his anxieties, and even his psychosis. His late-life struggle was made particularly difficult by his acute awareness of his declining mental capacities. His sensitivity and his ability to "notice everything," which were key to his creative genius, were by then fueling his torment.

His neurological and psychiatric conditions began years before the sixty-one-year-old stood at his worktable shuffling papers, unable to write the one sentence asked of him for a volume of well-wishes to be presented to President Kennedy. He had been delighted to receive the telegram inviting him to the inauguration but declined for the very health reasons that left him frustrated and frozen as he stared at the blank pages. The illness began with specific, inherited genes from both sides of his family. It was developing as the Red Cross volunteer lay unconscious in the mud of the Italian front during World War I, and continued to germinate with the slow poison of thousands of cocktails. His pathology was the result of the coalescing of genetic codes with trauma, untreated hypertension, diabetes, and lifestyle choices. And when his psychiatric illness was fully manifest, it eluded the finest doctors of his day.

Modern scans and testing would leave no doubt regarding the specifics of his diagnosis, and there are numerous treatment options available now that were not even theoretical in 1960. Even if he had received the correct diagnosis, there were few therapies available—but still, there were a few.

Though many excellent biographies of Hemingway have been written and his life has been extensively researched, no biographer to date has been able to make an accurate diagnosis, nor could one be expected to, without training and experience in the practice in neurology and psychiatry. Not until Verna Kale's 2016 Hemingway biography, the first by a woman, did any author consider that concussive injuries might have been a factor in his demise. What scholars instead have turned to, by default and out of sheer fascination, is psychoanalysis. Thus, there is no shortage of conjecture along psychoanalytical lines regarding Hemingway's mental state, with his fiction and many of his utterances, indeed, his very predictions of his demise, serving as a diffuse array of suicide notes to be mined for nuggets. Even as a young newlywed on the way to Paris with his bride he contemplated jumping into the wake of the steamer somewhere in the middle of the Atlantic, leaving behind only the mystery of his disappearance. His first major work, *In Our Time,* published when he was in his twenty-sixth year, is the usual starting point for psychoanalysis of his life through his fiction.

In the story "Indian Camp" (1924), he wrote of a country doctor modeled on his own physician father and of his young son, obviously a reflection of the young Ernest, as they are summoned to a difficult delivery. A Native American has been in labor for two days when they arrive. Hemingway writes of her screams as the doctor busies himself with a jack-knife Caesarean, necessary to save the breech baby, while his son, Nick, sort of looks on. Nick asks his father, "Oh, Daddy, can't you give her something to make her stop screaming?," only to be told the woman's screams "are not important. I don't hear them because they are not important." She has to be held still during the operation by "Uncle George" and three Indian men, and after she bites Nick's uncle on the arm, amusing one of three Indians, George curses her as a "Damn squaw bitch!"

When the procedure is a success and the newborn safe, the doctor boasts: "That's one for the medical journal, George." Yet his self-satisfaction is short-lived. With typical Hemingway sleight of hand, the obstetrical procedure has temporarily concealed the morbid punch line. The newborn's father was unable to leave his wife's delivery, as was the custom, because of an injury he had sustained days before from an axe—so he lay hidden on the top bunk while the screaming and drama unfolded beneath him. "Ought to have a look at the proud father. They're usually the worst sufferers in these little affairs," the doctor says. "He pulled back the blanket from the Indian's head. His hand came away wet. He mounted on the edge of the lower bunk with the lamp in one hand and looked in. The Indian lay with his face toward the wall. His throat had been cut from ear to ear. The blood had flowed down into a pool where his body sagged the bunk. . . . The open razor lay, edge up, in the blankets."[1]

"Why did he kill himself, Daddy?" Nick asks his father. "I don't know, Nick. He couldn't stand things, I guess." The doctor's answer is as satisfactory as any and remains applicable to any other case of suicide (real or fictional) since.

In an even more prescient story than "Indian Camp," Nick encounters Ad Francis in "The Battler." Ad is an ex-prizefighter who carries the scars and disfigurement of his past days, but not only physical ones—he also suffers from dementia pugilistica. He is not only grotesque but paranoid, volatile in mood and behavior and capable of violence with no provocation. Like Ad, Hemingway would one day find his brain forever changed in such a way and yet still somewhat insightful: "Listen, the little man said. I'm not quite right. . . . I'm crazy. . . . Listen, you ever been crazy? No, Nick said. How does it get you? I don't know, Ad said. When you got it you don't know about it." Ad's paranoia soon emerges, and his volatility erupts. He screams at Nick and threatens him. But in short order Nick is saved from harm when Ad is knocked unconscious by his companion and caretaker, Bugs, with his handy blackjack, carried for just such episodes.

Ad is "crazy" not only from the poundings he has taken in the ring, but also from an odd psychological trauma—the unpleasantness that followed from having married his sister. We learn, in Bug's explanation to Nick, that, though Ad and his wife are not really siblings, "there was a lot of people didn't like it either way and they commenced to have disagreements, and one day she just went off and never come back."[2]

A lifetime of such fiction is more than ripe for psychoanalysis and in perfect harmony with Hemingway's biography. Consider Ad's marital situation in light of a 1950 letter in which Hemingway elaborated: "When I came home after the first war, [my sister Ursula] always used to wait, sleeping, on the stairway of the third floor stair-case to my room. . . . She would drink something light with me until I went to sleep and then she would sleep with me so I would not be lonely in the night. We always slept with the light on except she would sometimes turn it off if she saw I was asleep."[3] In the unfinished story "The Last Good Country" Hemingway would revisit the theme of sibling partners. The teenage Nick escapes deep into the woods with his younger sister, Littless, to elude a vengeful game warden and the "down-state man" on his trail but also to elude their family ("the others"). "His sister was tanned brown and she had dark brown eyes and dark brown hair with yellow streaks in it from the sun. She and Nick loved each other and they did not love the others."

They sleep like any intimate couple, her head on his shoulder. When she sits on his lap, she asks, "Can I kiss you while you're making supper?" Hemingway even pounds us over the head with his symbolism: "We'll eat a couple of apples." Littless also brings another recurring Hemingway theme to the forefront after she crops her hair: "Now I'm your sister but I'm a boy, too."[4]

Sibling love and cross-gender themes are just the tip of the iceberg. The life and the fiction both contain seemingly infinite Freudian and Jungian facets. Perhaps there is no other literary life in which so much autobiographical information is wrapped into the fiction and so much fictional content appears as if in a crystal ball, eerily predicting the author's future. This is no ordinary two-way street; this is a multilane highway traveled for a lifetime. Fascinating as they are, none of these explorations can lead to the correct diagnosis—any analytical insight can exist only as theory. However, an examination of Hemingway's psychiatric case and a review of the extensive forensic data point to the very cells of Hemingway's brain. The deterioration of his central nervous system as the result of a collection of factors and the subsequent loss of his mental capacities and his sense of self—all with the demoralizing awareness of these losses—is ultimately to blame for his death. Though not the complete picture, the fiction and the memoirs serve their purpose too; their contents are the daily manifestations of a life in decline and a working man growing less competent. In short, they help to confirm the diagnosis.

This book grew out of two questions asked by Bill Smallwood, the coauthor of *The Idaho Hemingway*: why did Hemingway's mental illness get worse, not better, after two courses of electroconvulsive therapy? And what would modern psychiatry offer him today? The answer to the first is the subject of this book: patients who worsen after a course of ECT have organic brain disease. For them the ECT is not curative but a form of stress on the vulnerable nervous system that accelerates their decline. The following chapters elaborate on the exact nature of Hemingway's brain illness, a dementia caused by several factors, which was still progressing at the time of his death. The answer to the second is detailed in chapter 12.

As for Hemingway's profession, the last ten years of his life still involved international travel and a writing production that was at times as beautiful as ever, yet at others a bad imitation of his earlier work. And he was often paralyzed by anxiety, with writing a seemingly hopeless struggle that further compounded his anxieties.

In the last ten years of his life, he displayed a grandiosity of almost delusional proportions, moments of tenderness and humility, paranoia with specific and elaborate delusions, excessive alcohol intake with brief periods of self-control, volatility and abusiveness toward the ones he loved the most, frequent irritability, near-constant socializing, romantic infatuations, petty and grand disputes, and an acute self-awareness of his own magnitude—a puffing out of the chest and an endless display of a man all too full of himself, the expert on everything, all because of the spotlight.

He enlisted a celebrity entourage before it was fashionable. He repeatedly threatened his suicide, predicted his suicide, and even demonstrated (on more than one occasion) his "technique of hara-kiri with a gun" for dinner guests at his Cuban home. According to his friend Dr. José Herrera, Ernest would "sit in his chair, barefoot, and place the butt of his Mannlicher .256 on the fiber rug of the living room between his legs . . . leaning forward, he would rest the mouth of the gun barrel against the roof of his mouth. He would press the trigger with his big toe and we would hear the click of the gun."[5]

Until that July morning in 1961 when he loaded the gun, he was only performing. As Dr. Herrera further informs us, Ernest would lift his head off the gun barrel, "grinning." The precise reason *why* he was so compelled to perform is that by this point in his life he was trapped by his own legend. He was living out the "Hemingway role" because it was expected of him, or perhaps because he actually believed it, or, more likely, because at some point there was no difference.

An all-encompassing neuropsychiatric history must account for the fact that our subject is not interested in helping us. In fact, Hemingway disdained "literary detectives" and any analysis of living writers. And, as if to purposely confuse the issue, Hemingway leaves the most gifted of psychiatrists wondering if some of his reported exploits were delusional, mere exaggerations, or simply tall tales that were fundamental to the character of the greatest of storytellers (who, by the way, was narcissistic). Consider his detailed account of his romantic involvement with Mata Hari, the alleged World War I spy. Hemingway claimed that she had "more desire for what was done for her than what she was giving the man."[6] Yet, this is obvious fabrication. Mata Hari was executed by firing squad before the young Ernest ever left for Europe. This anecdote illustrates perfectly a recurrent dilemma—was it delusion fostered by illness and disinhibition or just a story of wishful thinking, meant simply to entertain friends who would never fact-check? The same impulses led to his famous story of dancing in a Paris café with Josephine Baker, nude under her fur coat. Not true, either, but so much fun that we wish it were.

Perhaps it's as simple as acknowledging than any life is complex; like the facets of a diamond, some aspects of life shine brilliantly at certain angles. Hemingway was forever showing different facets of himself in different circumstances, as we all do. The party-minded Hemingway who snuck cognac into a Milan army hospital and joked with comrades and the man who dined with Jean-Paul Sartre three decades later, quite seriously discussing contracts and royalty arrangements, were of course the same man, but the different snapshots in time are simply pieces of a much larger picture.[7]

One such snapshot took place on April 18, 1961, shortly before his death. The phone rang at Hemingway's home in Ketchum, Idaho. It was his long-time Man Friday, A. E. Hotchner. "Hotch" had been encouraged to place the call by friends at a New York cocktail party. Hemingway immediately brought up his much-anticipated work in progress, the fictionalized memoirs of his Paris years that would one day be titled *A Moveable Feast*. In a voice that Hotchner described as "dead" and in words that trailed off like "rocks falling down a well," Hemingway informed Hotcher that "It's gotten pretty rough. I can't finish the bloody book. . . . I know what I want it to be but I can't get it down."

His friend tried some encouraging words, but to no avail: "Hotch, I can't finish the book. I *can't*. I've been at this goddamn worktable all day, standing here all day, and all I've got to get is this one thing, maybe only a sentence, maybe more, I don't know, and I can't get it. Not any of it. You understand, I *can't*. I've written Scribner's to scratch the book. It was all set for the fall but I had to scratch it. . . . This wonderful damn book and I can't finish it."[8]

The genius who had written masterpieces such as *A Farewell to Arms* and "The Snows of Kilimanjaro" was now paralyzed, fully in the grip of a severe mental illness—an illness whose cruelest trick was to incapacitate the mind, yet all the while preserve insight into the sufferer's plight. This served to highlight the fact that his trade was ruined and that his greatest fear had come true: he couldn't work now and would never work again. He was, in his own words, "out of business." The more severe his symptoms of depression, anxiety, and psychosis, the more obvious this realization became. His decline confirmed his fears, and his fears worsened his symptoms—and he spiraled downward.

Many works on Hemingway are written from the perspective of bipolar disorder, which was not his problem, or alcoholism, which was just one piece of a larger puzzle. The neuropsychiatric journey that follows, a focus on the biology of Hemingway's brain and the traumas it endured, will, I hope, clarify much of the confusion and help make sense of many of his statements and behaviors. This aim of this book is to define for all future scholarship the specifics of the mental illnesses that shaped literary works that are household names and that destroyed one of our greatest writers.

Inheritance

Chapter 1

Mental illnesses can certainly pass down from generation to generation, but there was no hint of the trouble to come from the very sober and productive life of Anson Tyler Hemingway, Ernest Hemingway's paternal grandfather. He was born in Plymouth, Connecticut, in 1844, but Connecticut would not be the home of his descendants. He traveled with his family at the age of ten, making the nine-hundred-mile journey to Norwood Park, Illinois, when such travel was more than a little dangerous. He grew from youth to adulthood there, only eight miles from where he and, later, his son, Clarence Edmonds Hemingway, would die—in Oak Park.

Anson Hemingway volunteered to serve under the command of Ulysses Grant at the battle of Vicksburg, a city that President Jefferson Davis ordered held "at all costs." In February 1862 Forts Henry and Donelson, in Tennessee, fell, and New Orleans was in Union hands by April. If Vicksburg followed, then the Mississippi River would be completely under Union control, cutting the Confederacy in half. Lincoln also understood Vicksburg's strategic importance, labeling it the "key to victory." Capturing the city was so critical that during the campaign he even sent a spy to camp with instructions to monitor Grant's alcohol intake.[1]

Yet Vicksburg was more of a siege than a single battle, lasting just under fifty days. And Anson Hemingway would survive the abysmal conditions in the swamplands around Vicksburg. Malaria, smallpox, and dysentery claimed the lives of enough of his comrades to fill a mile-long trench of graves. And Hemingway proved especially useful to Grant, a proponent of enlisting the escaped and newly liberated slaves as Union soldiers, as he placed Officer Hemingway in command of many of these new troops. Grant also understood that this helped to solve the problem of exactly what to do with the hundreds of refugees who were descending on his camps in desperate need of food and shelter. In time Grant would win the protracted and muddy chess match and solidify his reputation. Anson would follow his General down into Natchez, Mississippi, where his duties involved more occupying than fighting, but by the time he retired from military service he had risen to the rank of first lieutenant. He was also an educated young man, thus a rare commodity in his day—a veteran who also possessed a college degree.

During his studies at Wheaton College in Illinois, he would meet and eventually marry his fellow student Adelaide Edmonds, and the young couple would settle in the Oak Park community, just ten miles from Chicago. Anson Hemingway would become a respected real estate broker with the reputation of being a deeply religious man. He served as a deacon in the First Congregational Church of Oak Park, and his opinion was valued when it came to local business or political matters. He also expected each of his children to receive a proper education, and all six would attend Oberlin College. His second child, Clarence Edmonds Hemingway, born September 4, 1871, would study medicine at the prestigious Rush Medical College, in Chicago, and settle into a general practice, a career he would one day encourage his son, Ernest, to follow. He specialized in obstetrics, and Ernest would pick up a level of medical understanding from his father's practice and discussions that would be evident in works such as *In Our Time* and *A Farewell to Arms*.

Dr. Hemingway's daughter (and Ernest's older sister), Marcelline, wrote in her memoirs that her father sketched the design for special forceps to be used in spinal surgery while sitting on the banks of the Des Plaines River (the procedure would eventually be termed a laminectomy). The idea "flashed in his mind," and he quickly drew the instrument design on the back of an envelope. He eventually took to sketch to Sharp and Smith, instrument manufacturers in Chicago, for further development.[2] This anecdote accurately sums up the public understanding of "Ed" Hemingway as a medical man, but also an avid outdoorsman, whose sprightly and brilliant mind never rested.

The medical volume on Dr. Hemingway's shelf titled *Nervous and Mental Diseases*, published when his son, Ernest, was twenty and a veteran of World War I, devotes only nineteen pages to "Mental Disease," twenty pages to the topic of "Psychoneuroses of the War," and just five to "Other Psychoneuroses." The majority of the text deals with epilepsy, movement disorders, meningitis, brain trauma, and various illnesses of the peripheral nerves. There are tips for discerning hysterical paralysis from the real thing (the hysterical being "caused by suggestion and cured by psychotherapy," often in one sitting) and a description of a new study detailing the mental deficiencies of a sample of Newport News prostitutes. There is also a new psychoanalytic theory on the origins of kleptomania that suggests that it is driven by the "instinctive desire to secure sexual excitation . . . by the stimulus furnished by the emotions of fear and anxiety that necessarily accompany the perpetuation of theft." But depression is not mentioned, nor is it mentioned in the index; neurasthenia (a nineteenth-century precursor to dysthymia, a form of low-grade depression, and chronic fatigue syndrome), though the fashionable diagnosis just three decades prior, gets only a passing nod.[3]

Despite the prominence of Freud's work, psychiatry had yet to be fully carved out from the hardware of the nervous system. Thus, when Dr. Hemingway began suffering from depression, there was little in his professional training or library to direct him in any attempt to heal himself. If he opened this volume at all in 1919, he was most likely reading about the brain injuries of contusion and "commotion" caused by the explosive detonations of war, as his son had experienced and written about from a Milan hospital the prior year. (Ernest's letter home, of July 21, 1918, detailed his traumas, which involved a mortar blast, concussion, and slugs in his leg. Under "Love Ernie" he had drawn a cartoon of himself lying flat, titled "Me drawn From life" and shouting "gimme a drink!" His stick-figured leg was bandaged from hip to toe, and a label read "227 wounds.")[4]

Like those of many patients with major depression, Clarence Hemingway's case was brought about by a stressful situation: he worried about his own health (he suffered from chest pains [angina pectoris] and diabetes). Neither were fatal illnesses at the time, but he also anguished over finances and his real estate investments. He and Grace had mortgaged their home (which was paid for in full at the time) in order to buy Florida real estate, taking part in the great Florida real estate boom of the early twentieth century. He had hoped this investment would secure his family's future. His brother George had encouraged the purchases, but the lots were not appreciating as they had been expected to. George then advised his brother to sell off some of them to stem the losses, but Dr. Hemingway balked, hoping for a future recovery rather than locking in the lower values and financial loss.

Psychiatrists would eventually view depression as an illness similar to many others in psychiatry: caused by a possible underlying genetic vulnerability compounded by some social stress and an excessive amount of anxiety that conspire to create the clinical disease. Patients describe an overall sadness, difficulty with sleep and energy (perhaps sleeping too much or too little, worrying into the night), anxiety, irritability, and appetite changes; everything seems a struggle, and even the activities of daily living are an effort. The longer a depressive disorder is left untreated, the harder it is to cure—even with modern therapies. For Dr. Hemingway, depression was a known symptom in the patient with manic-depressive illness or perhaps the hysterical patient and of course the emotionally weak, but not a topic to be found in the contents of his medical books. Though it had always existed, major depression was a black hole for Dr. Hemingway and his colleagues. With regard to recognizing and treating depression as a disorder, he and his profession were not in denial; they were simply in the dark. This particular science was unknown to them.

Biographers agree that Dr. Hemingway's situation was not as dire as he perceived—his house was still valued at more than he owed, three of his children (including Ernest) were financially secure, and he could practice medicine not only in Illinois but also in Florida, having obtained a Florida medical license. He even hoped to retire there in the near future. But depression often brings a catastrophic form of thinking to the sufferer, a type of "cognitive distortion" in which the patient sees things through a distorted prism as being much worse than they truly are—all negative situations and stressors, however minor, grow to catastrophes in the mind's eye. The patient may further see no hope for change. Indeed, hopelessness is viewed as one of the most problematic harbingers of suicidality in a depressed patient.

There is also evidence that Clarence's depression, like Ernest's, was tinged with paranoia. He had written to his wife in 1909 and again in 1920, detailing financial provisions he had made for his family in case of "his death under suspicious circumstances," even elaborating (in 1909) on how to create a "consistent and convincing story for a coroner's hearing." The 1920 letter anticipated his trip to Lake Walloon, in northern Michigan, to close up the family cabin, Windemere, for the season. The trip was also an excuse to rest his nerves and, he hoped it would permit him to return to his family in Oak Park less stressed and much less irritable. This letter also included a check for $1,000 and safe-deposit-box keys "in case of some unforeseen accident I should not return."[5] These were unusual concerns for a man who had no suspicious dealings or acquaintances and whose day-to-day life had certainly achieved the wholesomeness he strived for.

As his medical problems flared, he ignored his wife's advice. She insisted he visit a colleague when he woke with severe foot pain, but Clarence refused, no doubt fearing vascular complications from diabetes. His mind no doubt was ruminating on the worst of circumstances—neuropathy, injury, infection, and eventual amputation. He also refused to let his son Leicester (or any other family member) ride in his black Ford with him (by then he had graduated from horse-and-buggy house calls), fearing an angina attack would result in an accident and endanger others as well as himself. But Dr. Hemingway would never see himself as a patient who needed treatment, let alone analysis. These thoughts were not dismissed; they were simply never considered.

His oldest daughter wrote eloquently of her father's descent in her memoirs: "my father changed from his high-strung, active, determined, cheerful self—the self with a twinkle in his eye—to an irritable, suspicious person. He was quick to take offense, almost unable to let himself believe in the honesty of other people's motives. He began to spend long hours alone in his office with the doors closed. He kept his bureau drawers and his clothes closet locked. It was agony for my mother, who shared the bedroom with him, to think he must be distrusting her."[6]

His depression was noted in his own letters early as 1903, and he required a "rest cure" (when Ernest was just four).[7] Yet documentation from his professional career indicates that when he was at his "healthy" baseline, he handled stress masterfully. "Grace under pressure" will always be attributed to Ernest, but when, during the birth of Dr. Hemingway's first child, Marcelline (January 15, 1898), the attending physician suffered a heart attack, Dr. Hemingway was summoned and immediately returned home in a snowstorm. He not only cared for the critically ill doctor but continued to administer anesthetics to his wife and safely delivered his child, a complicated birth that required forceps.

Dr. Hemingway was regarded as one of the most skilled obstetricians of his time. Learning of the pregnancy of Pauline, Ernest's second wife, he wrote, "If you want to have me attend your wife at the Oak Park Hospital, I am glad to offer you my services." He was clearly looking forward to the opportunity, writing, in June, "We are anxious to hear what you are planning." Later in the month, he informed the couple that he was deferring plans to go to Windemere "until I hear from you."[8] Yet one of the last pieces of correspondence he ever received from Ernest noted that he and Pauline had chosen to have their son delivered in Kansas City and that thus, without directly stating it, they were declining Dr. Hemingway's offer to deliver his next grandchild. Perhaps it was their last meeting, in October 1928, that had convinced Ernest that his father was not the man for the job. When he and Grace visited Key West, Dr. Hemingway was anxious, tired, and possibly irritable. He had also gauged the value of his Florida real estate on the trip, a major source of his stress.

If this news hurt Dr. Hemingway, it was never documented that he expressed as much to anyone. Surely it was some bruise to his ego. Still, his professional composure and skills never seemed compromised as a result of his depression. He carried on silently as long as he could and eventually reached that strange point of no return and singular focus. On a day that his foot pain flared severely and caused him to ruminate once again on the worst of medical outcomes, he came home around lunchtime and asked how his son Leicester was doing, as he had been ill with a cold. He was better, his wife informed, but asleep. After burning some personal papers in the basement furnace, later thought to be financial records, he went to his bedroom, shut the door, and used his father's revolver, the very one carried by Anson in the Civil War, to end his life. He was fifty-seven years old. Uncharacteristically, he had left his checkbook unbalanced and bills unpaid for months. His fears were certainly exaggerated, as even in the week of his death he could have most likely sold the Florida property for a small profit—though the lots had declined from their peak prices, his original investment was still intact.

The medical report was stark and to the point: "The bullet pierced the brain looping under the skin, after shattering the bone of the skull in the left temple 5 cm. above and 7 cm. posterior to the external auditory meatus. There were powder burns at the point of entrance of the bullet. Blood was oozing out of the bullet wound."[9]

The young Leicester not only found his father's body but was the sole family member to speak to the coroner the next day at the inquest. Grace was too distraught and grief stricken and had to be heavily sedated. The thirteen-year-old had the sad and scarring duty of speaking in her stead. The eldest son, Ernest, was on a train from New York to Florida with his own son, Jack, when he received a telegram at the Trenton stop. It was from his sister, Carol, informing him of the grim news. He was already an established writer and halfway to the fullness of his stardom, working out his revisions of A Farewell to Arms at this point in time. In a letter to Ezra Pound, Hemingway would register his callous annoyance at his father's death: "I would have been glad to pay my esteemed father a good sum or give him a share in the profits to postpone shooting himself until the book was completed—Such things have a tendency to distract a man."[10]

His remark to Marcelline at the funeral, essentially that suicides are not welcomed into heaven,[11] reflected more than callousness. It grew primarily from the desire (unknown to Ernest consciously) to reject the new mantle of family patriarch. That would put him in the same struggle for power, the same losing battle with his mother, that had killed his father. Much easier to stay the rebellious son.

Leicester, the young teen who no doubt was traumatized by his discovery of his father on the bed expiring and making "hoarse breathing noises" and who then had to relive the experience at the coroner's interview, was instructed by his famous older brother: "At the funeral, I want no crying. You understand, kid?"[12] Leicester would also one day suffer from diabetes. His illness also resulted in vascular complications of the legs and, later, in peripheral neuropathy, a form of chronic pain from nerve damage. When tissue death occurs, many diabetics require amputations. And when Leicester was faced with the probability of more extensive surgery than he had already required, he too shot himself, like his father with a handgun. He was sixty-seven when he took his life.

To what extent a predisposition to suicide is inherited has been explored in many ways, from reviews of basic family history to the search for specific genetic markers. Suicides do run in families. A commonly reproduced Hemingway family photo from 1906 shows young Ernest wearing his page-boy haircut and looking to the left of the camera with a halfhearted attempt at a smile. Dr. Hemingway looks every bit the patriarch, with a stern demeanor but a gentle hold on his youngest, Madelaine ("Sunny"), balanced on his knee. The other two daughters, Ursula and Marcelline, are lovely, and Grace exudes maternal warmth. Perhaps the most remarkable aspect of those pictured is that three would die by suicide, Dr. Hemingway, Ernest, and Ursula (in 1966, overdosing while suffering with cancer), as well as the heart yet unborn at this time, Leicester (in 1982). A recently discovered letter by his namesake and maternal uncle, Leicester C. Hall, describes his depression and even catatonic symptoms, he considered might be a "foretaste of death."

There is something powerful lurking in a genetic code that not only conveys illness but self-destructive behavior. To measure the very strength of such a genetic connection, monozygotic twins (individuals who share identical DNA, or "identical twins") are often compared with dizygotic twins (who have the same genetic relationship as do nontwin siblings, thus "fraternal" twins). Monozygotic twins have a significantly higher concordance rate for completed (and even attempted) suicides than do sets of dizygotic twins. In fact, studies show that the chance that one monozygotic twin will make a serious suicide attempt is seventeen times greater if the co-twin made a serious attempt at any point in his or her life. What is also revealing is that adoption studies also confirm the genetic link. Adoption studies are particularly important because they can argue for genetic influence in the presence of different parenting and environments. The rate of suicide among biological siblings of adopted children who commit suicide is six times higher than the rate among controls (in this case, siblings of nonsuicidal adopted persons), even when the adopted siblings are raised separately.[13] Environment certainly plays some role, but the risk conveyed by DNA is undeniable. It has been estimated that as much as 43 percent of suicidal behavior may be explained by genetics, while the remaining 57 percent may be due to illness or environmental factors.

Yet what is most curious is that the genetic risk of a suicidal tendency can be transmitted completely independent of the genes for mental illness. The predetermined vulnerability for self-destruction is therefore sent along as its own potential time bomb, independent of the genetic risk for depression, bipolar illness, substance abuse, or any other psychiatric disorder. These findings challenge the notion that suicide is always the product of a specific illness, always the actions of a diseased brain, although this is commonly the case. Certainly schizophrenia is a risk factor for suicide (5 percent of schizophrenics die this way), as are bipolar illness (a 15 percent rate) and substance abuse (at least 50 percent of suicides are impaired at the time of their attempt). And anyone who commits suicide is by definition depressed. But the genetic variant that codes for self-destruction is separate from the genes linked to these illnesses.

Decades before this research, Hemingway, at some level, well understood this (either from intuition, wisdom guided by experience, or both). In 1936 he wrote to the mother of his second wife, Pauline, that the Pfeiffer bloodline was necessary for his children "to try to breed some if the suicide streak" out of them.[14] And some of the more insightful individuals he encountered detected this very streak in him, even in his younger days. The French writer (and Ernest's boxing partner in Paris) Jean Prévost described what he sensed as Hemingway's "obscure need for his own destruction." In his preface to the French translation of *The Sun Also Rises,* Prévost accurately predicted that "nothing would be able to strike down [Hemingway] but himself."[15] And the features editor at the Toronto *Star,* who met Hemingway during his stint there as a very young reporter, noted that "a more weird combination of quivering sensitiveness and preoccupation with violence never walked this earth."[16]

Though Clarence Edmonds Hemingway and his father, Anson, certainly warrant special genetic examination in connection with Ernest Hemingway's suicide, so does Ernest's maternal grandfather. Like Anson Tyler Hemingway, Ernest Hall served in the Yankee army. Hall was described as a tall, dark-haired gentleman with grey eyes, who crossed the Atlantic at age fifteen with his parents. After leaving their home in Sheffield, England, they eventually settled on the fertile land of Iowa. At the age of twenty-one Ernest Hall left the family cattle farm to join the First

Iowa Volunteer Calvary. He suffered a wound at the time of the battle at Warrensburg, Missouri, in 1862, and would carry the Confederate mini-ball in his left thigh for the rest of his life.

Hall never spoke of the war, and the circumstances of his wounding are vague and curious. According to his Civil War records, held at the National Archives, he was wounded during his term of service, "but not in the regular discharge of duty; though from an enemy in arms against the authority of the U.S."[17,18] The entry raises more questions than it answers, and perhaps this is why he never spoke of his war service.

His home was directly across the street from that of Anson and Adelaide Hemingway, so when his daughter, Grace Hall, married his neighbors' son, Clarence Hemingway, the young couple moved in with him. Ernest Hall had been a widower for a year, and he likely welcomed the attractive newlyweds' company. But Hall would eventually suffer from kidney disease, which would lead to his death when he was sixty-five. In a letter to Mary in 1945, Ernest wrote of his maternal grandfather's slow, painful demise. Hall had been diagnosed with Bright's disease, an inflammation of the kidneys, sometimes associated with kidney stones and all the more excruciating:

> My father married the daughter [of the Halls, who lives across the street] and as long as my English grandfather was alive it was all right because he exercised all discipline and controlled the daughter and her terrible selfishness and conceit. But I can remember when he died very clearly and how the pain of what he died of was unbearable and he wished to shoot himself and my father removed the cartridges from his pistol (which he had under his pillow) and he was allowed to shoot himself with an empty gun. I was a very little boy (six) but it still seemed to me the cruelest thing I could imagine, much worse than what God who they were always spooking us with, would do. My father was very proud of it. I could never forgive him for that nor for any of his other cruellnesses [sic] nor weaknesses.[19]

No six-year-old would fully comprehend or favor a grandfather's suicide. Nor would any six-year-old be intellectually equipped or likely to measure the foiling of a suicide against God's judgment. The tale is unverified in any other source and is clearly Ernest's inventive recollection, based on some fragment of memory or half-truth he recalled from childhood. Yet in 1945 Hemingway's theme was clear: if a suffering man wants to end his life, the well-meaning should simply get out of his way. And as Hemingway scholar Rose Marie Burwell concluded: "if he believed what he had written in this letter—as he frequently came to do with other tales he had told, then by the time he took his own life, he also believed that he was the third generation of suicidally intent men, and that they had come from both sides of his family."[20]

Beyond confirming the genetics of this scenario, this letter opens the door as well to the less objective and more elusive influence of "learned" or "modeled" behavior. Hemingway married his first wife, Hadley Richardson, in 1921. Her father had been deceased for eighteen years at that point, and, like Hemingway's father, he had committed suicide by putting a revolver to his head. Hadley was just twelve at the time (in 1903), and her future husband was only four. James Richardson's case was quite similar to Clarence Hemingway's, in that he was also tormented by financial worries, but, unlike him, he often drank to excess. Like those of his future son-in-law (whom he would never meet), his moods were visibly affected by alcohol, and the destructive influence was obvious even to his young daughter. The pistol shot was not instantly fatal, and the young Hadley watched her father die over the subsequent four hours.

Hemingway's sister, Ursula, born three years after Ernest, was also creative, but she preferred the visual arts. She resided in Hawaii during her adult life. Her suicide was by overdose in 1966 (women usually choose this method, while men are more likely to end their lives by more violent methods such as shooting or hanging). Yet, the female suicide in the family that received much more publicity was that of Hemingway's granddaughter Margaux.

Hemingway's eldest son, Jack (often referred to by his other nickname, "Bumby"), had three daughters, Joan (born 1950), Margaux (1954), and Mariel (1961). Joan has struggled with substance abuse in the past and has also been diagnosed with a bipolar disorder (she now resides in Idaho). Mariel was cast in Woody Allen's film *Manhattan,* as his seventeen-year-old girlfriend (the Allen character was forty-two). Her work is regarded critically as the brightest spot in this sea of pseudo-intellectual neurotic angst.

Jack's middle child, Margaux, was nearly six feet tall and able to pull off girl-next-door beauty with equal proportions of tomboy and glamour. She was the first fashion model given a million-dollar contract (by Fabergé). Her first movie, *Lipstick,* also starred her sister Mariel and was a disturbing and graphic story of rape, injustice in the courts, and, finally, revenge, or "true justice." But this critically acclaimed film was the high-water mark of her career. Her subsequent career setbacks were no doubt related to her struggles with depression, alcoholism, an eating disorder, and epilepsy. Though she was thought to be making a comeback, even appearing on the cover of *Playboy* in 1990, she overdosed on pheno-barbital (from a prescription that was not in her name) in 1996.[21]

Genetics are not the full answer but a piece of the puzzle. Though they constitute just one risk factor, adoption studies tell us that self-destruction is more than just learned or modeled behavior in a family but is in part caused by a specific set of genes that have been passed along. There are millions who have inherited such genes and never harmed themselves in any way, but, for a few, their genetics lay the groundwork, and additional risk factors may accumulate and finally overwhelm them.

Much psychological hay has been made of the photo of Ernest Hemingway as an infant, in a pink dress and a flowered hat, and his mother's penchant for dressing Ernest and his sister Marcelline alike. But he was only nine months old at the time, and in most other photos of Ernest in girlish outfits he is clearly under three years of age. Furthermore, Grace's "twinning" of Ernest and Marcelline went both ways, and by the time Ernest was five, the girlish clothing was in his past, but Marcelline's hair was cut to match Ernest's. Nor did the twinning end in childhood, but Marcelline was the one who suffered—she was even held back a year in school (kindergarten) and sat out another (eighth grade) just so that she and Ernest could be in the same high school class. Grace also insisted that Ernest take Marcelline to many high school dances as his official date. Male-female twinning and girls with boy's haircuts not only would show up in early stories ("Last Good Country") but would reappear in 1950. David and Catherine were Hemingway's fictional couple in *The Garden of Eden*. Catherine, one of the most psychiatrically disturbed of his characters, would become masculine by cropping her hair and tanning herself. The full exploration of these gender exchanges fascinates modern scholars, as they argue for a critical reexamination of Hemingway as far more experimental than his image and more popular works suggest.

Even in his last years, while working on *A Moveable Feast*, Hemingway would write some of his most sexually charged and yet quite tender passages. He and his first wife, Hadley, would cut their hair to be the same length and wake each other in the cold nights—each lover taking a turn dangling and swinging his or her hair in the other's face. And he was also working on the sexually charged manuscript *The Garden of Eden* during these last years.

Ernest's upbringing did plant various seeds, but not the one commonly assumed: the quaint Victorian holdover of dressing infants in a unisex fashion could never be the full explanation, as many have wished it to be, for macho overcompensation. It is rare for a child to store any memories before the age of three. Yet his machismo must have been shaken somewhat when Hemingway walked in on one of his sons in 1943 while he was trying on his mother's nylons. His boy was twelve years old at the time, and, like virtually all cross-dressers, he engaged in the practice from a very young age. He would later report "the look of horror" on his father's face at the discovery. And Ernest Hemingway's comment, several days later, about their coming from a "strange tribe" would eventually become the title of yet another Hemingway memoir, in 2007.

Gregory Hancock Hemingway was born in 1931, the younger of two sons Hemingway had with his second wife, Pauline. Gregory would train to become a physician, like his grandfather, but would live the most tortured and possibly the most tragic life, from a psychiatric standpoint, of any member of the clan. He struggled with bipolar illness, addictions, and gender identity issues. During a visit to Cuba, he stole some of his stepmother Mary's clothing and blamed the maid when the theft was discovered. After the incident, he described his cross-dressing in a letter to his father: "The clothes business is something that I have never been able to control, understand basically very little, and I am terribly ashamed of." Eventually he had a sex-change operation and presented himself as "Gloria" or "Vanessa" at various times thereafter, even altering his voice to a less-than-convincing female tone. But, as with his father, alcoholism would eventually take hold, and his medical license was not renewed in 1988 as a result. Because of the severity of his bipolar illness, he received even more rounds of electroconvulsive therapy than his father, and over a much longer span of time.

While in Miami, expansive and disinhibited from the manic phase of his illness, as well as possible intoxication, he caused a disturbance on a bus, which prompted the driver to pull over and call the police. He assaulted one of the officers and was subsequently arrested and booked but, once released, failed to show for his hearing. A second arrest in Miami followed in early September 2001. With Gregory noncompliant with his lithium and again well into a manic phase, his wife feared the typical out-of-control spending—and he soon discovered his accounts were frozen and his credit cards were useless. He was reduced to begging in front of a liquor store until by chance he was noticed by a friend. With this help, he was no longer destitute and was clothed and fed but still unstable mentally.

Toward the end of the month, "Vanessa" attended a party at the home of friends, wearing a long black evening dress and a blond wig. She danced and drank until four A.M. and then began walking, at some point stripping to just underwear and eventually sleeping on a park bench. Six hours later she was walking again, down the median of a highway, now without panties. The officer who arrested her was more than civil and described herself as a "big fan of Ernest Hemingway." They chatted cordially on the way to jail. On the back of the arrest affidavit, Gregory wrote "to the loveliest police officer i have ever met—greg hemingway."

His wife at the time hoped that the jail authorities would recognize the need for psychiatric treatment, and no bail was posted. It was obvious that Gregory needed psychiatric care, but the jail was unaware of his need for cardiac medications, and his heart went into fibrillation while he was in custody. He died on the concrete floor of the cell. Gregory's son, John, noted in his memoir that it was "fifty years to the day" of his mother Pauline's death. Perhaps alcohol withdrawal played a role in this sad end, triggering the arrhythmia; if so, like those of many alcoholics, his death may be considered a slow form of self-destruction.[22]

Ernest and his son Gregory would exchange many unpleasant letters. Gregory's illness and the resultant instability caused him to write numerous threats in letters that were laced with profanity and insults. Ernest certainly took offense and never backed down, but all the while he saw his son as quite ill and usually responded in a measured, matter-of-fact tone that satisfied his desire to stand firm without throwing gas on the fire. In 1957 he advised Gregory to have the electroconvulsive treatments that had greatly benefitted Gregory's older brother Patrick: "Even though you feel better now, the doctors have convinced me that it would be wise to take the same treatments Patrick had, and which did him so much good, so that you would not have a recurrence of that suicidal feeling and get rid of your anxiety state. They say that treatment cannot possibly do your brain any harm."[23] (Hemingway would one day take the opposite stand regarding shock therapy.) And Hemingway would not live to see his son transform himself into a strange imitation of the daughter he always wanted, but the theme of the son who disappoints his parents was very familiar to Hemingway.

Hemingway was wise enough to shield his parents from his first publication, *Three Stories & Ten Poems*, as it contained the story "Up in Michigan." Even the open-minded Gertrude Stein objected to it, calling it "inaccrochable," like a painting one cannot hang in public view. And true to the genius of Hemingway's sensitivity, the raw details of the central event of the story, the date-rape, seem less traumatic than the young lady's psychological torment. Dr. Hemingway did order six copies of *In Our Time* from Paris but shipped every one of them back to Three Mountains Press once he and Grace read the sentence "A short time after he contracted gonorrhea from a sales girl in a loop department store while riding in a taxicab through Lincoln Park." Such "filth" was not allowed in his home, no matter who wrote it.[24]

Exactly two years before Dr. Hemingway put the Smith & Wesson to his temple and just after the publication of *The Sun Also Rises* in 1926, he wrote to Ernest: "You are now a famous writer and I shall trust your future books will have a different sort of subject matter. . . . You have such a wonderful ability and we want to be able to read and ask others to enjoy your works."[25] Grace had wept at the vulgarities in the earliest of his stories and did not hide her anger when writing to him about his novel: "Don't you know any words other than 'damn' and 'bitch.' It is a doubtful honor to have produced one of the filthiest books of the year." Her final words fully negated his great accomplishment: "I love you dear, and still believe you will do something worthwhile to live after you."[26]

Hemingway was not only an adult; he was busy transforming twentieth-century literature and culture. Yet, to his parents, he was still the foul-mouthed teen, an embarrassment, and they prayed nightly that he would one day straighten himself out. (Grace reported she was too embarrassed to attend a public discussion on his "filthy" book.) It is significant that only after his father's death would Ernest Hemingway become "Papa," a nickname given to him by his second wife, Pauline, in 1929 that set up a paternal dynamic with whomever addressed him. The name fit, and it stuck for a lifetime. When Ernest inherited the patriarchy, he secured the persona of a "Papa": the sons were always in their youth. Thus, Father was not paranoid or suicidal, not harshly judging your great novels; he was forever the Papa who took you hunting and fishing at the lake and taught you to cook over the campfire.

As for his mother's possible genetic influence on him, Ernest claimed the only thing he inherited from Grace was poor eyesight. While suffering from a bout of scarlet fever at the age of seven, she apparently went blind, and the condition did not resolve for several months. The young Grace's blindness remains somewhat of a mystery, as acute scarlet fever is not associated with visual problems. Yet, scarlet fever can result in rheumatic fever, which it commonly did in the days before antibiotics. This autoimmune disease can indeed be associated with transient blindness, through a possible blood clot in a retinal vessel. But this is a very rare occurrence, and it is even more unlikely to involve both eyes. It is more likely that she suffered from another form of transient blindness in childhood and that its inception at the same time she had scarlet fever was merely coincidental. Though her blindness is generally accepted to have been a somatization disorder (that is, the result of psychological issues, not physical ones), whatever the etiology, once she recovered her sight she was forever light-sensitive. And this sensitivity crushed her performance dreams, as the bright stage lighting ended her opera career after just one performance. Grace studied voice in New York from 1895 to 1896 and was even offered a contract by the Metropolitan Opera. She made her debut at Madison Square Garden, but the eye pain associated with this one role sent her home to Illinois and her future husband.

Music always played a major role in the house (Ernest would play cello in his early teens for his school orchestra, no doubt at Grace's urging). And Grace had numerous students in and out of her home's music room. With a fee of $8 per hour, she was soon earning $1,000 a month. By contrast, Dr. Hemingway felt his patients would pay what they could when they could. Though on the surface this was noble in spirit, it was in reality a lofty defense against confrontation. And Grace felt her husband, Ed, was too frequently taken advantage of. Ed brooded about the earnings disparity, feeling emasculated and often arguing with Grace about money. After many such disputes, according to memoirs, she would retreat to her darkened bedroom and complain of a migraine. One of Hemingway's early stories, "The Doctor and the Doctor's Wife," presents a near-perfect reflection of their home life: the doctor struggles to keep his volcanic anger under wraps while his wife is "lying [in bed] with the blinds drawn" and quoting Proverbs to him ("Remember, that he who ruleth his spirit is greater than he that taketh a city").

Grace's conflicts with Ernest were typical of those between any adolescent boy and his mother, except that they never ended, no matter how successful Ernest became or how much he aged. An incident at Windemere Cottage would inspire Grace to write to her then twenty-one-year-old son that while a mother's love is like a bank account, rich with love and patience, Ernest was very much overdrawn: "For three years, since you decided, at the age of eighteen years, that you did not need any further advice or guidance from your parents, I have tried to keep silence and let you work out your own salvation; by that I mean, your own philosophy of life—your code of ethics in dealing with men, women, and children. Now at the age of twenty-one, and being (according to some of your best friends and well-wishers) so in need of good guidance, I shall brave your anger and speak this once more to you."

Grace continues for six paragraphs, elaborating on the theme of a mother's love as a bank account, "seemingly inexhaustible." But the child draws heavily on the account, particularly in adolescence. By the time the child reaches early adulthood, the bank is in need of some "good sized" deposits in the way of gratitude and appreciation. "Unless you, my son,

Ernest, come to yourself, cease your lazy loafing, and pleasure seeking—borrowing with no thought of returning—stop trying to graft a living off anybody and everybody—spending all your earnings lavishly and wastefully on luxuries for yourself—stop trading on your handsome face, to fool little gullible girls, and neglecting your duties to God and your Savior Jesus Christ—unless, in other words, you come into your manhood—there is nothing before you but bankruptcy: *You have over drawn.*"[27]

The incident that was apparently the last straw was a midnight rendezvous and picnic with the neighbor kids. Of the party of eight that set out by canoe and rowboat to the sandbar across the lake, three were Hemingways—Ursula and Sunny had actually planned the secret outing. But Ernest and his friend Ted Brumback, being the oldest, took the heat. Of course, the incident seems fairly typical for teens and young adults on vacation, and harmless enough. And the worst of the speculation in any biography has involved some possible "kissing the girls beyond the edge of the firelight."[28] Even Grace had to acknowledge that nothing "wicked" transpired.[29] She focused rather on the deceit involved. And it was clearly the latest of many offenses to Grace. She was so pleased with her letter that she drafted another copy for her husband and a third to keep herself. Her theme of unrepentance was by then quite familiar to Ernest. He played the role of prodigal son who never returned for a lifetime. He and his mother fit like two angry puzzle pieces.

Hemingway never spoke kindly of Grace throughout his entire adult life. His friend Buck Lanham wrote that he always referred to her as "that bitch": "He must have told me a thousand times how much he hated her and in how many ways."[30] He always blamed her for his father's death, and when she died, in 1951, he did not attend the funeral. Two years earlier he had written to Charles Scribner:

> My mother is very old, her memory is more than spotty and she
> is addicted to fantastic statements. Lately, because she is so old, I
> have played the role of a devoted son in case it pleased her. But I
> hate her guts and she hates mine. She forced my father to suicide
> and, one time, later, when I ordered her to sell worthless properties
> that were eating her up with taxes, she wrote, "Never threaten me
> with what to do. Your father tried that once when we were first mar-
> ried and he lived to regret it." I answered, "My dear mother I am
> a very different man from my father and I never threaten anyone.
> I only make promises. If I say that if you do not do certain sound
> things I will no longer contribute to your support it means factually

and exactly that." We never had any trouble after that. Except that I will not see her and she knows that she can never come here.[31]

The jabs went both ways, but Grace would score extra points for subtlety. Even during the last year of her life, before a dementing illness took over, she gave a newspaper interview in which she said: "Some critics and professors consider Ernest's books among the finest of our times, but I think the essays he wrote as a schoolboy were better."[32]

When Dr. Hemingway's suicide is discussed in the context of Ernest's writing life, the deleted passages from *Green Hills of Africa* are the primary touchstone: "My father was a coward. He shot himself without necessity. At least I thought so. I had gone through it myself until I figured it in my head. I knew what it was to be a coward and what it was to cease being a coward. Now, truly, in actual danger I felt a clean feeling as in a shower."[33]

The cowardice has been commonly interpreted as the act of suicide; however, for Hemingway, the cowardice he described in his father was his inability to stand up to Grace, allowing her to "force" him into this premature death, as Ernest made clear in his 1949 letter ("She forced my father to suicide. . . . I am a very different man from my father."). A suicide out of "necessity" would be that which Grandfather Hall plotted (even if it is apocryphal) when his kidneys were inflamed and his illness incurable, his situation akin to that of the fatally wounded man suffering on the battlefield. The henpecked did not qualify. His mother's dominance of his father was unforgiveable, and Ernest's defiance was a lifelong obsession—partly because it was a disruption in the assumed power structure. Hemingway never walked into a room where he was the weaker party, whether a defiant teen, or in a (fabricated) boxing match against a professional fighter, or even among falling shells in the Hürtgen Forest. He needed to command every situation, if not in rank, at least psychologically.

When he prevented his sons from visiting their grandmother, he told them that it was because of Grace's "androgyny."[34] Some biographers have concluded that Ernest projected homosexuality onto his mother, though historical investigations into this possibility are all dead ends (for Ernest and for Grace). But this was not the point he was making. Hemingway was a wordsmith, so his choice in this instance was very deliberate—he did not say his mother was homosexual, rather that she was androgynous. However confusing this odd accusation, Hemingway was behaving as a divorced parent might, speaking negatively about an ex-partner simply to drive a wedge between child and parent.

Ernest, however, would never be such a coward, certainly as long as Grace still lived. His father's life, as summed up by Ernest's stand-in, Nick Adams, was "both cruel and abused." Burying the gun his father used to end his life was a critical ritual. In classic Hemingway metaphor, he was now cleansed and safe, no matter what danger he might face, at least for the time being.

Trauma Artist

Chapter 2

Professors and critics still aptly described Hemingway as a "trauma art-ist," one whose life and thus whose writing were repeatedly informed by trauma—the celebrated World War I injuries being most central to the art. Though he disagreed, the theory was never news to Hemingway. But, more important, it was the critic's attempt to put him on the analyst's couch that he found intolerable. In his defense, few people know the dis-traction of having any and every detail from their lives uncovered (even their wardrobe from infancy and childhood) and then having their past and current work production analyzed for subconscious motivations.

Hemingway's personal injuries were the central theme of the 1952 book, *Ernest Hemingway,* by Philip Young, a professor at New York Uni-versity. Though Young's volume is essentially a work of literary criticism, Hemingway still fought to suppress its progress and release for a time. The book examines his fiction in the context of "wound psychology," and Hemingway wrote to Scribner's insisting that the publisher refuse Young permission to quote from any of his writing. He elaborated to his edi-tor: "Criticism is getting all mixed up with a combination of the Junior F.B.I.-men, discards from Freud and Jung, and a sort of Columnist peep-hole and missing laundry list school."[1] Hemingway felt "academic detec-tives" were always trying to "hang something on him," seeking Ph.D.s, and quipped that if he bothered to shoot Young, the man would "bleed footnotes." Hemingway eventually relented, but when writing to Young he still sought reassurance that the book was "not a psychoanalytical study of a living writer."

No doubt, Hemingway's male characters are defined, in varying de-grees, by their traumas. Jake Barnes, in *The Sun Also Rises,* is rendered impotent by his World War I wounds, and this fact dominates his daily life, though he openly denies that it does. He has indeed considered his trauma from every angle: "Of all the ways to be wounded. I suppose it was funny." This is an argument much more convincing when it applies to someone else's wounds. Harry Morgan (*To Have and Have Not*) loses his right arm from a bootlegging gunfight and eventually dies from wounds he suffered while killing four bank robbers in a shootout on his boat, concluding Hemingway's most violent book. The other fictional "Harry," the writer in "The Snows of Kilimanjaro," dies in the most inglorious fashion of all—from a mere scratch that becomes infected. At the other end of the spectrum is Francis Macomber's horrific death, which is described as lyrically as getting one's head blown off can possibly be.

And, of course, Hemingway drew on his recall of his own World War I injuries to elaborate Frederic Henry's traumas (*A Farewell to Arms*). Shortly after his arrival in Italy, he told his Kansas City friend and ambulance driver, Ted Brumback, that he was bored with the scenery: "I'm going to get out of this ambulance section and see if I can't find out where the war is."[2] He didn't have to look for long. And apart from the mortar blast, the one Hemingway survived on the front, all the traumas that followed for him were not the product of his being "accident prone," as is commonly thought, but the natural outcome of an adventurer's life, mixed with excessive drinking and a mindset of adolescent invincibility and recklessness.

His injuries and head traumas were frequent, random, and damaging. And, despite his lifelong protests at any attempt to link his art to these experiences, Hemingway would never escape personal trauma—in fact, head (and thus brain) trauma was a recurring event in his life. These repeated concussive blows did cumulative damage, so that by the time he was fifty his very brain cells were irreparably changed and their premature decline now programmed into his genetics.

Hemingway lettered in football at Oak Park High School, and, though six feet tall and 150 pounds, big for his time, he was slow and less coordinated than most of his teammates and played less than he and his father had hoped. He probably suffered no significant blows to the head, no more and no fewer than any other high school player of the day. Still, the equipment used in the early twentieth century was far from protective. And, though it is well known that he considered boxing a testament to his manliness at all points in his adolescence and adulthood, there is no evidence that he endured severe concussive injuries as a result. At sixteen he converted his mother's music room into a ring (the balcony made it a perfect venue). It didn't take long for Grace to ban the use of this arena for her teenager and his schoolmates, but they soon found that any backyard would suffice. He would brag later in life of learning to box before he was sixteen from a list of professional fighters in Chicago gyms, but there is no evidence that these sparring matches ever took place. The fabrication would gain some credibility from a detail he often cited, that his defective eyesight was the result of the dirty tactics used by his professional sparring partners (no doubt the professionals had to resort to cheating to beat the young upstart).[3]

The first major head injury Hemingway suffered occurred during World War I. He left his post at the *Kansas City Star* in 1918 to join the US Army Ambulance Service in Italy, first arriving at Bordeaux on June 3. While serving near the front, he would go down in history as the first American wounded in Italy after less than a month of service. Yet, he was not the first American casualty, just the first American to survive his wounds on the Italian front.[4] His own accounts of the injuries varied over time and were likely much less accurate than the initial report believed to have been written by his superior, Captain Jim Gamble: "Hemingway was wounded by the explosion of a shell which landed about three feet from him, killing a soldier that stood between him and the point of explosion, and wounding others."[5]

Hemingway was at the trenches of the front lines near the village of Fossalta di Piave, about twenty miles north of Venice, delivering chocolates to troops on July 8 when the Austrian mortar hit. It was a large, five-gallon bomb, full of scrap metal and explosives that knocked him unconscious and throwing enough dirt to half-bury him as well. Of eighteen Italians dead or missing on the Piave that night, Fedele Temperini likely saved Hemingway's life, taking the brunt of the explosion. This was the first of Hemingway's nine major head traumas, but there were additional injuries as well. Despite the shrapnel and concussion, Hemingway regained consciousness and picked up another man who was badly wounded and carried him, by his own account, 150 yards toward a first-aid dugout. He was soon "picked up by Austrian searchlights and took several big machine gun slugs bullets"[6] that he later wrote "felt like a sharp smack on my leg with an icy snow ball."[7] He never recalled the last hundred yards of his adrenaline-fueled run, during which he eventually fell, the wounded soldier tumbling with him, both unconscious. And accounts differ as to whether he actually carried the mortally wounded Italian infantryman. Such is the fog of war.

Hemingway was lifted onto a stretcher and taken by two bearers to the nearest dressing station, which was essentially a shed with no roof. He roused and for two hours felt an unbearable stinging in his leg. Near dawn, an ambulance took him to a makeshift triage shelter, a converted schoolhouse near Fornaci. There he received much-needed morphine and an antitetanus injection. He spoke to a fellow patient, whose wrist was now a bloody stump: "You're too old, Dad, for this war," he said to the fifty-four-year-old, who informed Ernest that he could "die as well as any man."[8] Ernest was so covered in blood that he was initially thought to have suffered a shot through the chest. The Florentine priest who made his way through the lines of wounded anointed him and administered last rites. Five days later, on a slow hospital train, he began his journey to Milan.

X-rays in Milan revealed a machine slug behind his right kneecap (entering from the side and leaving the patella bone unharmed) and another in his right foot. Both slugs were removed by his surgeon, Captain Sammarelli. Some publications still report that the surgical repair left him with a right kneecap fashioned from aluminum, but this was a classic Hemingway tall tale.

From the Italian government he received the Croce al Merito di Guerra (War Cross of Merit, given to all engaged in action) and the Medaglia d'Argento al Valore (Silver Medal of Military Valor), awarded for acts of exceptional bravery. But Hemingway's version of events would be inconsistent in retellings and was exaggerated over time. And it is noteworthy that he initially reported that he learned what had happened to him only the next day from an Italian officer who later recommended him for the honorable citation. He later said that Frederic Henry's wounds in *Farewell to Arms* were the most accurate description of his own, which explains why he claimed that two bullets had pierced his scrotum as well. It is very unlikely that he or anyone, no matter how robust, could carry a man even ten yards with machine-gun bullets in the knee and foot, and even more improbable is the report that two bullets might have traversed the scrotal sack of a running man without significant damage to the genitalia and thighs and leave him healthy enough to eventually have three children and numerous exploits. (He did not mention genital injuries in his letters from the hospital.) At least from the waist down, his injuries were exaggerated.

What is more likely is that he may have indeed acted while under the effects of a concussion and was therefore rendered amnestic for the subsequent actions. Perhaps he made efforts to assist the third soldier, perhaps even carrying him some distance before being hit by machine-gun fire, but the next day he reported no recall of these events. Later he claimed to have been informed that the soldier he "assisted" was already dead at the time he was attempting to carry him to safety. Even after stripping away the exaggerated heroics and undocumented and unlikely compounding injuries, Hemingway's brain had suffered its first major concussion. And he would eventually describe his own version of an "out-of-body" experience: "There was one of those big noises you some-times hear at the front. I died then. I felt my soul or something coming right out of my body, like you'd pull a silk handkerchief out of a pocket by one corner. It flew all around and then came back and went in again and I wasn't dead any more."[9] Studies of IED blast injuries of recent wars confirm that these concussions are commonly associated with out-of-body experiences.

The second major assault on Hemingway's brain occurred during his Paris years, in March 1928, while he was living with his second wife, Pauline, in the rue Férou. After dinner and drinks with Ada and Archie MacLeish, they returned at about 11, and by 2 A.M. Ernest entered the bathroom. The skylight had already been cracked when Hemingway con-fused its cord with the toilet chain and mistakenly pulled it. As Heming-way fumbled with the cords, the entire skylight fell onto his head, gashing him two inches above the left eye. Pauline summoned MacLeish, who managed to get his dazed friend into a cab, which reached the American Hospital at Neuilly, a suburb of Paris, just before 3 A.M.[10]

In contemporary photos, he wears the upside-down horseshoe scar as if every day were Ash Wednesday, his outward markings signifying inter-nal change. Biographers and critics find a direct link between the injury and his second major novel. The blood coursing down his face, his giddy concussive ramblings during the ride about his own blood's smell and taste, all precipitating a flashback to his ambulance ride in the Veneto ten years earlier—these were the accidental necessities. The writer was transformed, and a masterpiece of love and war flowed with an ease that amazed its creator. It was effortless, like a gambler's lucky streak. A short story going nowhere and essentially discarded then grew within six months into the first draft of *A Farewell to Arms*. He would write to his ed-itor, Maxwell Perkins, "My wife says that she will see that I'm bled just as often as I can't write—judging by the way it's been going this last week."[11] As one critic noted, "the blood had set him free," yet there was a cost. In the moment of his second concussive injury, more damage took hold.

Because Hemingway was already a famous author for *The Sun Also Rises,* wire services reported the episode, detailing the nine stitches, and the news reached his friend Ezra Pound. Pound fired off an amusing note from Rapallo, asking, "Haow the hellsufferin tomcats did you git drunk enough to fall upwards thru the blithering skylight!!!!!!!!"[12]

An accident that may have involved head trauma occurred in 1930, when he and John Dos Passos were still close. They were driving to Bill-ings, Montana, after a ten-day hunting trip, when the headlights of an oncoming car temporary blinded Ernest, and he drove right into a ditch.

Though Dos Passos and Floyd Allington, a ranch hand who had accompanied them riding in the rumble seat, were unhurt Hemingway broke his right arm so severally that he required three surgeries and several weeks to recover. Temporary nerve damage left him wondering if he would ever write or shoot again, and he grew frustrated and irritable as the pain was only partly relieved for brief periods.

Though he recovered remarkably well from the Montana incident, he would not escape the decade without another and even more bizarre injury. This one occurred during a fishing trip aboard his boat, the *Pilar*, once again with Dos Passos along with the other fishermen and crew. Hemingway was hoping to land a few large marlin and tuna. While en route to Bimini, he managed to hook a shark instead. He was ready to finish the creature off with his .22 Colt Woodsman, but while his friend Albert Pinder was gaffing the shark, it squirmed and twisted, snapping the gaff and causing Ernest's pistol to discharge. "I'll be a sorry son of a bitch, I'm shot" he said. The soft-nosed lead bullet split into pieces as it hit a brass railing; a fragment ricocheted into his left calf, and another entered behind his left kneecap (since a machine-gun bullet had lodged behind his right knee in Italy, he must have surmised by then that his patella bones were magnetized). Some smaller fragments managed to lodge elsewhere in his leg. Back in Key West, his doctor removed what he could but felt it wise to leave the largest fragment, which was lodged three to four inches deep in his calf muscle.[13]

During World War II, Hemingway suffered additional concussive injuries, the first of which occurred in much less noble fashion than his wounding on the Italian front. He was in London during 1944 and was invited to a party at the penthouse flat of Robert Capa in Belgrave Square on May 25. Capa would become famous for his photos made during the Spanish Civil War, where he first became close to Hemingway. Soon, he would photograph D-Day. But for now it was a time to party with his friends. Just after 2:40 A.M. Hemingway took the front seat in the car of a new acquaintance, Dr. Gorer, and they headed to the Dorchester Hotel. Gorer, at the wheel, was described as "no drunker than Hemingway" at the time (he had been drinking since 10 P.M.). The doctor's wife, a German refugee, took the back seat. London was blacked out during the Blitz, so none of them saw the steel water tank they plowed into. They had driven less than half a mile.[14] Hemingway's brain was again concussed when his head struck the windshield, and he also suffered a severe gash.

Capa was summoned to the hospital at 7:00 A.M. to find "215 pounds of Papa" on an operating table. "His skull was split wide open and his beard was full of blood." He thanked Capa for the splendid party and asked him to look in on Dr. Gorer and to notify Hemingway's three sons back in the States that no matter what they read in the papers, their father was safe and not badly hurt. After the hospital staff overheard Capa addressing Ernest as "Papa," he was known to them thereafter as "Mr. Capa Hemingway."[15]

Ernest required fifty-seven stitches across his scalp, and it took two and a half hours to close the wound. He was hospitalized until June 6, and not surprisingly, he ignored his doctor's orders. He held court, entertained visitors, and was found drinking whiskey and champagne specifically against medical advice. He was reliving his Milan Hospital days once more. It was amid this chaos that his third wife, Martha Gellhorn, decided she had taken enough of his volatility, his drunken rages, and his abuse and decided it was over. Irritability and angry outbursts are common after concussions, and alcohol indulgence is the best way to exacerbate this problem. Tinnitus, or ringing in the ears, also commonly follows a concussion, and this condition would stay with him for years (helped only slightly in the future by his antinausea medication).

Hemingway was technically a member of the press, but he was considered too important to military authorities to risk his death on the Normandy beaches. Yet, after the initial assault waves, he did board a landing craft, one of the LCVPs (or "Higgins Boats"), and reached the bloody shallow waters of Omaha Beach with troops before being ferried back alone to the transport ship (ironically named the *Dorothea L. Dix*). The first six assault waves had already landed in the shooting gallery before Hemingway's craft was allowed to depart, and he was forced to observe the rest of the invasion from the safety of the *Dix*. Just as well; he had only partly recovered from his May 25 injuries, and climbing the riggings into and out of the transport craft was a painful enough challenge (and risky, considering the disequilibrium that usually follows concussions).

Despite his official role as correspondent, after D-Day through the liberation of Paris and into the Hürtgen Forest, he would take up arms— strictly against the regulations that governed members of the press. So, in addition to being a correspondent, he was the self-declared leader of his band of "irregular" soldiers and an intelligence man operating in the theatre as well. To what extent he behaved bravely or recklessly and to what extent he actually fought and killed Nazis or just blustered and bumbled himself and his entourage into risky situations and later embellished his exploits are topics that will always be debated. What is certain is that he suffered at least one, and possible two, major concussions while in the field of combat.

Reuters reported that on August 3, 1944, six of "Hitler's supermen" surrendered to Hemingway and his driver, Archie "Red" Pelkey, when Ernest tossed a grenade into their hideout in the basement of a French country house. Two days later, on August 5, 1944, Ernest and his friend Robert Capa were on their way to find Colonel Lanham's command post in the area of St.-Pois. Hemingway had specifically gotten permission to retrieve Capa from Patton's Fourth Armored Division just twelve miles away and anticipated spending the weekend with him in Lanham's camp. He had even arranged for a captured convertible Mercedes (repainted olive green) to chauffer Capa in. But their next ride was less luxurious: Capa followed Hemingway's motorbike into hostile territory, ostensibly to find Lanham's headquarters, according to Hemingway's official biographer. However, according to Capa's account, "Papa said there was an interesting attack going on a few miles away and thought we ought to investigate. We put some whiskey, a few machine guns, and a bunch of hand grenades in the side car and set out in the general direction of the attack."

Capa warned against taking "lonely short cuts through no man's land," and made it clear he would follow Hemingway "only under protest," but still, as so many others had done and would do, he followed. Hemingway took the sidecar, his driver, Pelkey, was in control of the bike, and a photographer specifically assigned to Ernest (long before Capa arrived) sat directly behind Pelkey. Capa followed with Lieutenant Stevenson, a PR man also assigned to Hemingway.

Turning a corner, they unwittingly careened into the path of a German antitank gun. According to the news report, a shell soon exploded just three yards ahead of Hemingway (Capa's estimate was ten yards), and the explosion threw Hemingway into a ditch. The other four huddled "well protected" on the other side of the curved road. Capa is said to have continued snapping photos until a second antitank shell whizzed by too close for comfort. Tracer bullets coming for the light German tank kept kicking up the dirt just in front of Hemingway's helmet, which he gripped tightly, staying as low as he could. His headache was already throbbing, the London concussion rekindled. In Hemingway's account six years later, in a letter to Charles Scribner, he recalled: "A tank shell lifted me up and dropped me on head."[16] He also noted that his head slammed into a boulder in the ditch as well; thus, he likely suffered two successive concussions—one blast and a second on impact. Capa, Stevenson, the official photographer, and Pelky all hunkered down behind the road's bend opposite Hemingway as the Nazis obliterated the cycle and sidecar with machine-gun fire. Through the rest of the afternoon they could hear the German patrol talking between rounds. After two long hours, the tank drew back and drove off. At dusk, they were able to crawl back around the bend and head to the American lines.

Once out of harm's way, Hemingway and Capa were soon in a screaming match. Ernest accused Capa of retreating to the ditch across the road, well out of the German line of fire. In Capa's words, Hemingway "was furious. Not so much at the Germans as at me, and accused me of standing by during his crisis so that I might take the first picture of the famous writer's dead body."[17]

Hemingway had survived another brush with death, but this time, the postconcussive symptoms were quite significant: he reported double vision and memory trouble, while his friends noticed that his speech and thought processes were slower than normal and his verbal skills were noticeably lacking. His headaches "used to come in flashes like battery fire. But there was a main permanent one all the time. I nicknamed it the MLR 2 (main line of resistance) and just accepted that I had it."[18] Hemingway's symptoms are classic and typical for head injury and postconcussive patients. They report a baseline headache that never goes away and one that is superimposed when stress, insomnia, fatigue, or more trauma occurs.

Hemingway's postconcussive symptoms would soon be exacerbated by his D-Day experience, twelve days later. Coming in on the seventh wave, he had to climb nets to get in and out of the LCVPs, in "a more than moderate sea." He complained that "honest to God, nothing . . . hurt worse than going up and down those nets." Again, this is very typical of a postconcussive headache, which is excruciating when the patient is jostled, particularly by rough seas, and Hemingway already had disequilibrium and intermittent nausea. In addition, he felt continually lightheaded, his ears were ringing, and he was impotent from August to November. He was writing to Mary, his future wife, with all the details, reassuring her, but more likely himself, that his "abilities," sexual and otherwise, would soon return.

During 1945 and 1950 Hemingway notched his belt with two more concussions. On June 20, 1945, he ordered his chauffeur, Juan, into the back seat. Why he insisted on driving Mary to the airport, from which she would fly to Chicago and finalize her divorce from her second husband, is not known. But the road he took was spotted with clay that had leaked from construction trucks. Once mixed with rain, the clay made the road slippery and treacherous. The car skidded, and Hemingway warned Mary, "This is bad, Pickle. We have to go off." In the crash, Ernest cracked

four ribs and bloodied his forehead on the rearview mirror. Mary's lac-
erations required plastic surgery, performed fortunately by a very skilled
surgeon.[19]

The next major blow came on July 1, 1950, aboard his fishing boat.
Hemingway was climbing the flying bridge when the *Pilar* turned and
was rocked by a wave that hit it broadside. His heavy fall from the bridge
resulted in a gash so deep as to expose (but not fracture) his skull. He
had struck one of the large clamps that held the gaffs, and the wound
required three stitches. Two surgeons reassured him that only the "thickness of his skull had saved his life."[20] He would famously joke that being
labeled thick-headed was a form of literary criticism, but more lasting
than the flesh wounds was the recurrence of headaches and intermittent
irritability that followed, signs of the extent of the repeated brain injury
and more harbingers of future trouble.

The greatest damage occurred in 1954 when he and his last wife,
Mary, chartered a plane while on safari, hoping to view the spectacular
East African landscape. With Kilimanjaro in sight, the hydraulics of the
plane failed, and the passengers were indeed lucky to make it back to
Nairobi safely.[21] Mary and Ernest climbed into a Cessna 180 for the next
flight, which was scheduled to take them west over the southern end of
Lake Victoria and then north over Lakes Edward and Albert to the dramatic Murchison Falls of Uganda. They circled the falls three times as
Mary took photos. On the third pass, pilot Roy Marsh dove to miss a flock
of sacred ibis and the plane jolted and then reeled uncontrollably. The
skilled and composed pilot calmly informed, "Sorry, we're coming down
now. Get ready. Get ready."[22] With a badly damaged propeller and tail
assembly they crash-landed by the shore. Telegraph wires were initially
blamed, but a recent interview (of the son of the river boat captain who
eventually rescued them) indicates they likely struck one of the enormous
ant hills of Africa—that may reach up to 250 feet.

Mary was thought to be in shock for a time, and her pulse was 155
beats per minute.[23] Her anxiety subsided, but she had also suffered two
broken ribs. Ernest had sprained his shoulder.

A night in the open was punctuated by attempts at jokes and the fear
that a nearby elephant herd might get curious about the intruders. They
had crashlanded essentially in the herd's living room, and Mary woke
Ernest during the night to stop his snoring, which was a strange attrac-
tion for a few of the elephants.[24] By sheer luck, the next morning a boat
that had been chartered by a British surgeon from Kampala appeared
(interestingly, it had previously been chartered by John Huston while he

was filming *The African Queen*). The captain, an East Indian, actually charged the stranded group to climb aboard. The exact figure was one hundred shillings apiece, so high as to be nothing short of extortion. He dropped them near Butiaba, on the eastern shore of Lake Albert, where they were met at the dock by a policeman and the bush pilot who had been searching for them throughout the day in his twelve-seater, twin-engine de Havilland Rapide.

The pilot of the third doomed aircraft was Reginald Cartwright. The next day, his plane was gassed up and waiting at the Butiaba airport, where the runway was described as nothing more than a badly plowed field—rocky, furrowed, and bumpy—at best, a dangerous excuse for an airstrip. The trip would not take them to Entebbe as planned but would end in mere seconds, in a crash more violent and more fiery than the previous one. The plane bumped along for a while and lifted off only for a few seconds before it slammed down in explosive chaos. The cabin filled with smoke, and there were flames visible outside the windows. The starboard engine was on fire, and Mary found the door jammed shut. Cartwright, Mary, and Marsh all escaped after the pilot kicked out the front windshield, but Hemingway was too large for this exit, and his movement was limited by the pain from his shoulder injury the day before. He very unwisely chose to batter open the jammed door with his head, no doubt sustaining another major head injury. Staggering onto the port-side wing, he made his escape, but he sustained fractures of two vertebral disks and a dislocation of his right shoulder. There were first-degree burns on his head, face and arms, and, whether from the force of the impact, from his using his head as a battering ram, or both, his skull was now fractured. Cerebrospinal fluid drained from his left ear, and by the next day he reported the recurrence of his double vision, hearing that "came in and out like a radio in a thunderstorm," frequent vomiting, loss of vision in his left eye, and even complete loss of hearing on the left (fortunately, these last two symptoms were fairly short lived).

Mary and Ernest then endured what he called "the longest ride of his life," fifty miles to Masindi.[25] Though woozy, his head pounding, he told the press, "My luck, she is still good." He must have truly believed that, because he and Roy Marsh climbed aboard a small Cessna 170 to head for Nairobi, while Mary and Patrick (who had flown out to meet them) took a commercial airliner.[26]

In the 1950s, physicians had yet to define "postconcussive syndrome" (PCS), although it was well known that head injuries could result in a variety of neurological and psychiatric symptoms. To complicate matters, the symptoms can be variable and intermittent over time. The older a patient is, in general, the less resilient his or her brain is, the more severe the symptoms, and the longer they persist. Typical cases involve irritability and mood swings, memory and concentration deficits, noise and possibly light sensitivity, headaches, dizziness, fatigue, tinnitus (ringing in ears), insomnia, and impaired judgment. Hemingway had, at various times after his WWII concussions, all of the above.

When a commercial airliner spotted the wreckage of the first crash, the pilots radioed back that there were no survivors. Obituaries for Hemingway sprang up, and, once out of Africa, he read them late into the night with an intense fascination. Though it was a cliché, he was well aware of his reputation for romancing death in his life and work, and this time, in Africa, as in Italy and France, he had once again survived when the odds were against him. Perhaps this explains why he couldn't put the obituaries down. And after all, it was his best friend who wrote in *Ulysses,* "Read your own obituary notice; they say you live longer. Gives you second wind. New lease of life."

By contrast, twenty-one years earlier, when Scribner's mailed him galley proofs of *Death in the Afternoon,* with the tag "Hemingway's Death" across each page, he became so furious that he immediately fired off a telegram to his editor: "DID IT SEEM VERY FUNNY TO SLUG EVERY GALLEY HEMINGWAY'S DEATH OR WAS THAT WHAT YOU WANTED?"[27] He even wrote a follow-up letter to Perkins: "You know I am superstitious and it is a hell of a damn dirty business to stare at that a thousand times even to haveing it (in this last filthy batch) written in with red and purple ink. If I would have passed out would have said your goddamned lot put the curse on me."[28]

Post-concussion paranoia was probably a factor, as the perceived offense was essentially a function of his imagination, not an editor's attempt at dark humor. Yet he was so sensitive and superstitious that he found red and purple ink part of the jinx, and he was unable to even spell out the words "If I had died," writing only "If I would have passed out."

Though the plane crashes and the "greatly exaggerated" reports of his death are treated metaphorically by scholars, the second one in particular involved significant traumatic brain injury. This was his most severe concussive incident to date, partly because of his age, partly because of the multiplying effects of cumulative damage. None of his other accidents had taken such a toll, and friends agreed that after the crashes Hemingway was never the same man. He was just fifty-five, but his downhill slide was accelerating. And Hemingway had no difficulty in diagnosing his condition at the time. After the back-to-back plane crashes of January 22 and 23, he wrote in a letter from Kenya on February 2, 1954, "This is a funny thing. Maybe—concussion is very strange—and I have been study-ing it: Double vision; hearing comes and goes, your capacity for scenting (smelling something) can become acute beyond belief."[29]

It has been known since the 1920s that boxers suffer from a cognitive decline as they age. This condition was originally termed "dementia pugi-listica" and was the result of repeated head blows of subconcussive force, as the fictional Ad Francis would describe and further demonstrate. This form of dementia is usually associated with ataxia (balance and gait dif-ficulties), speech problems, tremors, and of course, a cognitive decline similar to that seen in Alzheimer's. In the 1956 film *The Harder They Fall,* a colleague tries to dissuade the Humphrey Bogart character, a sports-writer, from joining a group of corrupt fight promoters by showing him a film of a boxer with these exact symptoms. Of course, not all boxers develop the syndrome, but it has been a well-known possibility almost as long as there has been professional boxing.

The brain is suspended in a fluid-filled sac, and thus rapid accelera-tion-deceleration trauma will cause the brain to slam against the skull. The temporal lobes are particularly susceptible, as they sit above the rough structures of the petrous sections of the temporal bones. Tempo-ral lobes are critical for retaining visual memories, understanding and processing sensory inputs, storing new memories, and interpreting past memories and moment-to-moment emotional responses. From an ana-tomical standpoint, it is clear why so many head trauma patients have memory deficits and emotional dyscontrol once their temporal lobes have been battered against bone.

Side-to-side and rotational movements are thought to be more harm-ful than front-to-back movement. The damage found on pathological examination reads exactly the same as a list of the various mechanisms known to cause dementia: damage to the blood-brain barrier and the re-lease of neurotoxins (chemicals damaging to the brain cells), damage to the vessels that supply blood to the brain cells, disruption of the brain cell membranes so that calcium flows into cells (the accumulation of calcium inside cells is part of the mechanism of cell death in dementia), atrophy (or shrinkage) of brain structures, inflammation, and the release of cyto-kines (chemical messengers that attach to specific sites on the surface of brain cells and direct events inside those cells). In addition, a phenome-non known as "apoptosis" can also occur. Apoptosis is a form of DNA damage that acts as a time bomb, literally reprogramming the DNA of brain cells for premature death. In the laboratory setting, these trauma-induced mechanisms for accelerated cell death continue to unfold and affect DNA for up to a year after the initial injury has occurred.

One posttraumatic symptom that is commonly present is the persistent headache that Hemingway complained of during his World War II exploits. But brain cells have no pain receptors; the blood vessels that supply them do. So a persistent headache is the sign of vascular constriction, much like a migraine. This vascular constriction also compromises blood flow and can further impair memory and processing. After a trauma, the brain vessels often overreact, and their continual constriction can be easily seen on scans. The patient will simply say the headache never goes away and worsens with barometric changes or during flights (or in any setting in which air pressure changes). If the temporal vessels are constricted, the patient will lose memory and may even be accused of malingering, because long-term memories are absent even though short-term memory holds up well.

Hemingway famously exaggerated his traumas, particularly his first concussion and other World War I wounds. In one of his reports from the Spanish Civil War he wrote, "In the war that I had known, men often lied about the manner of their wounding. Not at first; but later. I'd lied a little myself in my time."[30] But lies were not necessary—the simple facts were damaging enough. The mortar explosion in 1918 had created vulnerability on a molecular and chemical scale, and when repeated concussions took place, his brain cells were more compromised with each successive blow—their demise was accelerated, and the areas of the brain affected were ever more diffuse. In Hemingway's case, these blows were adding more and more bricks to a load that was ever weighing down the life itself. By his mid-fifties, he had become a version of Ad Francis (and, with a tragic self-awareness, confessed as much to his associate Hotchner).

He had all the hallmark symptoms of postconcussive syndrome after his London car wreck and after his Africa plane crashes, but PCS can resolve. Every brain is different, every head injury unique, and we don't know why some of our patients recover fairly well or even completely and others have symptoms for years. Few patterns of recovery emerge, except that patients who suffer concussions at an older age and those with very severe traumas are more likely to have deficits for a lifetime. And individuals who suffer multiple concussions as Ad Francis and his creator suffered can progress from postconcussive symptoms to a form of progressive brain degeneration. However, the new terminology that replaced "dementia pugilistica" is "chronic traumatic encephalopathy," or CTE.

CTE is can result from concussive injuries like those Hemingway experienced but also from multiple "subthreshold" brain traumas, that is, numerous blows each of which is not so forceful as to result in a concussion but does damage nonetheless. After the Hemingway stand-in, Jake

Barnes, is knocked out in a Spanish café by the boxer Cohn in *The Sun Also Rises,* Barnes describes how "everything looked new and changed. . . . It was all different. I felt as I felt once coming home from an out-of-town football game. . . . It was all strange . . . my feet seemed to be a long way off, and everything seemed to come from a long way off, and I could hear my feet walking a great distance away. I had been kicked in the head early in the game."[31] Whether Hemingway really had such an experience in high school or borrowed it as was his gift, making it convincingly his own (such as the 1917 retreat at Caporetto), he was no stranger to the bizarre sensory changes that can accompany a head injury.

The National Football League's August 2013 settlement in which the league paid $765 million to former players with head injuries, as well as several other high-profile cases, has made this form of dementia a widely discussed topic in the media and in popular culture. Hall of Famer Mike Webster's CTE was highlighted in the 2013 *Frontline* episode "League of Denial: The NFL's Concussion Crisis" and the major motion picture *Concussion,* released in 2015. Webster was the center who anchored an offensive line that protected Terry Bradshaw for nine years. After hiking the ball, he usually slammed his forehead into the nearest defensive lineman trying to run through him. Tony Dorsett, the 1976 Heisman Trophy winner and Hall of Fame running back, spent twelve seasons in the NFL. Early in 2015, in tears, he discussed his symptoms. He gets lost when driving, and his daughters are afraid of his anger outbursts. And recently the family of Hall of Famer Frank Gifford revealed in November 2015 that he too had suffered from CTE, in hopes that this posthumous disclosure will further advance player safety.

Sadly, Hemingway's case is a textbook example. His own words describe the symptoms of postconcussive syndrome. The injuries from early blows resolved, but, with additional assaults, his brain developed CTE. This syndrome can develop years, even decades, after the traumas themselves. At autopsy, doctors find that the brain has atrophied and shows neurofibrillary tangles as well as deposits of tau protein and beta-amyloid, just as seen in Alzheimer's patients. But CTE is not the complete picture, just one of the largest pieces in the puzzle of Hemingway's illness. His brain cells suffered other, diverse forms of injury as well. Those additional insults on the cellular level, in addition to the repeated nature of his concussions and their cumulative damage, all propelled the pathology from PCS to CTE and, eventually, to a permanent dementia.

Giant Killer

Chapter 3

Hemingway famously described a life without alcohol as driving a race car without motor oil, and he lived his adult life determined to run a well-oiled race. Though numerous drinks have been named after him, probably only a few deserve the moniker. In Cuba, the Florida became famous for serving a Papa Doble, which consists of two and a half jiggers of Bacardi rum (white, not dark), the juice of two limes and half of a grapefruit, and six drops of Maraschino liqueur, all poured in a blender with ice chips and "whirled vigorously and served foaming in large goblets."[1] Still, a purist may point to *Islands in the Stream,* in which Thomas Hudson drinks gin mixed with lime and coconut juices (though the exact ratios were never clarified), with dashes of Angostura bitters. The fact that so many drinks around the globe in any number of oak-lined bars as well as numerous dives are named after him is a testament to the two-fisted drinking Hemingway—a part of the legend he seemed all too eager to live up to.

There is no shortage of drinking references in memoirs and biographies about Hemingway and, of course, plenty of references to his drunkenness—the flask in the pocket, the skin of wine on road trips, and the resultant volatility and arguments with spouses and others are noted throughout multiple biographies. Perhaps the most tragic and embarrassing alcohol-related incident occurred after a V2 rocket hit the neighborhood where Hemingway and other correspondents were staying in London during the Blitz; he was either too hung over or still too drunk to get up from breakfast and help his colleagues with the rescue efforts. Alcoholism, simply put, is the reason the term "bipolar disorder" does not apply in this detailed look at Hemingway's mental illness: the fact is that all of his affective (mood) instability and "bipolar" symptoms can be fully explained by the illness of alcoholism. What biographers have termed "bipolar" or "manic-depressive" disorder would more accurately be termed "alcohol-induced mood disorder." On paper, the symptoms of alcoholism—mood swings, volatility, depression, erratic sleep and insomnia, self-destructiveness, and even psychosis—are also hallmarks of bipolar illness. Contrary to popular myth, Hemingway never had a manic episode, and his name should be erased from every list of "famous bipolar patients."

Bipolar illness affects 1 percent of the population, and, as the name suggests, the abnormal mood states can be depressed or manic, thus representing two polar extremes. Of course the individual's mood state can be normal, or "euthymic," but long-term studies indicate that bipolar patients spend the majority of their lives in the depressed state. This is certainly risky, as the lifetime chance of suicide in the bipolar population is 15 percent, and opinion is now divided as to whether antidepressants are helpful and safe for bipolars. A patient may even present in a mixed state of mania and depression, such as being hyperactive and speaking rapidly but also crying and stating that she is depressed and perhaps even suicidal.

There are plenty of artists and writers who have suffered from this illness. Robert Lowell was a contemporary of Hemingway whose struggles with bipolar illness are well documented. His manic states were marked by hyperreligiosity and delusions ("I suspected I was the reincarnation of the Holy Ghost."), bizarre behaviors (standing in the street with outstretched arms to "stop the traffic"), and pressured speech—which even resulted in his arrest at one point. He termed the condition "pathological enthusiasm."[2] When a young Flannery O'Connor saw him in New York, as she was on his list to be canonized into sainthood, the naïve Flannery didn't understand the illness. She described herself as too inexperienced to recognize that he was mad; she just thought that was the way poets acted.[3]

Hemingway's behavior never reached a threshold of pathology that would qualify him for a diagnosis of bipolar illness, but his youngest son had documented manic episodes and, as discussed, suffered greatly. Still, no other first-degree relatives were ever in a manic phase as far as we know. Though some excellent biographies have been written with the underlying premise that Hemingway was "on a manic high" for discrete periods and "in a bipolar depression" at some other times, the premise is false. His stretches of productivity are best explained by the enthusiasm that success brings and as the result of a genius taking advantage of the visiting muse, knowing she may leave without warning at any instant. He felt exhausted when he had completed a major work, and the subsequent lulls caused him to ruminate about never completing another. Once he began writing again, a natural enthusiasm followed from realizing that his two worst demons—that he could not write and that he had nothing to say—were being exorcised. There is nothing pathological in these cycles; if there is, all artists are pathological to some degree.

To be complete, there are other forms of bipolar illness to consider. The traditional label refers to bipolar "type I," which involves classic manic episodes that last hours to days on end, along with bouts of depression and mixed states. When the mood state is abnormal, a patient may experience psychosis (delusions and/or hallucinations). Bipolar "type II" is a more subtle form. It involves bouts of depression but no true manias, just periods of "hypomania" that involve a level of hyperactivity, decreased need for sleep, and perhaps rapid mental activity but no symptoms that are sufficiently severe as to significantly impair day-to-day living. Type II is therefore a blunted form of bipolar type I. Type II is twice as common in women as in men, though type I is equally prevalent among men and women. The type II bipolar person may be harder to diagnose, as the symptoms of the illness may be mimicked by personality style or by symptoms of adult attention-deficit disorder or, as is very common, a substance abuse issue. And evidence does suggest that the type II patient is at higher risk for suicide than the general population, so the illness warrants careful monitoring and treatment as well.

Up to 60 percent of bipolar patients abuse alcohol or drugs, further muddying the diagnostic waters. Some patients are "self-medicating," but others may actually induce the abnormal mood states through their chemical abuse. These patients have mood disorder symptoms—depressive, manic, or mixed states—that are purely the result of alcohol (or other drug) intoxication or withdrawal and/or the psychological manifestations of addicting illness. This is distinct from the bipolar person who drinks to calm down or abuses stimulants to fend off a depression, that is, those who "self-medicate." Rather, for some people this is primarily a disorder of chemical dependency or abuse that results in marked alterations in mood and behavior. This was Ernest Hemingway. He was more vulnerable to alcohol-induced instability because of his head injuries (which make the brain more sensitive to the effects of chemicals, both prescribed and not prescribed), and these two causes of his mood swings comingled synergistically. And eventually, with more alcohol and more concussive blows, they blurred into the permanent damage of a brain with dementia.

Though chronic and excessive alcohol consumption will of course impair the liver, in many cases abstinence will result in normalization of liver tests over time. But the brain has fewer regenerative properties when damaged. Alcoholic dementia is similar in presentation to Alzheimer's, but the symptoms may occur much earlier in life and often involve pre-dominantly issues of impaired judgment and lack of inhibition. Small or moderate amounts of alcohol over an adult lifetime most likely confer some degree of protection from dementia; however, when the amounts are continual and excessive, the dementia may set in as early as a person's thirties. The mechanism may have to do with thiamine (vitamin B_1) depletion, as this and indeed all B vitamins are necessary for proper brain functioning.

Initially, patients with alcoholic dementia often present like those with frontotemporal dementia. The frontal lobes govern our morals and inhibitions and our emotions and behavior, and when synaptic loss occurs in the frontal lobes (loss of brain cell connections), one can expect inappropriate anger, outbursts of rage, emotional instability, and personality changes. The temporal lobes are essential for language skills, comprehension, verbal memory, and auditory and visual processing. They allow us to recognize familiar faces and understand what we hear—in short, to interface successfully with our world. Selective damage to these areas of Hemingway's brain would have no doubt compromised his skills and career and also his very personality and social presentation. Over time, the damage becomes more diffuse and involves all aspects of the brain; eventually, with continued alcohol induced damage, the dementia is indistinguishable from Alzheimer's.

During his early years, when he was famous only for his World War I injuries, and while recuperating in a Milan hospital, he would enlist the help of anyone (nurses, orderlies) handy enough (and willing) to supply him with alcohol, and when a cache of empty cognac bottles was discovered in his closet, the head nurse was described as less than amused.[4] By all accounts he very typically charmed his way out of trouble, but the scene would appear in *A Farewell to Arms*—although Frederic Henry was accused of attempting to induce jaundice and avoid the front lines. Still, almost twenty-seven years later, in London, Hemingway would once again pull off this gutsy move, albeit not exactly the toughest of the alcoholic's tricks, and obtain alcohol while in hospital. His drinking life most likely began when he was in his late teens, but he later claimed, probably falsely, that he was drinking by age fifteen. When he was eighteen he boasted in a letter to Bill Smith of downing his usual "18 martinis a day."[5] And, just a month shy of his twentieth birthday, he wrote to another pal of an enormous party at the Toledo Club, where "Your old pal Hem established the club record. 15 martinis, 3 champagne high balls and I don't know how much champagne then I passed out."[6] Whether true or not, the sophomoric idea that intoxication is the preferable method of entertainment for the truly cool was all too clear, and, unfortunately, it was never outgrown.

Hemingway biographers face a dilemma. If they ignore the alcoholism, then much of the story makes no sense. If they elaborate on the exact amounts and patterns of alcohol use, then they inevitably get bogged down by alcohol's metastatic influence—on relationships, marriages, writing, health, and depression. The biography then reads like a long and painful AA meeting. The exception is the masterful work of Scott Donaldson, *Hemingway vs. Fitzgerald*, in which he confronts Hemingway's alcoholism head on and explains the illness thoroughly and elegantly. In a 1950 letter Hemingway described alcohol as the Giant Killer that "I could not have lived without many times; or at least would not have cared to live without; it was straight poison to Scott instead of food."[7] He never experienced the insidious slow grip of addiction that so many describe, but alcohol was an indispensable part of the lifestyle and the life. To embrace, to use, to wrestle with—Hemingway's alcoholism was much in the spirit of Churchill's famous remark: "I have taken more out of alcohol than alcohol has taken out of me."

Donaldson, in his parallel biographical study of Hemingway and Fitzgerald, traces each man's drinking life, using his fiction, letters, and the memoirs of friends and doctors to flesh out the fullest picture. It is clear that Hemingway, unlike Fitzgerald, was a functional alcoholic for many years before the embarrassing public displays that were so prominent in Fitzgerald's short life began to figure prominently in his. Hemingway touted alcohol as a way of "changing his ideas" when stuck: "I have drunk since I was 15 and few things have given me more pleasure. When you work hard all day with your head and know you must work again the next day what else can change your ideas and make them run on a different plane than whiskey?" Donaldson concludes that "Alcohol, in short, was essential to his work and his well-being, as indispensable as food and shelter—and a source of great pleasure."[8] It was also medicinal. As Hemingway reported to Archie MacLeish, "Trouble was all my life when things were really bad I could always take a drink and right away they were much better."[9]

Hemingway expected his women to keep pace with him. He bragged about his first serious love in 1918: "the missus [Agnes von Kurowsky] . . . had heard about my hitting the alcohol and did she lecture me? She did not. She said, 'Kid we're going to be partners. And if you are going to drink I am too. Just the same amount.'" He also describes her pouring out some "damn whiskey" for herself.[10] The words are not typical of Agnes, and the story is more fantasy than fact, but his fantasy of lover-as-drinking-buddy came true more often than not. Of his wives, all but Martha Gellhorn generally kept pace with him.

During the Paris years, Ernest and Hadley would each have a bottle of wine with lunch and aperitifs before dinner, and then each would down another bottle of wine with that meal. He relied on exercise to "burn off the bad effects," a daily regimen he adhered to and wrote of in 1929 to his editor, Maxwell Perkins—it was the vigorous exercise, the boxing at the gym, the hunting, the fishing, the fresh air, that made it possible to "drink any amount." He went on to state that he "lunched with Scott and John Bishop . . . drank several bottles of white burgundy. . . . Knew I would be asleep by 5—so went around with Scott to get Morley to box right away . . . had a couple of whiskeys enroute. . . . I finally fought myself out of the alcohol." No doubt he was not in the best condition at the moment for a match. The fight was more damaging to him than to his friend Morley Callaghan. And controversy remains as to whether Scott Fitzgerald as timekeeper let a round go on far too long while Hem was losing out of incompetence, or whether, as Hemingway said, perhaps Scott was "so interested to see if I would hit the floor!"[11]

Technically, the body metabolizes ethanol to yield some energy, but these are expensive calories to take in—the natural muscle-relaxant properties, the sedation and depressant effects on the nervous system, as well as the dehydration, all argue that Hemingway would have been more vigorous without it. Protein or even complex-sugar-based calories would have been healthier.

Of course, his protagonists down spirits easily enough, and readers are often amazed at the amounts his characters consume. Throughout *The Sun Also Rises,* Barnes and company drink pretty much continuously, and, despite our narrator's occasionally mentioning that he is drunk and at one point convincing us with his perceived bed-spins, Jake still manages to appear throughout the text as the only sober member of the party. Colonel Cantwell (in *Across the River and Into the Trees*) is also a classic example and, like Barnes, is generally accepted as Hemingway's stand-in (both men are roughly the age Hemingway was when he created them). His typical drinking day is detailed by Tom Dardis in *The Thirsty Muse.* The Colonel drinks more than a quart of alcohol over just six hours or so. The afternoon starts with two Campari and gin cocktails, then goes on to six progressively dryer martinis, and finally he shares two bottles of champagne and three bottles of wine (one white, two red) with his lover. When the couple head to the gondola, they take another bottle of the red, a Valpolicella. There is no apparent compromise of the Colonel's intellectual or sexual energy, and he wakes with no hangover.[12]

In the 1940s, visitors to Hemingway's Cuban home, Finca Vigía, were greeted with absinthe, and at dinner there was abundant red and white table wine, with champagne flowing as well. After the meal, Scotch high-balls seemed "endless," according to one visiting couple, and for night-caps the absinthe bottles returned. Hemingway "never seemed drunk," according to guests, indicating great tolerance, and only later, when he mixed alcohol with sleeping pills, did he fall asleep in front of his company.

When Lillian Ross followed Hemingway and crew around New York for two days, in November 1949, she remained detached and reported each scene as a documentary filmmaker might. Her now infamous *New Yorker* article (May 13, 1950) was subtitled "How Do You Like It Now, Gentlemen?" It was Hemingway's catchphrase of the moment—essentially meaningless and probably quite annoying to hear over and over. The result of her detached stenography, recording Hemingway's "half-breed Choctaw" talk, as he termed it, was widely believed to be a hatchet job. The famous Hemingway, she suggested, was no genius, just a loquacious buffoon.

It was commonly thought that Ross and Hemingway were enemies, if not before certainly after her article. Hemingway scoffed at the idea, noting that they couldn't be enemies because no money or sex had ever been exchanged between them. But, to most readers, the piece was largely understood to be a deliberately destructive effort. Yet the article makes perfect sense once one realizes that Ross had been recording the actions and words of a man who began his trips with bourbon shots in the airport bar, started each morning with champagne, and sipped from his silver flask while strolling the Metropolitan Museum of Art. The camera recorded a self-important man on vacation, disinhibited by alcohol and rambling on, not the expected literary genius. As Hemingway wrote to one friend, "I had just finished a book and when you have done that you do not really give a damn for a few weeks." And he added, "There was no harm intended and much received. But I am still fond of Lillian."[13]

Only intoxication can explain some of the disjointed and inappropriate content of many of his letters, particularly since Hemingway knew his letters were being saved at least for posterity and certainly for scholarship. He wrote to Charles Scribner on July, 22, 1949: "we ought to keep copies of our letters like Mr. Lord Byron and [John] Murray [his publisher]. I know some funny things that could write you if wasn't so inhibited. Now I know the copywrite [sic] remains with me am liable to write you goddamn near anything."[14] A month later, he did write "-damn near anything": "In regard to the new medium sized book I want you to get it into the Book of the Month Club and start chopping down trees for the paper now. If it isn't good you can hang me by the neck until dead. I let Mary read 121 pages of it yest. and she hasn't been any good for anything since. Waits on me hand and foot and doesn't give a damn if I have whores or countesses or what as long as I have the luck to write like that. Have a lovely new whore so beautiful she would break your heart and three fine contessas in Venice. Three, I guess, is about the right number. But the finest one writes a lovely letter too. You would like her very much I think. Is an *admirable* woman. All this time I work at being a good and faithful husband to Mary whom I love. Think you will like the book."[15]

But eventually Mary had seen enough whores and countesses. Hemingway even invited an eighteen-year-old Havana prostitute he had nicknamed "Xenophobia" to Finca, but at least he waited until Mary was out of the country.[16] When she wrote to her husband the next year (May 1950) that she was leaving, she left no doubt that alcoholism was the reason: "Maybe it is ambiguous for me to explain my reasons for leaving. But I write them down because I think this time you should have the opportunity of knowing precisely how I feel about this marriage. It began in 1944 in bed in the Ritz Hotel in Paris and my own reasons for it were two: I thought you were a straight and honorable and brave man and magnetically endearing to me. And because, although I was suspicious of your over-drinking, you said so often that your chief desire was to be GOOD and adult and to live your one and only life intelligently, I believed you and in you . . . you could if you want to, be a companionable and considerate husband—as well [as] gay and charming and sturdy in spirit, which you are when you are not drunk. . . . Your principle [sic] failure is that, primarily because of your accumulating ego and because of your increasing lapses into over-drinking, you have not been the good man you said you intended to be. Instead you have been careless and increasingly unthinking of my feelings, at times to the extent of brutality." He is also described as remorseless, scoffing, petulant, and irritable and as believing that his "infallibility" should not be questioned.[17]

Mary never left. She was as determined as ever to be the last "Mrs. Hemingway." But the themes are certainly familiar—the substance abuser who promises to straighten up and fly right, the woman who understands her role as the catalyst for his transformation, her belief that new love will be all he needs to do so, and, of course, the inevitable (and repeated) disappointments. No doubt, her frustration was compounded by the realization that when her husband wasn't drunk, he was a classic dry-drunk.

It was also around this time that José Sotolongo, Hemingway's Cuban doctor, removed the guns from Hemingway's home. The Cuban lifestyle he had carved out not only included Papa Dobles at the bar but also pitchers of martinis at home. He and Mary were fighting very frequently, and the tension was fueled by Hemingway's infatuation with his young Italian muse, Adriana, who came to stay in Cuba for an extended visit. "On one occasion I had to interfere bodily," Sotolongo explained. "I left the house at four in the morning when I saw that the danger was over. They had threatened each other with firearms, and each of them had a shotgun. I had to take their guns away and hid them in my car. . . . That night I wrote to tell him, that our friendship was over, but he called me the next day and asked me to help him dry out."[18] During those Cuba years, Hemingway was "always" intoxicated, according to Dr. Sotolongo, who had already warned him that "If you keep on drinking this way you won't even be able to write your name."

By the time he was fifty-seven, and only after further and stricter medical orders (because of an enlarged liver and hypertension), Hemingway did reduce his intake to two glasses of light wine at supper. It was at this point that he found himself and his surroundings boring and made the famous comment that equated the sober life with racing a car without motor oil. Yet there is evidence that his intake eventually crept up to its former level again. One researcher discovered a bill from March 1958 labeled "Papa's Liquor" and added that "the bill for the month was $95 for wine and $45 for whiskey; Mary's was $95.69 for vodka and gin. Throughout the summer, the liquor bill varied, but Hemingway's personal consumption was averaging four to six bottles of whiskey a month and two or three cases of wine."[19]

Though he did successfully limit his intake for a period of time, he was well on a downward slide by then. The damage caused by his alcoholism to cells that had suffered multiple concussive injuries was largely irreversible. The brain damage from chronic alcohol comes not only from vitamin deficiency, though this can be one mechanism, but also from a variety of other effects. As with any toxin a body ingests, the liver can deal with only so much. When the liver's capacity to "detoxify" a chemical is overwhelmed, the toxic effects on brain cells lead to synaptic loss, just as in other forms of dementia: the brain cells literally lose their connections to one another.

Alcohol was not the only chemical Hemingway's body and brain were dealing with during the 1940s and 1950s. He took a variety of medications and supplements, including high doses of vitamin A, which he thought would help his eyesight, thiamine (vitamin B1), and vitamin E because he believed it would improve his libido. He used the potent sedative Seconal, a barbiturate, to sleep and took Reserpine for hypertension; this medication is known to cause depression by preventing the transport of serotonin, dopamine, and norepinephrine to cells. At times he was pre-scribed Ritalin (methylphenidate) for low energy when he complained to his doctors that after he had lunch he was sleepy and unable to write. He was also prescribed testosterone at one point.[20] These latter two therapies are still in common use and were probably good ideas. Indeed, many pa-tients today are prescribed testosterone when this hormone is found to be depleted, especially if the patient has mild depression or libido changes. And Ritalin has also been commonly used as a part of the therapy mix for older depressed individuals. But the potential benefits were likely drowned by the whiskey, wine, and Papa Dobles.

Hemingway's personal physician for the last years of his life went on record in a rare interview with William Smallwood (coauthor of *The Idaho Hemingway*). He was asked his opinion about the discrepancy be-tween the Hemingway of the biographies—"a liar, braggart, back-stabber" and an "immodest philanderer"—and the Hemingway everybody knew in Idaho—"a kind, humble, generous, sensitive, playful, mischievous, loyal, polite gentleman." Dr. George Saviers believed that the difference was alcohol. In the summer of 1959, he had joined Hemingway in Spain to attend Hemingway's sixtieth birthday party, an elaborate affair arranged with great effort by Mary. According to Smallwood's notes (retold by Til-lie Arnold), Dr. Saviers "told how Papa was drinking around the clock in Pamplona and how his personality was so different than what we had seen. He said that he was loud, that he pontificated as an expert on every-thing, and that he told stories about himself that were obvious lies. George was especially disgusted with how Papa had treated Mary when she broke her toe at a picnic on the Irati River. He said that Papa was down-right cruel to Mary and he did not know how Mary put up with it."

Dr. Saviers also referenced some long rambling passages from *Green Hills of Africa* and elaborated on the influence of alcohol on Hemingway's writing, his correspondence, and even his tendency toward paranoia. But the doctor ultimately believed that it was an oversimplification to divide the life or the work into the "drunk or sober" Hemingway: "Hemingway," he concluded, "was a complex man."[21]

Dr. Saviers's point about complexity is accurate, as alcohol was not the only answer to Smallwood's question about the contradictions in how Hemingway was seen by people in different settings. The friends that Hemingway had and made during his last years in Idaho saw a man who was humble, polite, sensitive, and even mischievous (implying childlike), because he was regressed. With illness, particularly a dementia when one is aware of one's limitations, comes a childlike regression that was evident in his every interaction in the community.

Of course, Hemingway did not have a monopoly on alcoholism among his fellow writers. Scott Fitzgerald's addiction did not destroy his talent, as Hemingway thought, so much as ruin his production. The novelist and poet Malcolm Lowry (who was ten years younger than Hemingway) began drinking by age fourteen. He was amazingly productive despite a short, volatile life of near continual drinking. James Dickey's alcoholism was well known and also socially disruptive. When asked by an intern during a hospital admission for detox how much he drank, Dickey responded, "As much as I damn well please."

And William Faulkner, the contemporary whose stature is most commonly equated with Hemingway's, also met the criteria for a diagnosis of alcoholism. Yet, by contrast, Faulkner's alcoholism would best be described as binge-type—not like Hemingway's functional steady intake. Faulkner would completely incapacitate himself at random intervals and require hospital detoxification. Saviers's assessment that alcohol compromised Hemingway's craft is debatable. In works such as *Green Hills of Africa*, Hemingway, in his free-form writing and his pontificating, sounds roughly the same, drunk or sober. (Yet his more disinhibited, abusive, and rambling letters make it clear that many of these letters were written while he was experiencing some level of impairment.) Some biographers insist that Faulkner always worked sober, though the basic observation that his fiction is rambling and his train of thought often difficult (or impossible) to follow argues against this.

And, like Hemingway, Faulkner was compromised not only by alcoholism but also by repeated head trauma that would also play a critical role in his demise. On December 29, 1961, the horse he was riding stepped in a hole, throwing him. Nearly all falls from horses are awkward and can result in the head striking the ground. Faulkner's postconcussive symptoms included amnesia and headache, and this was in fact the worst in a series of falls. He would be dead in seven months.[22]

Both alcoholism and traumas were referenced by *The New Yorker*'s brief mention of Hemingway's much-anticipated 1926 novel. After first elegantly summarizing the author's effortless mystique and magnetism, the review continues: "'The Sun Also Rises' . . . is a new novel by that already almost legendary figure in the Parisian group of young, American authors. This is a story of exquisite simplicity built on the sensational theme of a love affair between an American who has been sexually incapacitated during the war, and a credible and living counterpart of the jejune *Iris March*. The author of 'Torrents of Spring,' who has only to publish to be read by a certain circle of the intelligentsia, and not even to publish to be discussed, has written wittily and with a smooth deliberateness astonishingly effective in numerous passages of nervous staccato. An unconscious sense of security in the author carries the reader from episode to episode with mounting curiosity and no fatigue."[23]

The review ends: "Related in the first person with a fierce flippancy rarely seen in the sober and surely never in the casually drunk, the book is the verbal expression of anguish not wholly of mind nor of body, unless it is of an alcoholic mind in a tragically maimed body." Perhaps no other review was ever more prescient and applicable to the "already almost legendary figure," even if accidentally so.

Dementia, Disinhibition, and Delusion
Chapter 4

Hard living takes its toll. The concussions, alcohol, hypertension, and prediabetes all contributed to the changes in Hemingway's brain. As his sixth decade progressed, Hemingway's volatility worsened; he grew more and more paranoid and became irretrievably depressed. And by the time he presented with psychiatric symptoms so severe as to warrant hospitalization, his brain had been dementing for years, and, sadly, the damage was irreversible. Yet the severe bout of depression that led to his two Mayo Clinic admissions was not his primary illness; rather, it was a manifestation of the larger process of brain dementia—as were his delusions and his cognitive decline. The illness of dementia, seen with the benefit of hindsight, clarifies much of the biography of his last decade—including not only the character of his professional writing but his eventual inability to write. It also explains the escalation of his abusive behavior and the internal torment of paranoia.

Dementia, in the medical sense, is a general term—like pneumonia or cancer—a disease that may have one of many different causes or, as in Hemingway's case, multiple comingled causes that overwhelm the body's defenses. Dementia is further diagnosed as a specific type on the basis of its underlying etiology. Alzheimer's disease, named after its discoverer, Dr. Aloysius Alzheimer (who first examined his dementia patient in 1901), was one of the first categories of dementia described in the medical literature. But strokes can also cause dementia. The illness can result from a single large stroke or from an accumulation of smaller ones. This syndrome is termed "vascular dementia" and is second to Alzheimer's in prevalence. These patients often decline in a "step-wise" fashion; that is, their confusion worsens and their functioning declines suddenly—seemingly overnight, in response to a medical stressor, such as a fall, or an infection.

Parkinson's disease may also involve a progressive dementia as well. And, of course, chronic alcoholism is a common cause.

A particularly disabling form of dementia that is often rapidly progressive is frontotemporal dementia, also termed "Pick's disease" after its discoverer (who described the condition in 1892). Frontotemporal dementia patients are often younger than the average dementia patient, sometimes in their late forties or early fifties. Because frontal lobes of the brain govern our morals and inhibitions, this form involves personality changes, and often inappropriate behaviors and speech are prominent. And a newer category, termed "Lewy body dementia" (which is named for the describer of the specific protein deposits seen in the brain tissue under the microscope), has appeared in the past two decades. Lewy body patients report vivid hallucinations, very detailed delusions, and symptoms of Parkinson's disease—often atypical and asymmetrical, such as a tremor affecting only one hand, not both. Curiously, when Lewy body patients are given medication to treat their hallucinations, their symptoms often become much worse. Thus, one way of telling early on if the dementia is of the Lewy body type is by observing that antipsychotics worsen the patient's psychosis.

Another newer category of dementia is associated with HIV infection, which also involves its own form of dementia, characterized by apathy, sluggishness, slowed and dysarthric speech (poor articulation due to neurological damage), clumsiness, and cognitive difficulties (for example, memory and concentration impairment). Finally, patients may present with any mixture of these types; for example, the alcoholic may develop Alzheimer's or suffer from an accumulation of small stokes that also contribute to dementia. A recent study showed that, at autopsy, 77 percent of patients with vascular dementia had enough pathological evidence to diagnose Alzheimer's as well. And as our ability to discern the various types of dementias continues to improve, we are discovering that combined dementias are the rule, not the exception (or at least the various types share many of the same mechanism of brain cell demise and death and thus many of the same pathological findings).

To be diagnosed with dementia, a patient must have memory deficits as well as impairment in one or more other cognitive domains, such as planning, organizing, mental processing, or abstraction. Other areas that may be affected include language, an inability to recognize and name objects ("agnosia"), and motor skills, or "apraxia." A thorough neurological exam and various motor tests, such as to assess finger and hand coordination, are performed in patients suspected of having any form of dementia. We always examine the patient in detail, looking (and hoping) for any sign that the dementia may be reversible, such as dementia caused by a thyroid condition or a vitamin B-12 deficiency, which can cause difficulties with concentration and memory. But, unfortunately, these reversible cases are rare.

A PET scan (or Positron Emission Tomography study) is the best way to definitively diagnose dementia. This test involves injecting radioactive glucose into the venous system and then measuring exactly where in the brain the glucose is being utilized. Thus, it's a real-time look at which brain cells are working and using energy and which ones are not. A PET scan is different from tests to measure blood flow; certainly one needs blood flow to the neurons to see metabolism, but even when there is adequate flow, metabolism can still be impaired. The brain cells in patients with dementia are simply not functioning properly; even if the cells are alive, they cannot uptake and utilize glucose normally, and over time they die sooner than they should.

By simply writing a basic medical history of Ernest Hemingway, one is listing all the known risk factors associated with developing a dementia: repeated severe head injuries and concussions, alcoholism, hypertension (especially if untreated or poorly managed), and prediabetes. His weight during the last decade of his life is associated with elevated glucose levels, even if he was never formally treated for diabetes. Neuropathy and vascular injury associated with diabetes can occur in patients months or years before their glucose levels rise to a threshold that qualifies for the diagnosis (much like his father's condition).

One of the curious aspects of dementia is that patients who have never experienced psychosis can begin suffering from delusions and hallucinations as the brain is progressively affected. As mentioned, Lewy body dementia patients often have very vivid hallucinations and elaborate, well-organized, or "systematized" delusions (when patients explain them in detail, they may involve great complexity). Hemingway's delusions are well documented during his last years in Ketchum, Idaho. He feared he would be arrested for hunting on private land despite repeated explanations (including from the land's owner) that it was perfectly fine. And one evening, in 1959, simply noticing lights burning after business hours in Ketchum's First Security Bank triggered his paranoia. Lloyd and Tillie Arnold had just picked up the Hemingways and were heading back to their home for a roast beef dinner. A snowstorm was moving in that night, and, with chains on the tires, Lloyd's car crawled through town, past the ski shop, and then the bank. Ernest nudged Lloyd hard. "They're checking our accounts in there," he said, in all seriousness.

Tillie believed it was just the cleaning women, and Mary insisted that she and Ernest weren't active enough clients at that particular bank to have any records to check, but Ernest had no doubt. He had suspected as much for some time; now he "was sure." He believed "they were trying to catch us . . . they wanted to get something on us." "They" was the FBI. At the Arnolds' home, Ernest kept looking through the large living room window, staring down on the dim light at the bank in the distance. Lloyd made drinks and tried his best to reassure Ernest. The bank manager was putting in overtime, likely protecting Ernest's assets. "Yeah," he responded, "but you don't know how the big outfits work, absolutely none of it [money] your own anymore, no matter how hard you try to play straight with 'em . . . you can't win, they won't let you." His friends now realized how seriously ill he was and feared that the Hemingway they had known for years was gone forever. Tillie went to bed that night crying.[1]

Another telling delusion involved his young Italian muse, Adriana Ivancich. She was a month short of nineteen when she met Hemingway when both were on a hunting trip in northern Italy in 1948. Adriana conveyed an elegant presence, and Hemingway found her enchanting. The fact that she had descended from Italian nobility impressed him very much, and he was no doubt smitten with her the instant his hunting party found her standing in the rain by the side of the road. She was waiting for their mutual host (and friend of her brother), Count Carlo Kechler, to pick her up in the large Buick that was chauffeuring Hemingway around Europe. He was impressed during the ride by what he described as her "quick mind." She refused a drink from his flask of whiskey, and as the conversation progressed, she apologized for not having read any of his books. Hemingway explained that she could learn "nothing good" from them, but Adriana disagreed, saying that there is "something good" in everything.

The next day was damp and dreary as well, and the shooting was equally disappointing. After the men had finished their partridge hunt, they gathered to drink and warm up in the hunting preserve's home. In the kitchen, Ernest found Adriana rain-soaked and thoroughly worn out from her less than successful day with the rifle. He chatted sympathetically with her in front of the large fireplace, broke his plastic comb in half to share with her, and was more than charming—he was conversant, warm, and very kind. The self-possessed young woman combing out her long dark hair in the firelight knew nothing of Ernest's hair fetish. Of course he made plans to see her again, inviting her to his favorite Venetian watering hole, Harry's Bar.[2]

Adriana was hazel eyed and thin and had a narrow pale face that "went shadowy under the cheekbones."[3] By their next meeting, a luncheon, he was calling her "daughter." In letters he also addressed her as

"Daughter," and he signed them "Mister Papa," but the words between are tender and imply more than a paternal affection:

> First, daughter, I think you write beautifully in Italian and I under-stand it. The style is clean and good and you never get florid (flow-ery) unless you are angry. I never mind when you are angry because I think when I was twenty I was angry nearly all the time. Also I remember that when we have a chance to see each other neither one is very angry very long. . . .
>
> I am lonesome for you and do not want to say these things to anyone else. . . .
>
> Am prejudiced about you because I am in love with you. But in any situation, under any circumstances where it was my happiness or your happiness I would always want your happiness to win and would withdraw mine from the race. . . .
>
> I love you very much. Mister Papa[4]

He professed his love many more times, in many other letters: "I cannot do anything but love you"; "I will love you always in my heart and in my heart I cannot do anything about it." He even wrote (the day after Valentine's Day, 1954) that perhaps Mary would understand that what had happened to him when the two met at the crossroads in Latisana "was just something that struck him like lightening." When Adriana heard the false reports of his death in Africa, she wept for the entire day, her heart "heavy like a stone." When he wrote to her after having survived the crashes, he claimed he had never loved her so much as "in the hour of his death."[5]

In his letters he also addressed her at times as "Adriana Hemingway," while he was "Ernest Ivancich." This private experiment with gender and identity exchanges had played out in some of his short stories and would also figure prominently in his (unfinished) manuscript, *The Garden of Eden*. As Hemingway's last decade progressed and his mind and its asso-ciations loosened, Adriana and the idea of Adriana would play multiple roles.

She appears as Renata, the eighteen-year-old lover of the fifty-year-old Colonel Richard Cantwell, in Hemingway's sixth novel, *Across the River and into the Trees*. In fact, the age gap between the fictional and the real couples was almost identical, and, not surprisingly, the Colonel addresses Renata as "Daughter." In the book, Cantwell spends much of the last day of his life recalling his time with the Contessa Renata and reminiscing about his past. As with Hemingway's connection with Adri-ana, the sexual relationship between Cantwell and Renata is ambiguous early in the novel, but later, in the Gritti Palace Hotel, Renata says, "I can be your daughter as well as everything else." The Colonel responds, "That would be incest." Hemingway knowingly fueled the myth that he and Adriana were lovers by forbidding publication of the novel in Italy for a period of two years after its release elsewhere (ostensibly to protect her reputation). Despite the critics' universal dislike of the work, it remained on the best-seller lists for twenty-one months, as would anything with Hemingway's name on it.

Carlos Baker has suggested that Hemingway was attempting a poetic metaphor "of greater complexity than he had ever tried before." Renata, which means "reborn," represented the spirit of youth and renewal in both Ernest and his fictional stand-in Cantwell.[6] As with much of Hemingway's work, the reader is rewarded by not becoming distracted by the autobiographical backdrop. The short novel is a profound meditation on coming to terms with one's life in its last few hours. Cantwell is a man with a firm hold on the control column of a crashing plane, self-consciously managing its descent. And the Colonel would have his intimate rendezvous with his young friend, under a blanket in a gondola, yet Hemingway would never consummate his affection for Adriana. At Hemingway's invitation, Adriana, along with her mother, did stay at his Cuban home for almost two months. But she spent the final month on the island in a hotel, in response to the rumors of intimacy.

From a psychiatric standpoint, Hemingway was simply expressing his fantasy life in his fiction, which was nothing new. But years later, he agonized over the delusional belief that he was going to be arrested for intimacy with a minor. (Adriana was eighteen, and technically he had nothing to fear even if they were intimate, but, by definition, a delusion is an unrealistic belief, unshaken by facts and reason.) Furthermore, no evidence has surfaced since his death that he and Adriana were ever lovers, though this was accepted folklore in Italy. Adriana's protective mother, who chaperoned her during her trip to Cuba (with her brother), in addition to Mary's jealousy and watchfulness, would have been enough to prevent that. Her brother always insisted when interviewed that the relationship was not sexual but rather one of father and daughter. But in Hemingway's private thoughts, he persisted in the fantasy life after his book was complete. He continued to express himself in letters with almost Shakespearian level of double-speak: love-struck language couched in paternal greetings and farewells. He even spoke of a creative partnership with her, White Tower. Adriana would be the full partner and artistic genius behind his dust jackets. (The White Tower is an obvious reference to the tower built at his Cuban home; however, it was in the White Tower restaurant that he had courted Mary in London in 1944—thus, the name of this fictitious company was possibly another private dig at his wife. And he dedicated *Across the River,* the work inspired by Adriana, to Mary.)

The dementia that exacerbated his abusiveness, vulgarity, and insults in his last decade was the same process that also propelled his fantasies into unrealistic fears that finally distilled into delusion. He had met Adriana in 1948, and before ten years had passed their relationship was the focus of his paranoia. The sicker he became, the more demented his brain, the more he obsessed he became with the idea that he would be arrested at any moment for taking "indecent liberties with a minor." Thus, the fantasies that he earlier described in elegant fiction became a source of psychological torment.

Adriana was roughly Gregory Hemingway's age (they were one year apart), so she could have indeed been the daughter Ernest and Pauline had hoped for, but perhaps Adriana's psychological needs fit like a missing piece into the puzzle of Hemingway's world as well. Her father, Carlo, was planning on running for mayor of Venice at the end of World War II. But in the bitter and chaotic months after the war, he was murdered by his political enemies. His body was discovered by his son on June 12, 1945, in the rubble of San Michele.[7]

Adriana's older brother, Gianfranco, would win Hemingway's admiration as well, but for different reasons. He was wounded by the machine guns of a British Spitfire while serving as an officer in the Italian armored regiment at the battle of El Alamein, under the command of Erwin Rommel.[8] After recovering, he joined the OSS as chief of partisan activity in the Veneto region. He later served as a translation officer after the German surrender at Trieste. His heroics also included conducting a mafia-like vendetta that targeted his father's murderers. Despite this heroic and battle-tested résumé, Gianfranco was shy, unassuming, and quiet. After earning a law degree at the University of Padua (in 1947), he was off to Cuba in November 1949. He stayed as Hemingway's guest, sleeping in Finca's "white tower." Though he did take a job with a shipping company, he was also there to assist with the manuscript of *Across the River,* mainly correcting Italian names and geography. Hemingway arranged the financing of a farm in Cuba for Gianfranco and, in order to further help him financially, gave him a manuscript of *The Old Man and the Sea* in 1953.[9] He lived in the Hemingways' guest house for nearly three years and became quite close to Mary.

While Ernest addressed Adriana as "Daughter," Gianfranco was Mary's "Bunney" (mainly because of his short stature, but the affection is clear). And he proved more than just psychological ballast to Ernest's infatuation with Adriana, as one of Mary's notes to him reveals: "Bunney—Bunney—It is curious how it doesn't get any better—the hurting and longing in the bones and blood and skin and eyes and ears and nose. Sometimes, hurting strong, I ask myself 'Was it worth this—that joy, this misery?' And the answer is always 'Yes.' Dearest Huomino [little man]." Mary gave instructions that this note could be made public only after her death.[10]

Hemingway believed Adriana a successful artist in her own right. She illustrated "The Good Lion" and "The Faithful Bull," fables he wrote in 1950 for her small nephew and which appeared in *Holiday* magazine.[11] And her cover drawings for *Across the River* and *The Old Man and the Sea* appeared on their dust jackets. Yet they were submitted and accepted at Ernest's suggestion. The advertising and promotion director at Scribner's explained that "the jacket drawings for both these books as executed by 'A' were so bad that we had to have them skillfully redrawn. So what was on the jacket was not actually her original art, which was pretty abominable."[12] She published a book of her own poetry, *I Looked at the Sky and the Earth,* a work passed over by several publishers before she took the manuscript unannounced into the offices of Alberto Mondadori, who looked at it over the next few weeks and eventually agreed to its publication. Mondadori was one of Hemingway's two Italian publishers, and it's hard to accept that her work made it to press on the basis of its merits, as her poetry could have been written by any high school girl with a crush.

The last letter of Hemingway's to reach Adriana before the false reports of his death in Africa spoke of his desire to write another story of Venice: "the real story of their love," a difficult story of Venice, one that would be a truer account of their love, more sensitive, and certainly more discreet.[13] But *Across the River* had done enough damage. Adriana did indeed suffer from the scandal and gossip that resulted from being Hemingway's muse and the real Renata. She met him for the last time in his hotel room in Venice in 1954. He apologized for the trouble the book had caused her: "I am sorry about the book. You are the last person I would have done any harm to." He insisted she was not Renata and he was not the Colonel. On this last day, he again spoke tenderly of his affection for her and concluded "Probably it would have been better if I had never met you that day under the rain." By the end of the visit, both were in tears.[14]

Adriana would write her memoir, *La Torre Bianca* (The White Tower), in 1980 and, tragically, would hang herself from a tree on her family's farm near Capalbio at the age of fifty-three. She had attempted suicide two prior times, and her last attempt was not immediately successful. She was cut down and taken to the hospital, only to die a few hours later.

Hemingway would revisit his Adriana infatuation when he hired the nineteen-year-old Valerie Danby-Smith as his secretary; he insisted on her company at meals and bullfights throughout his travels in Spain and France in 1959. And, once again, his involvement with her would become a springboard for his dementia-driven paranoia. The young Irish girl with a light complexion and dark hair had been sent to Spain specifically to interview Hemingway. Her initial attempt at the interview was embarrassingly unsuccessful, so Hemingway gave her instructions on how to better conduct one. Afterward, he invited her to the Pamplona festival in July, and from then on she was officially part of his entourage.

Valerie did not have Adriana's pedigree or elegance, yet he found her attractive, and, unlike Hemingway's association with Adriana, there is evidence of his intimacy with Valerie beyond his usual paternal doting on young women. There was an obvious romantic intensity between them in public, and when Hemingway's Idaho friend and hunting buddy Forrest MacMullen was interviewed, he left no doubt that Ernest and Valerie were lovers.[15] It is understandable that Valerie would believe herself the subject of his later delusions of "indecent liberties with a minor," but there is no way of knowing if Hemingway was paranoid because of his affection for Adriana or Valerie or both. Whichever romance he was ruminating on, he was convinced that an arrest warrant was coming, sooner or later.

Whether or not they were lovers, by the summer of 1959 Valerie agreed to their tentative agreement and stuck by his side as a "secretary" at $250 per month. Mary questioned the arrangement, inquiring just exactly what she was expected to do. Eventually Valerie grew tired of the late nights and the heavy drinking, but, like Adriana, she would journey from reality to delusion in Hemingway's mind (unlike Adriana, she was bypassed in his fiction). Hemingway would obsess about her immigration status—believing that somehow he was the one responsible for her presence in the United States "illegally"—and this would become another major source of mental torment in his last two years. Though she was never in violation of immigration law, he feared he would be arrested for her situation at any moment.

She would eventually help Mary pack up the Cuba house and sort Hemingway's papers after his death. Valerie also spent time with his youngest son, Gregory, at Hemingway's funeral, and eventually married him (she was the third of his four wives). And, in 2004, she wrote her own memoir, *Running with the Bulls: My Years with the Hemingways*.

Between Adriana and Valerie, another young lady would capture Hemingway's attention, speaking volumes about his state of mind. The fantasies that were acted out and that were ignored by his wife and companions displayed a lack of inhibition consistent with a severe mental illness.

On safari in 1954, Hemingway announced to Mary at dinner that she was depriving him "of his new wife," a girl of Wakamba ethnicity from a nearby village. Mary took the issue in stride and, after inspecting her, suggested only that the young native girl needed a "proper bath." She then left Kimana by plane for two weeks of Christmas shopping in Nairobi. When she returned, she found that Ernest had shaved his head and begun hunting with a spear, had dyed his suede jackets and shirts the orange-rusty shades worn by the Maasai nomads of Kenya, and overall "had gone native" with a vengeance. He ignored the dangers of spearing a leopard out of a tree and chased it into the bush with a shotgun. The new wife, whom Ernest called "Debba," was on hand for all Christmas festivities (at one point she was chaperoned by her aunt).[16]

In Mary's writing about Ernest and Debba, it was her turn to be ambiguous, stating that the Christmas celebration at camp had gotten so "energetic" that the couple had broken her bed while she was away.[17] Ernest enjoyed his reputation as a polygamist among the natives, who recalled Pauline from his last safari. They assumed Mary was his fair "Indian wife" and Pauline his dark one. They even assumed he was married to "Miss Marlene" Dietrich, whose voice they heard on his portable phonograph and who worked for him in a "small amusement Shamba I owned called Las Vegas."[18] The title of Honorary Game Warden for the Kimana Swamp further fueled his narcissism, and he was soon out "half the night prowling with a spear."[19]

Five years later, Hemingway would report to his confidant, Hotchner, that he had "an African son" and added that he had gifted the bride's family a herd of goats, but Hotchner dismissed these statements as "typical EH fabrication."[20] In the original manuscript of his "Africa Journal," which would eventually be edited and published as *True at First Light,* Ernest's desires are certainly on full display: "I . . . went out to see Keiti . . . thanked him for the action he had taken as an elder and told him that I would approach the father of the girl Debba formally. He smiled very happily. Then I told him that if I had a child from the girl Debba he would have a choice of a career as a soldier, a doctor, or a lawyer or that he could go for his upbringing to the Kingdom of Mayito. If he wished to stay with me as a son and not have to make a career he could be my true son and we would hunt together."[21] The "Africa Journal" is indeed a fictionalized memoir, where lovely descriptions of Africa's landscape and wildlife are sparse and relationships and dialogue take center stage. On this platform for Ernest's fantasies, he projects a condescending acquiescence onto Mary, who says, "I think it's wonderful that you have a girl that can't read nor write, so you can't get any letters from her. . . . But you don't love her do you? . . . Maybe you like her because she's like me. . . . I like you more and I love you."[22]

As for Debba's appearance, the only description we have of her says that she was "a masculine-looking sturdy young woman—short of hair and square of face."[23] She was around fifteen years old and not nearly the Beatrice that Hemingway fantasized she was. One safari companion, Denis Zaphiro, a ranger with the Kenya Game Department, described her as "an evil-smelling bit of camp trash."[24] No matter, as it was the *idea* of a Debba that propelled Hemingway, regardless of the specifics of her physical presence. All that really mattered about her physically was that she existed. Perhaps Mary understood this at some level, as she had with Adriana.

But Hemingway's psychological need for a second (fertile) wife drove his disinhibited, head-first dive into native attire, custom, and ritual courting, as was spelled out plainly enough in a letter just a few weeks before he put away his "Africa Journal" for the last time: "Miss Mary who can't have children can have Debba to help her as a second wife. Debba can have children and they can be doctors, soldiers or lawyers as they decide. This all was cleared with the elders."[25] Desire and motivation were spelled out, like his journal, unedited. And Mary was his second in-fertile wife, following Martha, her predecessor. Hemingway claimed she had never shared this fact with him before or during their marriage and that he learned it only through a slip of the tongue by Charles Scribner. Ernest was furious, insisting that Charles should have told him this fact about Martha *before* they were married or simply never shared this fact. Scribner wrote to Ernest in 1950, essentially telling him that his memory was selective: "she [Martha] told me that you would not believe that it was possible for her not to have a baby when married to you, *no matter how much she explained it*" (emphasis added).[26]

As with any patient with disinhibition, unspoken and even uncon-scious desires are often pursued, as if the patient were propelled by forces he or she cannot articulate. Though Hemingway could articulate in letters his ideas regarding the fertility of each lover, it does not necessarily follow that he was insightful. What also speaks to the fact that his behaviors, and their documentation, reflect disinhibition in the pathological sense is his specific writing concerning Debba in his "Africa Journal" (later heavily edited and published as *True at First Light*). When she asks to hold his rifle after a killing, she says, "It was so cold. . . . Now it is so hot."[27]

As they ride next to each other in the Rover, he elaborates on how she enjoys pressing his pistol and holster against her thigh.[28] Hemingway's overt focus on libido more likely than not simply leaves his readers embarrassed for him. And at this point in his life he was worldly, presumed to be mature, and long accepted as one of history's greatest writers. Such adolescent sexuality would, one hopes, never have seen the light of day if the "Africa Journal" had not been published after his death. He never expected the manuscript to be published in this form. One might expect, or at least hope, that he would have deleted these passages, but the fact that they are there in the rough draft is worrisome enough.

But do these behaviors reflect disinhibition to a pathological degree or simply a man indulging in himself and his freedom and exploring unabashed desires? Certainly alcohol played a role. He was drinking two or three bottles of hard liquor a day and wine with meals.[29] At one point he was so drunk that he fell out of a "fast-moving" Land Rover.[30] Whatever the mixture of motivations, it was clear that no matter how inappropriately or even bizarrely he acted, there were no negative consequences. No one, not even a man as respected and mature as Philip Percival, who had led safaris for Teddy Roosevelt and Churchill, among others, was willing or able to put limits on his behavior.

Just as discrete amnestic episodes (periods with sudden onset but lasting a only brief time during which a person in his fifties or sixties simply goes blank, becomes confused, and cannot recall what he is doing, such as where he is driving) are harbingers of a dementia to come, similar periods when one becomes disinhibited and oblivious to social norms and appropriate behavior are also harbingers of a future decline into dementia.

Another display of social inappropriateness occurred in September 1956, after Ernest and Mary had made the trip across the Atlantic on the *Ile de France*. His friend the screenwriter Peter Viertel arranged a luncheon with some of his Hollywood friends. At a sidewalk café, he dined with Audrey Hepburn, Rita Hayworth, and Mel Ferrer. An older gentleman approached the famous group and asked for autographs to give to his daughter, and all complied except Hemingway, who said, "Sir, you look to me to be a c--ksucker." No laughs, only a cold silence from the sophisticated ladies, forcing Hemingway to at least offer an apology.[31] Either blasting Mary or ignoring her was one thing, and even erupting at friends was not uncommon, but vulgarity directed at an elderly stranger was a different matter. Perhaps the worst crime was subjecting the doe-eyed and eternally innocent Audrey to such unpleasantness.

A recurrent theme in Hemingway's late-life paranoia was the FBI and its continual "surveillance." The G-men enjoyed great power and stature in the minds of Americans in the first half of the twentieth century—the FBI men of newsreels and movies were the ultimate authoritative and stealth operatives in the collective unconscious of Hemingway's generation. Robert Oppenheimer was another contemporaneous genius who was tormented by near continual FBI surveillance. But, unlike Hemingway, Oppenheimer was not delusional.

Since Hemingway's FBI file has been made available thanks to the Freedom of Information Act, it has become commonplace to argue that he was *not* paranoid, just astute and observant. But the mere fact that he had a file was not unusual for a celebrity of his era, particularly given his connections during the Spanish Civil War. With a terrible case of stage fright that even an afternoon of drinking could not quell, he took the stage at Carnegie Hall on June 4, 1937, at an event sponsored by the communist-dominated League of American Writers. The audience was also going to see the film *The Spanish Earth* (at that point, without a soundtrack). The only other speakers that night were Earl Browder, secretary of the Communist Party USA, and Joris Ivens, Stalin's operative, who was posing as an independent filmmaker.[32]

But what he feared was not the existence of a file containing information or associations but that he would be arrested for indecent contact with minors, for Valerie's immigration violation, for his undeclared gambling winnings, and for less well defined crimes he termed "the rap on him." He also feared surveillance—that FBI men were recording him. Later in life he even feared that they were doing so from his bathroom.

Thus, the existence of a file does not negate his paranoia. His delusions were independent of its existence, and he was not under surveillance. Yet, since the issue is Hemingway's paranoia, it is worth examining his FBI file in detail.

The first entry in the file is a memo to Director Hoover, dated October 8, 1942, reporting that Hemingway had been residing in Cuba almost continuously for two years and that he was on "friendly terms" with Consul Potter and the Second Secretary of the Embassy and had met the ambassador on several occasions: "At several conferences with the Ambassador and officers of the Embassy late in August 1942, the topic of utilizing HEMINGWAY's services in intelligence activities was discussed. The Ambassador pointed out that HEMINGWAY's experience during the Spanish Civil War, his intimate acquaintances with Spanish Republican refugees in Cuba, as well as his long experience on this island, seemed to place him in a position of great usefulness to the Embassy's intelligence program. . . . The Ambassador further pointed out that HEMINGWAY had completed some writing which had occupied him until that time, and was now ready and anxious to be called upon."

The memo's writer also noted that "any information which could be secured concerning the operations of the Spanish Falange in Cuba would be of material assistance in our work, and that if HEMINGWAY was willing to devote his time and abilities to the gathering of such information, the results would be most welcome to us." Hemingway must have been delighted—he was officially a spy.

The next memo reported that, while in attendance at a jai alai match with Hemingway, the agent was introduced to a friend of Hemingway's as "a member of the Gestapo." The agent quickly told Hemingway he didn't appreciate the remark, "whereupon he promptly corrected himself and said I was one of the United Sates Consuls." The FBI men proved to have long memories, and the Gestapo remark is reiterated several times in the documents that follow.

A memo from 1942 focused on his possible communist leanings, explaining that Hemingway "engaged actively on the side of the Spanish Republic during the Spanish Civil War" and also that "Hemingway, it will be recalled, joined in attacking the Bureau early in 1940, at the time of the 'general smear campaign' following the arrests of certain individuals in Detroit charged with violation of Federal statutes in connection with their participation in Spanish Civil War activities." While in Spain, Hemingway was on the antifascist side of the fence. By default, that meant he (like so many other artists) was acting out the script of Stalin's operatives in the conflict. *The Spanish Earth,* the film he screened with President and Mrs. Roosevelt and for which he was proud to be the public face, was made by Joris Ivens, an operative from Stalin's Comintern. Yet, with regard to Hemingway's current communist leanings, a memo from December 1942 states that "Hemingway has been accused of being of Communist sympathy, although we are advised that he has denied and does vigorously deny any Communist affiliation or sympathy."

But, as that memo continued, it was clear the bloom was off the rose: "Agent Leddy stated . . . the extreme danger of having some informant like Hemingway given free rein to stir up trouble such as that which will undoubtedly ensue if this situation continues. . . . Hemingway is going further than just an informant; he is actually branching out into an investigative organization of his own which is not subject to any control whatsoever." Hemingway had "apparently undertaken a rather involved investigation with regard to Cuban officials . . . including . . . [the] head of the Cuban National Police . . . the Cubans are eventually going to find out about this if Hemingway continues operating, and that serious trouble may result."

In another letter, the "organization" created and controlled by Hemingway was described as "unknown for its reliability or trustworthiness." Two days later, J. Edgar Hoover sent a letter consisting of five brief paragraphs in response to his agent, Ladd, who had warned of the risks Hemingway posed: "Certainly Hemingway is the last man, in my estimation, to be used in any such capacity. His judgment is not of the best, and if his sobriety is the same as it was some years ago, that is certainly questionable. However, I do not think there is anything we should do in this matter, nor do I think our representative at Havana should do anything about it with the Ambassador. The Ambassador is somewhat hot-headed and I haven't the slightest doubt that he would immediately tell Hemingway of the objections being raised by the FBI. Hemingway has no particular love for the FBI and would no doubt embark upon a campaign of vilification." In retrospect, Hoover's insights were impressive.

Hoover next read that "The Legal Attache at Havana expresses his belief that Hemingway is fundamentally hostile to the FBI and might readily endeavor at any time to cause trouble for us. Because of his peculiar nature . . . Hemingway would go to great lengths to embarrass the Bureau if an incident should arise." The agent further cited Hemingway's prestige as a literary man and his influence on public opinion. Hoover responded, "I see no reason why we should make any effort to avoid exposing him for the phoney [sic] that he is." He was prepared to "meet him head-on" if it meant protecting the Bureau's interests.[33]

By 1943 the last of these memos was written. One interesting entry stated, "A clique of celebrity-minded hero worshipers surround Hemingway wherever he goes. . . . To them, Hemingway is a man of genius whose fame will be remembered with Tolsty [sic]." The remainder of his file includes newspaper clippings, a brief description of a petty dispute he had with a columnist, and a great deal of information on Gustavo Durán, who had commanded a brigade in Spain and was described as an "active member of the Communist Party . . . during the Spanish Civil War." Durán first met Hemingway in Paris, where Durán was studying music in the 1920s. Hemingway even shared a hotel room with him in New York prior to turning over his manuscript of For Whom the Bell Tolls to Scribner's. Durán was entrusted with correcting his Spanish and critiquing the plot (while suitemates, he noted Ernest's early breakfasts of gin and tea). Years later, Hemingway recruited him for a major role in his "intelligence gathering" in Cuba. Hemingway trusted Durán without reservations, but it was obvious the FBI had concerns.

The FBI also understood that Hemingway's hunts for Nazi subs in Caribbean waters were nothing but quixotic drinking parties at sea, during which grenades were tossed into the water for sport. He never encountered a submarine but had unwisely stockpiled an impressive arsenal in the *Pilar*'s holds that he eventually had to jettison after the Cuban revolution (as he realized he no longer had a good explanation for the stash of weapons).

Thus, the information in the file as it existed was certainly not news to him. He could have guessed its contents on the basis of his own experience and contacts with the FBI men. And the surveillance he feared was related to delusions that began fifteen years after these entries were made. What is lacking (or perhaps largely blacked out) in his FBI file is an extensive discussion of his support for Fidel Castro shortly after what Hemingway called "a good revolution," an "*honest* revolution." Castro claimed, "We took *For Whom the Bell Tolls* to the hills with us, and it taught us about guerrilla warfare." When Castro won a fishing tournament in May 1960, Hemingway presented the prize to him. He told journalists he hoped for the best, that the people of Cuba, the "people who are being shot," deserved it. And "This is a very pure and beautiful revolution so far—Naturally I do not know how it will come out."

These statements did prompt the American Embassy in November 1959 to notify the State Department of Hemingway's words to the press: "1. He supported [the Castro government] and all its acts completely, and thought it was the best thing that ever happened to Cuba. 2. He had not believed any of the information published abroad against Cuba. He sympathized with the Cuban government, and all *our* difficulties. 3. Hemingway emphasized the *our*, and was asked about it. He said that he hoped the Cubans would not regard him as a *Yanqui* (his word), but as another Cuban. With that he kissed the Cuban flag." When asked to kiss the flag again for the cameras he quipped, "I said I was a Cuban, not an actor."[34]

But Hemingway was no true fan of Castro. He was simply a man trying to protect his Cuban home, his art collection, his boat, and the most valuable thing he had—a stack of unpublished manuscripts.

Another noteworthy absence from the file is a report on the two-hour visit from the Soviet minister of trade, Anastas Mikoyan, to Hemingway's home, the Finca, in February 1960. The Soviets were courting Castro, and courting Hemingway seemed like a good PR move. The minister had brought Russian translations of Hemingway's writing and promised royalties that had been long frozen in the Soviet Union. Hemingway insisted he could not accept such payment unless all other American authors were paid for their work that had been translated for Soviet readers. Though certainly well into his downward spiral, he could still sniff out when he was being used, and he wanted no part of it.

The only entry in his FBI file that coincides with the treatment of his mental illness is a well-meaning but fumbling gesture by his own psychiatrist, who, unbeknownst to Hemingway, one day contacted the agency to help dispel his patient's delusions of FBI surveillance.

There are many delusions that are hallmarks of dementing illness. One interesting form of psychosis is a version of "Capgras Syndrome." This involves the delusion that family members or others close to the patient have been replaced with imposters or body doubles and that the "real" individual is missing somehow. This bizarre concern is seen in some patients with head injuries as well. Perhaps the mind is trying to make sense of the fact that things do indeed seem very different through the prism of illness. For all of the delusions already discussed in connection with Hemingway's demise, this one is certainly absent, which is in some ways surprising. For a period of time in the 1930s, Hemingway did in fact have an imposter. There was a doppelganger of sorts, a man who traveled the country, reading and signing books and presenting himself as the one and only Ernest Hemingway. He even left unpaid tabs in Hemingway's name. According to Leicester's memoir, he didn't look very much like Ernest and even showed up at the family home in Oak Park, nervously asking to see Grace. Hemingway didn't seem particularly troubled at the time by his antics, until many of the bills he incurred were forwarded to Key West.[35]

Patients with severe depression may hear a voice call their name or think they hear someone at the door—any number of minor hallucinations can occur, and they resolve with adequate treatment of the depression (usually without requiring an antipsychotic drug and often with just an antidepressant and psychotherapy). When very severe, the delusions associated with depression are quite bizarre; for example, patients may assert that they are "already dead." These delusions are "mood congruent," meaning that their content is overall in keeping with the illness of depression. Hemingway's delusions were quite diverse and more typical of his dementia than of the depressive illness of his final two years. And there is no evidence that he ever suffered hallucinations.

Though not yet incapacitated by his illness, the ever-observant old newsman was quietly keeping tabs on his demise through the 1950s. While in Venice after his Africa plane crashes, Hemingway met with the Italian poet Eugenio Montale, who left an elegant snapshot of the great man, all too aware of the slippery slope he was treading:

> Farfarella, the garrulous porter,
> loyal to his orders,

said it was forbidden
to disturb the man, the lover
of bullfights and safaris.
I beg him to tell that
I'm a friend of Pound's (exaggerating somewhat)
and deserve special treatment.
Who knows . . . he picks up the phone,
talks, listens, talks again,
and Hemingway the bear takes the bait.
He's still in bed.
From the fur of his beard pierce only
eyes and eczema.
Two or three empty bottles
of Merlot, avant-garde of the many
to come. Down at the restaurant
they are all at the table.
We do not speak of him, but of
our dear friend Adrienne Monnier,
Rue de l'Odéon. Sylvia Beach, Larbaud,
the roaring thirties and the braying
fifties. Paris, London
a pigsty, New York stinking,
pestiferous. No hunting
in the marsh, no more wild ducks, no
more girls, not even the idea
of such a book.
We make a list of mutual friends,
whose names I don't know. All's rotten,
decayed. Almost in tears
he asks me not to send
any people of my sort, still less
if they are intelligent. Then he gets up,
wraps himself in a bathrobe
and shows me to the door with a hug.
He lived a few more years, and
dying twice, had the time
to read his obituary.[36]

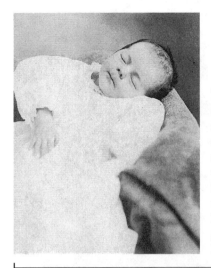

The newborn Ernest weighed nine and a half pounds and measured twenty-three inches, with thick black hair and dimples. His mother wrote that "The robins sang their sweetest songs to welcome the little stranger into this beautiful world." Photograph copyright unknown, reproduced courtesy of the Ernest Hemingway Collection Photographs, John F. Kennedy Presidential Library and Museum.

Of the Hemingways in this 1906 family photo, three would commit suicide: Dr. Hemingway, Ernest, and Ursula (and eventually Leicester, born in 1915). Ernest understood his genetic burden, writing to his mother-in-law when he was thirty-seven that the Pfeiffer bloodline was needed to "breed some of the suicidal streak out of" his children. Photograph copyright unknown, reproduced courtesy of the Ernest Hemingway Collection Photographs, John F. Kennedy Presidential Library and Museum.

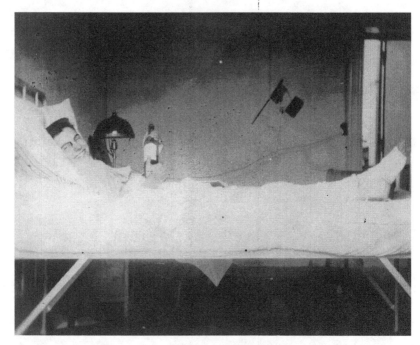

Hemingway proudly displaying his stash of booze while recovering from his World War I injuries. The Red Cross hospital occupied the fourth floor of an elegant mansion near the cathedral in Milan, and the head nurse was less than amused when his wardrobe was discovered to be filled with empty cognac bottles. The pattern of alcohol intake was set at a young age. Always a complex mixture of contradictions, Hemingway was described by nurses as "impulsive, very rude, 'smarty,' and uncooperative," yet he was also relying on his good looks and charm to help excuse nearly any mischief. Photograph copyright Henry S. Villard, reproduced by permission of Dimitri Villard, courtesy of the Ernest Hemingway Collection Photographs, John F. Kennedy Presidential Library and Museum.

Elizabeth Hadley Richardson was nearly eight years older than Ernest when they married, and she was matronly in appearance even as a young woman. Writing *A Moveable Feast* at the end of his life forced him to reconsider Hadley and his infidelity. Hemingway described her as the heroine of the book, and this final work can be viewed as his last act of contrition. Photograph copyright unknown, reproduced courtesy of the Ernest Hemingway Collection Photographs, John F. Kennedy Presidential Library and Museum.

On the basis of its grouping in the Hemingway Archives, it appears this elegant nude of Hadley from their Paris years was still in Ernest's possession at the time of his death. Photograph copyright unknown, reproduced courtesy of the Ernest Hemingway Collection Photographs, John F. Kennedy Presidential Library and Museum.

Pauline, Hemingway's second wife, was four years older than Ernest. At times, she looked more adolescent boy than young woman. Androgyny was a recurrent theme in Hemingway fiction. Photograph copyright unknown, image reproduced courtesy of the Ernest Hemingway Collection Photographs, John F. Kennedy Presidential Library and Museum.

Hadley and Pauline were close and for a time knowingly shared Ernest's affection. Pauline liked to crawl into bed with the couple at Shruns and Juan-les-Pins in 1926. Pauline would later befriend Mary as well. As the Hemingway expert Burwell noted, only Martha, married to Hemingway for five years (November 1940 to December 1945), "would not engage in the gender-bending antics that he found erotic." Photograph copyright unknown, reproduced courtesy of the Ernest Hemingway Collection Photographs, John F. Kennedy Presidential Library and Museum.

Hemingway had no qualms about displaying his scar from the Paris skylight accident. He believed that the injury was transformative and freeing, that it had unleashed his pent up creativity: *A Farwell to Arms* followed the trauma. Photograph by Helen Breaker, reproduced courtesy of the Ernest Hemingway Collection Photographs, John F. Kennedy Presidential Library and Museum.

Though referred to by archivists as "Hemingway with an unknown African woman," this photograph is likely the only known image of his "Wakamba wife, Debba." She was believed to be sixteen, and, unlike his attachments to his other late-life female companions, Adriana and Valerie, his affection for Debba was more archetypal than romantic. Photograph by Earl Theisen, © 2014 Roxann Livingston/Earl Theisen, used with permission, reproduced courtesy of the Ernest Hemingway Collection Photographs, John F. Kennedy Presidential Library and Museum.

On safari in 1954, Hemingway "went native," dying his clothes like a local, hunting with a spear, and pursuing Debba. In hindsight, that is, with the benefit of a correct neuropsychiatric diagnosis, he was disinhibited because of his use of alcohol and the early phase of dementia. Photograph copyright unknown, reproduced courtesy of the Ernest Hemingway Collection Photographs, John F. Kennedy Presidential Library and Museum.

This photograph of Hemingway, Robert Capa, and their driver, Olin Tomkins (center), was taken near St. Lo. Hemingway suffered three more concussion during his World War II days, one in London and two in France. The photograph was contributed to the Hemingway Archives by Captain John Ausland, who had a distinguished military and postwar career and published *Letters Home: A War Memoir* in 1993. The photographhgraph is reproduced courtesy of the Ernest Hemingway Collection Photographs, John F. Kennedy Presidential Library and Museum.

This Yousuf Karsh photograph, more than any other, solidified Hemingway as iconic and provides for millions the mental imagery conjured when his name is mentioned. Photograph copyright Yousuf Karsh, used by permission of Julie Grahame, North American Representative, Estate of Yousuf Karsh, and reproduced courtesy of the Ernest Hemingway Collection Photographs, John F. Kennedy Presidential Library and Museum.

Mary and Ernest were closing out their 1954 safari with sightseeing, and while they were photographing Murchison Falls, their plane struck abandoned telegraph wires and crashed. This was the first of two crashes, the second more fiery and violent, that left Ernest with multiple injuries. He was assumed dead after the second crash, and many of his obituaries mentioned he had always "sought death." Hemingway asked, "Can one imagine if a man sought death all his life he could not have found her before the age of 54?" (6). Copyright unknown, reproduced courtesy of the Ernest Hemingway Collection Photographs, John F. Kennedy Presidential Library and Museum.

Battered and burned, Hemingway is recovering after his Africa plane crashes. What no camera or x-ray could show was the cumulative damage to his central nervous system. Image reproduced courtesy of the Hemingway Collection Photographs, John F. Kennedy Presidential Library and Museum.

Mary Hemingway and Castro during her 1977 return trip to Cuba. She was pleased with her negotiations that rescued Ernest's manuscripts shortly after his death, but she burned letters and manuscripts that she believed would have embarrassed him. Copyright unknown, reproduced courtesy of the Hemingway Collection Photographs, John F. Kennedy Presidential Library and Museum.

Gianfranco and Adriana Ivancich pictured in Cuba. Gianfranco lived in the guest house at the Finca for nearly three years and rushed to Mary's side upon learning of Ernest's death. Copyright unknown, reproduced courtesy of the Hemingway Collection Photographs, John F. Kennedy Presidential Library and Museum.

Ernest and Adriana in a lighthearted moment. Copyright unknown, reproduced courtesy of the Hemingway Collection Photographs, John F. Kennedy Presidential Library and Museum.

Hemingway was drawn to the majesty of Kilimanjaro, and begins *The Snows of Kilimanjaro* with a reference to its sacredness. Copyright unknown, reproduced courtesy of the Hemingway Collection Photographs, John F. Kennedy Presidential Library and Museum.

Free Fall

Chapter 5

Scott Fitzgerald once described Hemingway as having the quality of a stick that's been hardened in a fire. Of course, if left in the fire too long, the stick will crumble. The last four years of Hemingway's life were certainly his least content and his most stressful, and easily the most difficult for Mary as well. He was crumbling. But there was still the international travel, the writing, the quasi-employees hanging on, and very little peace of mind. And all the while the restless mind still propelled the body, sometimes purposefully, sometimes in anxious circles.

In 1956 he was off to Spain, crossing on the *Ile de France* again and drinking far too much. When friends brought their concerns to Mary, she responded, "What can I do? He didn't marry a policeman. It's better if I let him alone."[1] She knew instinctively (or at least by this point in their marriage) that exorcising a devil was much more difficult than living with one. Nagging or not, he did what he chose—why stir up more trouble? In order to survive as the last Mrs. Hemingway, she accepted her role as the quiet enabler—and the more Ernest incapacitated himself, the more he needed her. The flask he was carrying, full of "splendidly aged Calvados," was engraved "From Mary with Love."

Not long after arriving in Spain, Ernest paid a visit to a writer he had always admired—the Basque novelist Pío Baroja y Nessi. He owned seven of Baroja's novels and believed the 1954 Nobel Prize had been awarded to the wrong man. He told him as much when he visited his deathbed: "I am convinced that you deserve the Nobel Prize much more than many writers who won it—myself first of all, for I am more or less just another of your disciples." Hemingway brought the dying man a bottle of Scotch, as well as some socks and a sweater, both made of cashmere. He also gave him an inscribed copy of *The Sun Also Rises*. When Baroja died, three weeks later, Hemingway followed the funeral procession through the flower-lined streets—it was October 30, and the flower sellers were readying for All Souls Day.[2]

Hemingway had played his role perfectly—he was the grateful student and admirer paying homage and humbling himself. He wrote a touching description of the burial in a letter to Harvey Breit dated November 5, 1956, and couldn't resist including a dig at his old friend and enemy, Dos Passos: "We buried Don Pio Baroja last Tuesday. It was very moving and beautiful. I'll tell you about it. Thought Dos Passos or *some* Americans could have sent some word. . . . He was a hell of a good writer you know. Knopf dropped him, of course, when he did not sell. The day was misty with the sun breaking through and burning off over the bare hills and on the way out to the un-consecrated ground cemetery the side of the streets were jammed solid with flowers, the flower sellers stands for Nov 2—All Soul day, and we rode out to the cemetery through the country he wrote about. . . . There were not too many of us. He was buried in a plain pine coffin, newly painted black so that the paint came off on the faces and the hands of the pall bearers and on their coats."[3] Ernest was particularly moved by this last detail, which ends his letter.

Though not nearly as robust as he had been only two years earlier, and with the travel taking its toll, he nonetheless began planning another safari. He was also hoping to take along his favorite matador for the six-week Africa trip, as well as his son, Patrick. But Hemingway's health continued to deteriorate.

His blood pressure was 210/105 (which was actually an improvement from his Cuba reading of 215/125), and he suffered nosebleeds. X-rays showed "an area of inflammation around the aorta," and his Spanish doctor told him to reduce his alcohol consumption.[4] He was also instructed to eliminate fatty foods, and his doctor forbade sexual activity. He also forbade the Africa trip—yet Hemingway ignored the dictate and continued his planning anyway. Only when Gamal Abdel Nasser, the president of Egypt, closed the Suez Canal was the trip cancelled, as a journey around the Cape of Good Hope would prove far too lengthy—and result in a poor ratio of travel to hunting.

And so, it was on to Paris as a consolation prize. And though the Lost Generation had long scattered, the Ritz Hotel had a surprise waiting for him—two trunks had been sitting in the hotel's basement, reportedly since 1928, stuffed with newspaper clippings, notebooks filled with Ernest's longhand, pages of typed fiction, even books, sweatshirts, and a pair of sandals. The stash is thought to have inspired the series of sketches that would become *A Moveable Feast.* "It's wonderful," he said to Mary, looking up from one of the trunks, and added, "It was just as hard for me to write then as it is now."[5] He knew his skills had regressed to the point at which writing was again a struggle—not from inexperience, as in the early 1920s, but from a decline in cognitive functioning—a mental decline on which he was quietly keeping tabs.

Ernest had forgotten many of the names from the café days when he and Hadley were "very poor and very happy" and became careless with dates and geography, yet he plowed ahead on his Paris sketchbook from the fall of 1957 to the spring of 1958.

He had been thinking about this very work at least since 1933, when he wrote to Maxwell Perkins in his typical grandiose way, "I'm going to write damned good memoirs when I write them because I'm jealous of no one, have a rat trap memory and the documents. Have plenty to write first though."[6] In fact, Hemingway had been forming the work over the ensuing decades, recalling and revising (both consciously and subconsciously) his Paris history and his literary apprenticeship. He had no idea that there would be trunks in Paris awaiting his return more than twenty years later, yet these newly found documents, and even their very *existence*, would be debated for decades.

Despite the inspiration of the Paris trunks, real or imagined, as 1957 progressed his obsessions about his health would turn fatalistic. When an elevated cholesterol level was reported (at 408), he was sure his death was imminent. His inflamed aorta progressed to an enlarged aorta, no doubt the result of his erratic blood pressure. He became more ruminative and fearful and more depressed. The cycle was obvious: stress and worries about his ailments further compromised his health, leading to more anxiety. On the *Ile de France,* crossing the Atlantic homeward, he was given cholesterol-lowering medication, high doses of B vitamins by injection, treatment for his eczema, and blood pressure medication by the *Ile*'s doctor, Jean Monnier, who also instructed Ernest, "You must *stop drinking alcohol. . . .* I understand that it might be harsh, even painful at the beginning, but you must gradually reduce your drinking to nothing." His new doctor in Havana concurred: "Rest, mild exercise, restricted diet, altered medication, and no alcohol."[7]

By March 1957, irritable, depressed, and with an enlarged liver, he was forced to give up liquor, but he continued to drink wine. His famous quip about a life without alcohol being akin to driving a race car without motor oil dates to this period, and he also remarked that it was "a bore not to drink, and very hard to take bores without something to drink."[8] Hemingway echoed a complaint that is not uncommon in the newly sober.

It was in this state of strained semi-abstinence that the Armenian-born photographer Yousuf Karsh found Hemingway in 1957. He had been sent to Cuba by *Life,* whose editors had hoped to coax an autobiographical article from Hemingway that would accompany his photos. Karsh described his subject as "the shyest man I ever photographed."[9] Such a demeanor more than likely indicated a depressed state of mind. Only in his last few years, with dementia and depression progressing, was he ever described as "shy." But the photo that resulted was instantly iconic. In fact, the mental image most have of Ernest Hemingway is this very photo or is at least partly influenced by Karsh's portrait: Ernest in his burly turtleneck sweater with the suede front. Mary had purchased the sweater in Paris the year before from the Christian Dior boutique as a Christmas gift.[10] One result was that Karsh's future subjects demanded that they too wear sweaters for their portraits. The portrait has been described as "biblical" and "Moses-like," and its weighty presence is undeniable. Yet the clues to his demise are also evident: the famous scar on his left forehead is still visible, there is a heaviness above his eyelids, and his eyes peer out at slightly different angles, indicating a degree of neurological damage. It is challenging to view and consider a familiar photograph with a fresh eye, but Hemingway conveys a profound sadness, which is only partly veiled by the distraction of the image's recognizability.

By the fall his cholesterol was down to 208 from the peak of 428, and his weight had dropped 17 pounds, down to 203. He had stuck to his pledge of only wine for about two months, but he still ruminated about his finances, and as the violence led by Fidel Castro and Che Guevara came closer to his doorstep, Hemingway's stress level understandably rose. The whisky returned, and the wine limit was gone. The alcohol, combined with the Doriden, a barbiturate, left him sedated and falling asleep in his chair in front of guests by early evenings.[11] And Mary, also in need of antianxiety medication, was taking one Doriden to Ernest's two pills per dose. It was more than clear that it was time to leave Cuba. He was not being unduly frightened, he would explain to Patrick, given the murders he saw around him every day. The rebels, when they took over, would be no better than the dictator's Fulgencio Batista's henchmen. He and Mary were off to the safety of Ketchum.

He was in his fifty-ninth year when the cross-country ride to Idaho began. The Hemingways rode with their friends Betty and Otto Bruce and stopped frequently for food at local grocery stores. His preferred drink during the ride was Scotch and lime juice. The 1958 World Series was their entertainment. The couples heard the play-by-play action as the Yankees become only the second team in history to rally from a 3-1 deficit to win a Series. Whitey Ford and Warren Spahn squared off for the first game, and the names of other baseball greats and future Hall of

Famers—Mantle, Berra, Aaron, Larson, Bauer, and Mathews—helped pass the miles. All the while, Ernest nibbled on cheese and pickles and sipped his Scotch.

Paranoia struck in Cody, in an unlikely spot. As the car pulled into a motel one night, which seemed safe enough and certainly clean, Ernest was spooked. He insisted they move on but never fully explained what he had found so ominous about the place. In a lighter moment, but not a particularly amusing one for Hemingway, a group of children at a restaurant was asked who the famous bearded man was. "Burl Ives!" they announced.[12]

Once in Idaho, he began hunting, usually daily. He was able again to swing with the birds, and, unlike during his recent Africa shoots, when his heavy drinking had compromised his marksmanship, he was back to impressing others with his skill. Initially they rented a home but soon found one to purchase. It was on a hillside flanked by tall aspens and cottonwoods. Another photographer visited him while in Idaho, though his official assignment was to get some shots of Mary in her kitchen. She had become skilled at cooking the various fish and game Ernest and his friends brought home, and *This Week,* a syndicated Sunday supplement magazine, hoped to get one of her wild-game recipes and a picture of her preparing the dish.

The photographer, John Bryson, felt very welcome and stayed on in Ketchum for several days rather than fly back to L.A. after his shoot. He even walked with Hemingway to the Sun Valley Lodge, where he observed him holding court in the bar. On one of these walks, he caught Ernest kicking a beer can down the road, which playfully told the world that there was still some life in the old man. Hemingway liked the picture and asked for several copies to send out as gifts. But more telling than this sprightly image is the photo from either late 1958 or early 1959 (Bryson had stayed over five days around the New Year holiday).[13] It shows the same neurological features as the Karsh photo a year prior, but the hint of sadness has evolved into a vacant stare.

While Bryson was enjoying the Hemingways' hospitality, before sunrise on New Year's day 1959, Batista flew out of Cuba for the last time with somewhere between $300 and $700 million. Hemingway wished Castro luck—fortunately, a friend had written to inform that so far Finca was safe. But, despite the peaceful country life in Idaho, Hemingway couldn't stay put for long—he decided that he must again spend the summer in Spain. The official excuse was a bullfighting article commissioned by *Life,* but for another Spanish summer, another "dangerous summer," he needed little prodding. And he was feeling better physically, his weight, cholesterol, and blood pressure had all dropped, and he was limiting his alcohol—but he was still declining mentally.

He and Mary left in mid-March and first rode across country with Hotchner at the wheel. Ernest even drove between New Orleans and Key West. Next they flew to Cuba, where the victorious Castro was planning an American tour for April. Ernest even lunched with Tennessee Williams at the Floridita in the older section of Havana. Williams came late, confessing later that he feared Ernest "usually kicks people like me in the crotch."[14] Yet Hemingway was more than civil, and both enjoyed the time together and the conversation. In Spain they were the guests of Bill Davis, a wealthy expatriate whom Hemingway had known for twenty-five years. His estate, La Consula, would be their home base. Ernest and Mary were given adjoining rooms on the second floor, and Ernest's balcony overlooked the gardens and the courtyard. The estate had a sixty-foot swimming pool. Ernest's room was equipped with a writing table and his preferred stand-up-style desk. "Anyone who couldn't write here couldn't write nowhere," he said.[15]

Hemingway planned to follow the bullfights of Antonio Ordóñez and his rival, Luis Miguel Dominguín. The two were actually brothers-in-law. It was during this trip that he met Valerie Danby-Smith and dragged her into his entourage, carousing into the night. His language was unusually obscene, and his anger outbursts and cruelty toward Mary would also peak. Perhaps his worst display was at his sixtieth birthday party, which Mary had arranged on the Davis estate, an extravagant affair with an orchestra, flamenco dancers, fireworks, and even a shooting gallery. He ridiculed Mary and blamed her for spending too much money on the party (though he knew she had paid for most of it with *her* article for *Sports Illustrated*) and even erupted at his old World War II pal Lanham.

The bullfighters were both gored, first Dominguín, then Antonio, and both were hospitalized. After visiting Antonio, Ernest and Valerie set out from San Sebastian for Madrid, with Davis at the wheel. They crashed when the right front tire blew out, demolishing the front of the Lancia. Though no one was hurt, Hemingway was badly shaken. By the next day, he decided that he had had enough. The country life was again calling.[16]

During the voyage back he received a note from a thirty-seven-year-old writer who was working on a biography of Scott Fitzgerald. He hoped to interview Hemingway or at least chat with him about his old friend. Like Fitzgerald, Andrew Turnbull had also attended Princeton, and he first saw his subject when he was only eleven. His biography would begin, "One evening in the spring of 1932 I was walking with a friend down the

lane of my family's country place outside Baltimore. As we approached
La Paix, the old house on our property that had just been rented again,
we noticed a man sitting motionless on the high front steps. Alone and
pensive . . . the stranger was the new tenant my parents had been talking
about; he was Scott Fitzgerald." The famous tenant obviously liked the
young boy and even took him to Princeton football games and encouraged him in his sports and writing. It's not surprising that the boy became
Fitzgerald's second biographer, but he received no help from Hemingway.
He ignored Turnbull's request for most of the trip, as he was nursing a
cold (and a slight fever) in his cabin, but he finally consented to a meeting
on their last day at sea.

Turnbull had one kind recollection of Hemingway, that "a great dignity flowed from his tall lurching frame and his sad mask of a face,"
and his other remarks were also telling. Hemingway's official biographer,
Carlos Baker, summarized the meeting as follows: "Turnbull shared the
view of another passenger that there was something 'staged and put on'
about Hemingway. . . . Like many others he was struck by the 'meager-
ness' of the bare forearms, the 'delicacy' of the features 'above the froth
of beard,' and the whites of his eyes, which were veined with red. His
conversational manner was shy and wistful, he was not very helpful about
Fitzgerald, and his eyes flicked over Turnbull with 'a kind of grazing dif-
fidence.'"[17] During the trip he had even informed Turnbull by a note that
he was "trying to write a little about him [Fitzgerald] when I knew him."
Hemingway's worn-out briefcase contained the manuscript that would be
edited to A Moveable Feast, which at this point contained at least three
sketches on Fitzgerald. None were flattering. Still, this was the treasure
Turnbull was seeking. Hemingway was always secretive about his writing, and now he was paranoid—there was never a chance he would have
shared.

Hemingway docked in New York and lodged in a fourth-floor apartment on the Upper East Side, at 1 East 62nd, with a view of Central Park.
He isolated himself, expressing the fear that he was "being tailed." Next
he was off to Cuba for the famous flag-kissing episode, then a drive to
Idaho with Antonio and Carmen Ordóñez, showing off America along
the way. Antonio was especially impressed with Las Vegas. Ernest had
hoped to take the bullfighter hunting, but his sister needed him in Mexico. The frantic message relayed some unspecified domestic crisis (as it
turned out, Antonio's sister was separating from her husband), and the
couple quickly departed, leaving their Jamaican cook behind. Soon after,
Mary fractured her left elbow in a fall while duck hunting with Ernest
and Dr. Saviers, and the break was so severe that it required an extensive

two-hour operation. On the way to the hospital, the pain was excruciating, and Mary began to groan. Ernest callously said, "You could keep that quiet. . . . Soldiers don't do that."[18] And once Ernest was her caretaker, he never let Mary forget it. He grumbled about the errands and assistance he was forced to provide and all the while plotted yet another trip to Spain.

Prior to leaving for Europe, he stayed in New York in late July 1960. He was again literally penned up in the East 62nd Street apartment, fearing that "They're tailing me out here already. . . . Somebody waiting out there."[19] He set up a flimsy card table in a corner of the main room and used it as his office, and he rarely left. He received Charles Scribner there but did venture out to lunch with Lenny Lyons and Hotchner. And he did manage a visit to an eye doctor, but he was essentially a prisoner of his delusions. He also began obsessing about Valerie's immigration status and repeatedly called the Office of Immigration in Key West, assuring them she was only a "visitor" in the country. When Hotchner discussed the offer of $100,000 from Twentieth Century Fox to adapt the Nick Adams stories, Ernest insisted he should hold out for $900,000.[20] His once impressive business savvy had deteriorated, and he was possibly having grandiose delusions as well as paranoid ones.

Once again, the same writing assignment, the bullfighting installments for *Life,* was his justification for a trip he shouldn't have planned and never should have taken. Still, he kept insisting that the matador, Ordóñez, simply "needed him there." For this trip he flew to Lisbon and then on to Madrid, and just the time change was extremely disruptive— Ernest found himself overly fatigued and struggling. The body requires time to recalibrate to a new time zone; the general rule is one day per hour. Even if Hemingway was fully adjusted to East Coast time when he left, he would need five days to adjust to the Spanish time zone. His circadian rhythm, his body's early-morning cortisol pulse, and his level of alertness and energy all needed time to adjust. Dementia made the shifts delayed, partial, and disjointed—it was a significant psychological and biological shock to his damaged brain. He was struggling even before the plane landed.

While in Europe, he was extremely depressed, as his friends noted; his memory was shot, he was consumed with guilty ruminations, and he complained of cramps and nightmares. He wrote to Mary that he wished she were there to protect him from insanity. He further wrote: "I don't know how I can stick this summer out . . . am so damned lonesome . . . only thing I'm afraid of, no, not only thing, is complete physical and nervous crack-up from deadly overwork." She must have surmised that the other "things" he feared were driven by his delusions. He concluded, "I wish you were here to look after me and help me out and keep [me] from cracking up."[21] He agonized over the installments of the bullfighting articles for *Life*, which were expanded and published posthumously in book form as *The Dangerous Summer*, and genuinely felt he had made a "mess of it." When he saw the September 5, 1960, issue of *Life*, with his forced but pleasant grin, he described it as "the horrible face on the cover" that "made him sick."[22]

His paranoia surfaced again with a vengeance. He was inquisitive and suspicious of everyone and everything. Even bullfighting was corrupt and "unimportant." His installments were criticized for seeming to favor Antonio in the ring, and for the first time he seemed very affected by a negative reaction to his work. The bad karma spread, Antonio suffered a concussion in the ring, and Carmen suffered a miscarriage. As for his longtime friend and host, Bill Davis, he was repeatedly trying to murder Hemingway, or so the delusion went. A car wreck in 1959 proved as much; Bill was at the wheel again for this trip, with Ernest in the passenger's seat, wide-eyed and hypervigilant, aware of the "death by motor vehicle accident" plots. Valerie was sent to help as best she could, but Ernest insisted, "Did you notice how Davis is driving? He's trying to kill me."[23] And the ever trustworthy Hotchner soon made the journey, but even his calm presence failed to reassure Ernest. In public, he could not control his irritability; he railed at waiters at his favorite restaurant, the Callejón, and stormed out before the luncheon with friends was over.

Whether he lodged at the Davises' estate, La Consula, or in a hotel room, he stayed in bed for days, and his delusions, when he expressed them, had become essentially random. He feared he would not be allowed to board the plane with all of his luggage, and he was so convinced of this that Hotchner had to get a signed statement from the airline to reassure him (he and Mary tended to travel with extensive baggage, of course, at a time when no limits were imposed by airlines). His friends wanted to send him home, the sooner the better. But Hemingway delayed his return for four days, unable to even get out of the bed—he was paralyzed by fear and exhaustion. To the relief of all, he finally agreed to a midnight flight home.

The word most often used to describe Hemingway in the weeks that followed was "fragile." The vigorous man was gone, and a pale, thin-limbed, tentative shadow of his past self was what friends and visitors were so shaken by. He must have felt some relief being home at last, but soon the delusions, particularly of FBI surveillance, would bore in again on his depressed and compromised brain. He refused to talk to Hotchner inside, as all the rooms were surely bugged, so he insisted they speak only outdoors, away from the FBI's listening devices. The delusions were multiplying—he expressed to his confidant Hotch that undeclared gambling winnings were causing him trouble with the IRS, that hunting on private land would bring the sheriff any minute, that the government was aware of Valerie's immigration status—and then there was a persistent fear of arrest for "taking indecent liberties with a minor," a sad and tender hangover from the Adriana days.

When he grazed a car in a parking lot, he was sure he'd be arrested at any moment, despite the owners reassuring him the damage was minor and telling him not to worry. He told Mary he couldn't afford the hillside home they desired, with its spectacular mountain views, owned by Dan Topping, because he had no way to pay the taxes. She reached one of the bankers on the phone to reassure her husband that he did indeed have a substantial balance, but he refused to believe it. The vice president at Morgan Guaranty in New York "was confusing us. . . . He's covering up something," he told Mary.[24] When she asked what he could possibly be hiding, like a true paranoiac he replied, "I don't know. But I know."

A letter he had posted to his bank must have been taken as a prank: he explained that he did not have much opportunity to visit the bank as much as he should, though he had held an account with Morgan Guaranty for around thirty years. He also noted that all future calls would be identified with his serial number, o–363, because it was easy to remember and was "not the correct one which a con man might have. A con character would say 364. So we will make it 363. . . . This is getting too much like OSS so if anybody wishes to know whether it is actually Hemingstein speaking I will answer that I am a friend of David Bruce." He signs it "Ernest Hemingway o–363." The postscript reads: "This letter, of course, opens it wide for any con man to destroy us so please commit it to memory and destroy it. EH."[25]

What is remarkable is that this letter is dated March 11, 1955, *more than five years* before Mary found it necessary to call Morgan to reassure Ernest. Clearly his illness was an ongoing process, not an acute event. By 1960 he even believed his mail was being read by postal authorities. Even his favorite project, and perhaps the only work that qualified as an obsession, *The Dangerous Summer,* was a source of anxiety, as he feared it would only bring libel suits. The photographs used for the second installments were somehow unfair to the matadors, and they exposed Hemingway as a "double-crosser" and a fool.

There was no doubt he needed treatment, but where he should get it and how to get him there secretly were the questions. The fact he would receive psychiatric care not only was to be kept from the public but would have to be withheld from the patient himself. When Dr. Saviers discussed the possibility of Hemingway checking himself into the Menninger Clinic, he refused: "They'll say I'm losing my marbles."[26]

International Trips during the Last Decade of Hemingway's Life

November 19, 1949: New York to Le Havre / *Ile de France*

March 22, 1950: Le Havre to New York / *Ile de France*

June 24, 1953: New York to Le Havre / *Flandre*

August 6, 1953: Marseilles to Mombasa / *Dunnottar Castle*

March 1954: Mombasa to Venice / *Africa*

Late May or early June 1954: Genoa to Havana / *Francesco Morosini*

April 1956: Havana to Peru / air

May 1956: Peru to Havana / air

August 1956: New York to Le Havre / *Ile de France*

January 1957: Le Havre to New York and Mantazas, Cuba / *Ile de France*

Late April or early May 1959: New York to Algeciras / *Constitution*

Late October 1959: Le Havre to New York / *Liberté*

August 1960: New York to Madrid / air

October 1960: Madrid to New York / air

(Adapted from Meyers, *Hemingway*, 578)

Stigma

Chapter 6

The stigma attached to mental illness was powerful during most of the twentieth century. Hemingway was born at the end of the Victorian era, when a common pastime was a walk through an insane asylum to gawk at the random antics of warehoused psychotics, for whom effective treatment was decades out of reach. In the 1800s, London's Bethlem Royal Hospital, known as Bedlam, would open its doors for Sunday strolls, charging one penny per entry; so popular was the viewing that the usual take was £400 per year. Hemingway showed a sensitivity toward psychiatric difficulties (not only in his writing but also in his life) *only* if that illness was the result of combat service. The stigma attached to other forms of psychiatric illness resonated in his letters and fiction. As the shell-shocked Nick Adams put it in 1932, "It's a hell of a nuisance once they've had you certified as nutty. . . . No one ever has any confidence in you again."[1]

Hemingway had written elegantly of battle fatigue, or shell shock, the precursors to posttraumatic stress disorder, or PTSD. And, in every decade of his writing life, he displayed in his works flawless insights regarding women with borderline personality disorder (Brett Ashley, Margot Macomber, and, in his forties and fifties, while creating Catherine Bourne of *The Garden of Eden*). Still, one's own "nuttiness" was another matter altogether. In his defense, until about 1925, once a patient was admitted to a psychiatric facility, there was only a 25 percent chance that the person would ever be released. Many Americans of Hemingway's generation knew of townspeople who had suffered psychotic symptoms and been sent to asylums, never to be seen again.

By his sixtieth year, two of his sons had received electroconvulsive therapy, or ECT, Patrick in 1947 and Gregory in 1957. And many of his friends had suffered tragic deaths—Capa had stepped on a landmine in

Indochina in 1954 and died in a field hospital, still clutching his camera. A girlfriend from his Michigan youth, Katy Smith, who married John Dos Passos, was described by Hemingway just after her death in a letter as "an old girl of mine, had known her since she was 8, and Dos drove her into a parked truck and killed her last Sat. . . . Looks as though our Heavenly Father was perhaps dealing off the bottom of the deck."[2] Katy was almost completely decapitated in the horrific wreck, and Dos lost an eye. And a pal from Paris, Evan Shipman, died of pancreatic cancer in 1957; the unique smell of cancer was noted in Hemingway's memoirs during Shipman's last visit with him in Cuba.

One of the more dramatic deaths was that of Harry Crosby, whom Hemingway had met during his Paris years and who had accompanied him to Spain in 1927. Crosby had driven an ambulance in World War I and survived Verdun and battles near Orme, after which he was awarded the Croix de Guerre. After the war, he plunged headfirst into a lifestyle of extreme hedonism, one that has probably never been rivaled since. He abused cocaine and hashish and became addicted to opium, and his near continual sexual exploits sadly sometimes involved underage individuals. Crosby was the heir to a fortune made in Boston banking, and he spent it lavishly. He edited and published some of the Left Bank writers in the 1920s, including Hemingway (his Black Sun Press published an edition of *Torrents of Spring* in 1932), but the two were never particularly close. Still, Hemingway referenced his bizarre end in a letter to Fitzgerald in 1929: "Did you know Harry Crosby who shot himself yest? He told me about this girl before he went to N.Y. Mac Leishes introduced her to him. He was a hell of a good boy and I feel awfully bad today about him."[3]

The "girl" was his mistress, Josephine Bigelow, whom he shot (or who shot herself) as they lay in bed, fully dressed, in a borrowed apartment at New York's Hotel des Artistes. Two hours later, Harry put a bullet through his right temple. He was found with the pistol still in his hand and a picture of a thireen-year-old North African girl, a victim of his past exploits, in his wallet. Crosby had made a suicide pact with his wife, Polly, and strangely equated true love with such an arrangement; the day before his death, his final journal entry was "One is not in love unless one desires to die with one's beloved."[4]

Scott Fitzgerald wrote Hemingway in November 1940, "It's a fine novel [*For Whom the Bell Tolls*], better than anybody else writing could do. . . . I'm going to read the whole thing again. . . . I envy you like hell and there is no irony in this." He even mentions Martha Gellhorn in an overly generous manner: "I hear you are marrying one of the most beautiful people I have ever seen."[5] And he signs it "With old affection." Scott was living in Hollywood with the gossip columnist Sheilah Graham at the time. Six weeks after he wrote to Ernest, Scott collapsed in their apartment and died from his third heart attack.

The way Hemingway processed various tragedies was documented in his letters. And he once claimed his analyst was his "portable Corona No. 3."[6] Yet when those in his past or present circles suffered from the insidious tragedy of mental illness, his response ranged from silence to derision. Not only did Hemingway meet Fitzgerald, Shipman, Crosby, and Dos Passos during the Paris years; he also met James Joyce, who died after surgery for a perforated duodenal ulcer in 1941 in a Zurich hospital. In 1953 Hemingway described Joyce as "the best companion and finest friend I ever had."[7] Once he read *Ulysses*, he voiced the opinion that Joyce was the "greatest writer in the world."[8]

During their last night in Paris, Ernest and his new wife, Pauline, dined with Joyce and his wife, Nora, a meeting famous not only for the unique meal (they dined on venison and pheasant Hemingway had shot just the day before in the Sologne) but for the conversation.

A melancholic Joyce asked Hemingway his opinion of his work: were his books too "suburban? . . . that's what got him down sometimes." Before Ernest could answer, Nora chimed in: "Ah Jim could do with a spot of that lion hunting." Joyce replied, "The thing we must face is I couldn't see the lion."[9] These words have keep Lost Generation scholars busy for decades—with regard not to the superficial understanding of Joyce's ever-failing eyesight but to his metaphorical blindness in comparison to Hemingway, who wrote as he lived and lived what he wrote about. But Joyce's primary distraction that night was not his "suburban" books (an unusual self-indictment for a modernist) but rather his daughter, Lucia.

At the time of the dinner party, Lucia Joyce, a schizophrenic, had been unstable for months. She was at times mute and catatonic and at other times violent. Twice she set fires, once in her Geneva hospital room (because her "father's complexion is very red and so is fire") and once while staying at an aunt's home (this time simply because she "wanted to smell burning turf"). She moved in and out of various sanatoriums or stayed with nurses or sometimes with extended family. She even was examined by Carl Jung, who was her twentieth psychiatrist. But in the days before antipsychotic medication, even his analysis was of limited benefit. Joyce, like many parents in his situation, was often in denial. He spoke of Lucia in public as if she were fully sane, and, further, he convinced himself that she was clairvoyant, citing evidence that her psychotic utterances were predictions of future events rather than disorganized ramblings.[10] Joyce suffered depression, insomnia, and even auditory hallucinations under the strain of his daughter's instability. If Hemingway was aware of Lucia's struggles, he never commented on them, but he could see the toll they were taking on his finest friend.

Sherwood Anderson, the accomplished writer who recommended Hemingway move to Paris to begin his literary career, turned to writing full time after a psychotic break. Despite being a successful businessman and seemingly in complete control of his manufacturing company, he arrived at his office one day, mumbled something to his secretary about his feet being wet and "getting wetter," and walked out. He was found amnestic and confused four days later in a drug store and was checked into a hospital.[11] Roughly a decade later, he had three novels and two collections of short stories in print and was about to meet the unpublished Hemingway, who was dreaming of similar success.

The influence of Anderson on Hemingway's fiction and on his very path in life is well known. Hemingway had read *Winesburg, Ohio* in the summer of 1920, before they ever met. That meeting took place in Chicago when Ernest was basically freeloading at the expense (and at the mansion) of their mutual wealthy friend, Y. K. Smith in 1921. Anderson encouraged him to live and write not in Italy but in Paris and provided him with letters of introduction to Gertrude Stein, Sylvia Beach, Lewis Galantière, and Ezra Pound. It is also well known that Hemingway parodied Anderson's style in his novel *Torrents of Spring*, a work written primarily to extricate himself from his contract with Anderson's publishers, Boni and Liveright.

Many biographers assume that his parody of Anderson's style was a typical Hemingway double-cross—a knife in the back of a friend. Yet Hemingway tried to hedge his gamble and kept Anderson informed of the strategy—it was simply too early in his career to burn this important bridge. And at the end of May 1926, the very month *Torrents* was released, he wrote to Anderson from Madrid: "It goes sort of like this: 1. Because you are my friend I would not want to hurt you. 2. Because you are my friend has nothing to do with writing. 3. Because you are my friend I hurt you more. 4. Outside of personal feelings nothing that's any good can be hurt by satire."[12] After this series of contradictory and convoluted excuses he observed, "Anyway I think you'll think the book is funny—and that's what it is intended to be—"

Much to Hemingway's relief, they dined together in Paris eight months later, and "He was not at all sore about Torrents and we had a fine time."[13] For three decades Hemingway never disparaged Anderson and never called attention to his history of psychosis. His silence on the matter was Hemingway's version of gratitude. But by 1953, he broke his silence, writing that "Sherwood Anderson was a slob. Un-truthful (not just inventing untruthful; all fiction is a form of lying) but untruthful in the way you *never* could be about a picture. Also he was wet and sort of mushy." Still, these harsh judgments are essentially about the man's work, not the man, but (as with his self-contradictory statement from 1926 when he seemed to be describing how he was not hurting Anderson while he was busy hurting him) he further added, "He had very beautiful bastard Italian eyes." In this instance, in much the way he would later disparage Scott Fitzgerald, he feminized Anderson (and still managed to sneak in the word "bastard"). "From the first time I met him I thought he was a sort of retarded character." And a few days later, Anderson was still on his mind as he wrote, "Sherwood was like a jolly but tortured bowl of puss turning into a woman in front of your eyes."[14]

It was 1956, and Hemingway was well into his decline. Though he could not articulate it, he was in the early stages of dementia. His fears were obvious, and at this moment he was about to begin work on his Paris sketches, which turned his mind to the mentor who had sent him to that city. Hemingway's denial was so entrenched that he avoided terms such as "crazy" or "psychotic"; rather, he conflated Anderson with one of his (Anderson's) characters, a grotesque.

The only variety of mental illness for which Hemingway seemed to have any compassion, and even reverence, was shell shock. Upon returning home after the war, he was able to convince a Boyne City doctor in 1919 that he was "badly shell-shocked." Ernest did report some difficulty sleeping, but if he claimed to be experiencing nightmares and anxieties, he was really just claiming stories heard during his Milan hospital days as his own.[15] Lying is too harsh a judgment; he was simply practicing his lifelong vocation of fictionalizing his life. His attitude was expressed well in a passage from "The Education of Mr. Bumby," in *A Moveable Feast*: "'It would be no disgrace if he had been demolished mentally by the war,' I said. 'Many of our good friends were. Later some recovered to do fine things. Our friend André Masson the painter.'"[16]

After the war, Masson would share a Paris studio with Miró, and the three forest landscapes Hemingway acquired from him now hang at the John Fitzgerald Kennedy Presidential Library and Museum in Boston. No doubt Hemingway felt some kinship with Masson, who also served in World War I and who managed to survive a bullet that pierced his chest— and in the delirious state of shock that quickly followed he saw the sky as "a 'torso' of light," the world around infused with "wonder." Masson didn't fall but stood dazed and feeling no pain, thinking, "I fear nothing any more." He was dragged to the safety of a hollowed-out bomb crater by another soldier. He huddled next to a dead German, whom he called "Ramses II," as he had been there so long that he appeared mummified. When nightfall came and he was finally taken to a hospital, he was still too psychotic to allow treatment. "Then began the long succession of hospitals, fits of rage, revolts, refusal to accept treatment, and finally the psychiatric hospital where he was confined," according to his biographer. As with Hemingway, critics would cite Masson's war trauma as central to his art: "The war scarred him deeply. . . . The art of Masson was to be a meditation on this disorder."[17]

In a deleted fragment of writing Hemingway expressed his full sympathy for any soldier so affected: "In those days it was no disgrace to be crazy, but, on the other hand, you got no credit for it. We, who had been at the war, *admired* the war crazies since we knew they had been made so by something that was unbearable. It was unbearable to them because they were made of a finer or more fragile metal or because they were simple and understood too clearly" (emphasis added).[18]

This passage, in context, contrasts Fitzgerald's ignoble mental anguish with that of the warrior, even if a simpleminded one. Thus, Hemingway was no stranger to mental illness. It is likely that as a child he heard his father speak of patients who suffered from psychiatric conditions, and he may have even encountered them during his father's workday. General practitioners see numerous psychiatric comorbidities, as they are ubiquitous in their patient populations (and were especially prevalent at a time when there were so very few effective treatments). His father's specialty of obstetrics no doubt involved cases of postpartum depression (which affects around 20 percent of women after delivery) and possibly postpartum psychosis (which affects one in one thousand). But, of all of his friends and acquaintances who quietly (or publicly) struggled with psychiatric issues or who seemed bent on outdoing one another with dramatic endings, there were four specific individuals whose lives and difficulties helped solidify the adult Hemingway's denial of his own illness.

It was September 1931, while sailing to the States on the *Ile de France*, that Ernest and Pauline met Jane and Grant Mason. Pauline was into her seventh month of pregnancy with their second child, Gregory. Grant Mason was a Yale graduate who ran Pan American Airways in the Caribbean and who held a substantial interest in Cuban Airlines as well. His wife, Jane, was just twenty-two, with a model's beauty; she was described as having "a perfect oval face . . . strawberry-blond hair parted in the middle and drawn back . . . large blue eyes."[19] She was also an avid sportswoman. She loved fishing for marlin off Cuba and hunting big game in Africa, dabbled in art and sculpture, and could hold her liquor—even keeping pace with Hemingway, according to mutual friends. To sum up Jane and Ernest, each was the moth, each was the flame.

As if Jane's being young, vivacious, beautiful, and fond of the same sporting life as her husband wasn't enough for the tired and pregnant Pauline to be concerned about, the Masons also lived in Cuba. They resided just thirty minutes west of Havana, on an elegant estate in the Jaimanitas suburb, and employed nine servants (including a Chinese cook, an Italian butler, a Cuban chauffer, and a German gardener). Their "pets" included not only dogs, parrots, flamingos, and peacocks but also a fox, a honey bear, and a monkey. Grant traveled frequently as his job demanded and, being generally unassertive, didn't try to rein in his wife in any way. During the 1930s, Pauline was often with her sons at the Key West home, where the peacocks that strutted around the yard were a gift from Jane. Ernest, according to one of his sons, "used to cuckold Mother unmercifully in Havana with an American lady friend."[20] They first made love one spring evening in 1933. Ernest and Jane were both staying at the Ambos Mundos hotel, and Hemingway had just started knocking out a piece for *Esquire* about marlin fishing when he heard a gentle taping on his window. He was staying on the top floor. Jane had walked the fifty-foot-high ledge (that stuck out two and a half feet) to climb through his window and wasted no time sprawling on his bed, claiming she was "just in the neighborhood."[21]

Pauline tried to compete, even dying her hair blond like Jane's and writing to Ernest that she was "having large nose, imperfect lips, protruding ears and warts and moles all taken off before coming to Cuba. Thought I'd better, Mrs. Mason and those Cuban women are so lovely."[22] Pauline was easily the most attractive of Hemingway's four wives, but, as with most affairs, it's about not wanting what you already have (and the corollary). Despite Pauline's awareness, the rendezvous continued.

While Jane was driving her Packard with two of Hemingway's sons and her own adopted child as passengers near the airport in Havana, a bus ran them off the road, and they rolled down a forty-foot embankment. The car landed on its wheels, and no one was seriously hurt. But a few days later, Jane jumped from her second-story balcony. It seemed unrelated to the car incident; in fact, it seemed completely unprovoked. Grant believed it was more a manipulative act than a real suicide attempt; he referred to it as her "jumping out of our home in Jaimanitas at an altitude, all her friends agreed, which would be reasonably impressive as an effort at suicide but not high enough to cause death or serious injury. . . . As I remember it, she went off a second story balcony. . . . I do not think the accident was directly related to anything currently happening with Ernest or me or with anyone else but just one of her changeable fits of elation and depression. In case she tried another such stunt, I arranged for constant nurse attendance and then shipped her to New York on a Ward Line vessel with special bars on the portholes."[23] Hemingway couldn't resist, privately joking to Dos Passos that Jane was the girl who "fell for him literally."[24] This was at least her third suicidal gesture.

Jane suffered vertebral fractures, and after spending five months in hospital she wore a back brace for a year. Of course, these circumstances prohibited any relationship with Ernest, but, even when she had recovered, he had seen enough of her instability. Curiously, her psychiatrist, Lawrence Kubie, had been hired by the *Saturday Review of Literature* to write psychoanalytical reviews of some of Hemingway's books (those written between 1924 and 1933). He naively wrote to Hemingway, in an oddly bombastic fashion, thinking the writer would somehow approve and aid in the effort.[25] Even before the American Psychiatric Association published a Code of Ethics, it was obviously a violation of boundaries and trust to explore Jane's intimacy with Ernest and to use the evidence to discuss Hemingway's "sexual conflicts." Fortunately, Kubie's work remains less than a mere footnote, as the literary analysis he did produce is not only worthless but also embarrassing to the psychiatric profession.

When Jane and Ernest parted ways for good, in April 1936, the end of the relationship was described as a "violent and bitter break." Just four months earlier, in January, Ernest had complained of "facing impotence, inability to write, insomnia and was going to blow my lousy head off."[26] By the spring, he had recovered enough to participate in a fishing tournament (and Jane chartered a boat to compete with him). He was also, by then, well into "The Short Happy Life of Francis Macomber." Jane, of course, was the physical and psychological basis for Margot Macomber, who cheats on her husband, mocks him as a coward, and "accidentally" blows his head off. There are several theories as to why the affair ended; mainly it's speculated that Pauline had had enough. But Ernest was a quick study, and by this time it was obvious that the risks outweighed the rewards.

During the 1950s, as Hemingway's illness progressed, he was often reminded of the psychiatric struggles of another friend as he was repeatedly lobbied to support Ezra Pound's release from St. Elizabeth Hospital in Washington, D.C. Pound was confined for more than twelve years, and to this day his exact diagnosis remains elusive. What makes Pound's case so difficult for physicians to categorize is that his full-blown psychosis was seemingly the result of ever-evolving eccentricities, rather than a discrete, neatly categorized episode. Hemingway appreciated this aspect of his illness, elaborating on "our knowledge of how he went nuts, how gradually and steadily he became irresponsible and idiotic." And both Hemingway and Joyce noticed the worsening of Pound's erratic behavior as early as 1933. They concluded that their former mentor and the tireless champion of their work had lost his grip on reality.

The three men had arranged a dinner together, and it was the last time Pound would see Joyce. According to Hemingway, "Joyce was convinced that he was crazy then and asked me to come around when Pound was present because he was afraid he might do something mad. He certainly made no sense then and talked as utter rot, nonsense and balls as he had made good sense in 1923."[27]

During the 1930s, Pound voiced his support for Mussolini and his brand of fascism. Hemingway wrote to his friend, trying his best to dissuade him from a political stance that could only end up as a public humiliation or worse. Though Hemingway's letter was sincere, accurate, and thoughtful, Pound was too ill to accept the advice. He fired back, insisting Hemingway move his money to Italy and ridiculed him for "killin . . . pussy cats, however titanic, that ain't got no guns to shoot back with, you god damn lionhunter." He wanted Hemingway to save his ammo for usurious financiers, "the buggars back at the Bank of Paris."[28] There was no stopping Pound—he was manic and obsessed, and these conditions robbed him of the insight that he was ill. He began making shortwave radio broadcasts from Italy. His rants were characterized as anti-American and anti-Semitic. In practical terms, few if any people heard them, fewer understood them, and any rational listener would have concluded that the speaker was deranged.

Once the Allies controlled Italy, Pound was taken into custody by the U.S. military, which, misunderstanding his situation, was actually quite eager to help. Though he was handcuffed, he believed he was headed for a plane to the States, where he would aid his government by sharing his intimate knowledge of the Italian situation. He was instead imprisoned and charged with treason. When he was taken to his holding cage, he thought it was just a temporary stop. And, as he realized over the next few weeks that he was there to stay, he was truly mystified. The military had constructed one of its Disciplinary and Training Centers, or DTCs, outside Pisa, for its most recalcitrant offenders. It also served as a temporary jail for the most violent criminals, such as rapists and murderers who were awaiting transfer to the United States for federal trials.

Pound was held in a primitive "tiger cage," which was essentially a dog kennel of only 100 square feet. It had a concrete floor and a sloped roof, so there was minimal protection from the elements. Though he was not a violent man, his cage was reinforced with metal strips used in the construction of runways. Other prisoners were given basic army pup tents to protect them from the rain and sun, but for a period of time Ezra was denied even this flimsy shelter, and he slept on a stack of rain-soaked blankets. The sun scorched him during the day, and searchlights kept him up at night. He was already delusional, and the brutal conditions forced a complete psychotic break. His head, he later reported, simply felt "empty."[29]

Pound was eventually brought to U.S. soil. Though his holding conditions were more humane, he never fully recovered, and he still faced a serious charge. Many of the colleagues he had helped in the 1920s did not forget or betray him, and once Archie MacLeish had arranged for Robert Frost and T. S. Eliot to support Pound's release, Hemingway also agreed to sign the letter. MacLeish then pleaded his case to the attorney general: "Sure I signed it," Hemingway said. "Pound's crazy. All poets are. . . . They have to be. You don't put a poet like Pound in the loony bin. For history's sake we shouldn't keep him there."[30] But Hemingway was too astute to accept the myth that all poets are by necessity psychotic, though this is a common defense of Pound—that his genius was so eccentric as to be otherworldly (even one of his psychiatrists described him as having been a "peculiar individual for many, many years").[31]

Hemingway realized that Pound's support of Mussolini and his misguided cheerleading for fascism were clear signs of illness, and the medical vocabulary with which he defined it was no less accurate than that of Pound's own psychiatrists. In 1943, Hemingway wrote to MacLeish while Pound was still in Italy, engaged in rambling "anti-American" broadcasts, and asked MacLeish, "Will you please send the photostats of Ezra's broadcasts that you have? Whenever the damned business comes up we will probably be called on, or should be called on, and I think should know what it is all about. If Ezra has any sense he should shoot himself. Personally I think he should have shot himself somewhere along after the twelfth canto although maybe earlier. He has certainly lived with very little dignity for a man who gave his allegiance to a government simply because under that government he was treated seriously. But it is a *pathological business all the way through* and he should not be punished on any other basis" (emphasis added).[32]

When MacLeish had complied with Hemingway's request, he wrote back, "Thanks for sending the [photo]stats of Ezra's rantings. He is obviously crazy. I think you might prove he was crazy as far back as the latter Cantos. He deserves punishment and disgrace but what he really deserves most is ridicule. He should not be hanged and he should not be made a martyr of. He has a long history of generosity and unselfish aid to other artists and he is one of the greatest of liveing poets. It is impossible to believe that anyone in his right mind could utter the vile, absolutely idiotic drivel he has broadcast. His friends who knew him and who watched the warpeing and twisting and decay of his mind and his judgment *should defend him and explain him on that basis.* It will be a completely unpopular but an absolutely necessary thing to do. I have had no correspondence with him for ten years and the last time I saw him was in 1933 when Joyce asked me to come to make it easier haveing Ezra at his house. Ezra was moderately whacky then. The broadcast are absolutely balmy. . . . But you can count on me for anything an honest man should do" (emphasis added).[33]

Hemingway's stance is clear. Being an "honest man," he had not forgotten his debt to Pound, and ultimately he made good on his promise, signing MacLeish's letter. But he also fully understood Pound to be psychotic and understood that his behaviors were driven by his illness. Hemingway even knew this was essentially Pound's only defense. Yet, despite these insights, he wrote that Ezra was still deserving of "punishment, disgrace, and mostly ridicule."

Hemingway also wrote to Pound's lawyer, Julien Cornell, in 1945, telling him that he had known for many years that Pound's mental condition was far from normal. Pound was deemed too psychotic to participate in his own treason trial and was never expected to recover. Thus, he was held for more than a decade on the basis of the Kafkaesque argument that he was awaiting a trial that could never occur because he would always be too insane to participate. Given the charge of treason, he simply couldn't be released, though everyone involved agreed he posed no danger to the public. Pound suffered from a bipolar disorder, and he was one of the 5 percent of bipolar patients who spend their lives in a "hypomanic" state, an abnormal and expansive mood but still a blunted form of mania. He did have bouts of mania, as well as delusions, and his obsessions were more fodder for his pressured, restless mind. Later in Pound's life, the manias burned out and left him facing depressive and catatonic phases. Though not a member of the Lost Generation, he functioned as Manet did for the Impressionists—as the older mentor. Yet he outlived Joyce, Eliot, and Hemingway.

One year and nine months after Hemingway penned his reply to MacLeish, Pound would be caged, warehoused, and suffer more punishment, disgrace, and ridicule than Hemingway could imagine. Pound would sit for more than a decade in what Hemingway called "the loony bin." However, true to his word, and helping in any way he could, Hemingway sent

Pound a check for $1,000 in 1956. Pound had it set in Plexiglas to use as a paperweight. He said he didn't need the money.

And, of course, there was Zelda Fitzgerald, who said she heard flowers talking to her and whose psychosis was evident to Hemingway from their first encounter; after spending time with her at the Fitzgeralds' Paris apartment in 1925, Hemingway didn't even wait for Scott to return. As they passed in the hallway of the building, he said, "But Scott you realize, don't you, that she's crazy?"[34] He saw Zelda as poison to Scott: "A man who suffers from a woman . . . has a more incurable disease than cancer. . . . A woman ruined Scott. It wasn't just Scott ruining himself. But why couldn't he have told her to go to hell? Because she was sick. It's being sick makes them act so bloody awful usually and it's because they're sick you can't treat them as you should. . . . You can always trade one healthy woman in on another. But start with a sick woman and see where you get. Sick in the head or sick anywhere."[35]

Ernest had no difficulties trading in perfectly healthy women for newer models. And, curiously, he had first elaborated this same theme as an even younger man, three years before meeting Scott and Zelda, when writing to his friend Ezra Pound in 1922. He knew that Ezra and T. S. Eliot were close. He also knew that Eliot had been recovering from depression and writer's block in Lausanne *and* that Eliot's wife suffered from a psychotic disorder (probably schizophrenia) when he wrote: "I am glad to read of Herr Elliot's [sic] adventure away from impeccability. If Herr Elliot would strangle his sick wife . . . he might write an even better poem."[36]

Zelda's brother, Anthony, committed suicide by jumping from a hospital window in Mobile, Alabama, when Zelda was thirty-three.[37] He had been hospitalized specifically for psychiatric treatment. And Zelda was frequently suicidal, attempting to throw herself in front of a train on one occasion and at times catatonic; she required multiple hospitalizations through her life. To Hemingway, she was the ruin of Scott, forever trying to "put him out of business," and not just because she was psychotic. He wrote to Scott just after the publication of *Tender Is the Night*, telling him that "I liked it and I didn't like it." And also: "Of all people on earth you needed discipline in your work and instead you marry someone who is jealous of your work, wants to compete with you and ruins you. It's not as simple as that and I thought Zelda was crazy the first time I met her and you complicated it even more by being in love with her and, of course you're a rummy." It seems a letter from Ernest was worth a year of therapy.

And Zelda was no fan of Hemingway either, his machismo being a caricature to her (she even told Scott that his friend was "a phony").

Yet, when suffering from psychotic episodes, she often expressed her delusional belief that her husband and Ernest were guilty of an ongoing homosexual affair—perhaps fueled by the fact that Ernest and Scott frequently teased each other in public with homosexual innuendos in mock-effeminate voices.

The shorthand understanding of the Fitzgeralds was that Scott drank because Zelda was psychotic and that Zelda was psychotic because Scott was a drunk. Scott stated this plainly in a letter from 1932: "Perhaps fifty percent of our friends and relatives would tell you in all honest conviction that my drinking drove Zelda insane—the other half would assure you that her insanity drove me to drink. Neither judgment would mean anything. The former class would be composed of those who had seen me unpleasantly drunk and the latter of those who had seen Zelda unpleasantly psychotic. These two classes would be equally unanimous in saying that each of us would be well rid of the other—in full face of the irony that we have never been so desperately in love with each other in our lives. Liquor on my mouth is sweet to her; I cherish her most extravagant hallucination."[38]

Zelda's psychotic disorder would have manifested itself with or without Scott's alcoholism, and Scott needed no excuses to lift a glass. The last sentence represents denial of delusional proportions. Scott was pretending he was not the very caricature of the drunkard who is alternately disruptive and pathetic—and he strangely romanticized his spouse, who had one of the most torturing of illnesses. In 1933, Scott told one of Zelda's doctors that "I am perfectly determined that I am going to take three or four drinks a day." If he followed doctors' advice and quit drinking altogether, he explained, Zelda and her family "would always think that that was an acknowledgement that I was responsible for her insanity."[39]

Zelda wrote to her sister in 1947: "I have not been well. I have tried so hard and prayed so earnestly and faithfully asking God to help me, I cannot understand why He leaves me in suffering." That same year she again sought treatment at a sanatorium familiar to her, Highlands Hospital, in Asheville, North Carolina.[40]

Her last doctor, Robert Carroll, had pioneered certain unique "therapies" such as administering a lumbar puncture in order to inject the spinal fluid of his patients with honey, placental blood, horse blood, and even hypertonic solutions (liquids with a greater salt concentration than normal bodily fluids).[41] His patients who managed a recovery did so despite the odd toxic and physiological stressors he placed on their nervous systems. But he also administered insulin coma and electroconvulsive treatments. We know that Zelda received some ECT therapy while in

Asheville, and though Dr. Carroll declared her well enough for discharge in early March 1948, she decided to stay on a bit longer to be sure of her recovery.

Normally she slept in an unlocked room, but on the night of March 11, she was given sedatives and was drifting off in a locked room on the top floor when a fire broke out in the kitchen. The same nurse who had minutes before given Zelda her medication noticed the blaze and began evacuating patients on the lower floors. She called the fire department forty-five minutes later, but by that time the fire had spread upward through the dumbwaiter shaft, setting each floor ablaze all the way to the roof. The *New York Herald Tribune* reported that only one patient on the top floor was able to break out a window and leap to safety, while Zelda and the others perished. Her remains were identified only by her slippers.

Hemingway was aware of this tragedy, but it didn't soften his opinion of Zelda. After his marriage to Martha Gellhorn had deteriorated, in 1948 he wrote to Charles Scribner, blasting Martha in a number of ways, but concluded, "[I]f she were ever burned alive like Scott's poor bloody crazy career destroying wife I would just hope she took a good deep breath quick of the flames and think no more of it."[42] (A line from *Brideshead Revisited* explains perfectly Hemingway's sentiment: "When people hate with all that energy, it's something in themselves they're hating.")[43] It has been suggested that Zelda and her destructive psychosis possessed archetypal power in Hemingway's mind—and simply noting how many times her career-destroying abilities are mentioned in his *Selected Letters* makes this a convincing idea.[44]

Scott's mental difficulties were viewed no more sympathetically than Zelda's by Hemingway. Shortly after Scott published the second of his three essays concerning his depression in *Esquire* ("The Crack-Up" and "Pasting It Together" were the first two, with "Handle with Care" on the way), in which he described how he had mortgaged himself "physically and spiritually up to the hilt," Ernest wrote to Maxwell Perkins: "Feel awfully about Scott . . . he seems to almost take pride in his shamelessness of defeat. The Esquire pieces seem to me to be so miserable. There is another one coming too. I always knew he couldn't think—he never could—but he had a marvelous talent and the thing is to use it—not whine in public. Good God, people go through that emptiness many times in life and come out and do good work."[45]

Perhaps his cruelty toward Scott in *A Moveable Feast* can be partly explained by this resentment. Scott was gifted with the greatest of talent, a talent that Hemingway had had to earn. Scott's talent could be liberating and profitable, and his work should have been his therapy and cure.

Instead, he bellyached openly and became a public martyr. The lifelong relationship between the two was complex. Artistically, Fitzgerald was Pissarro, technically beautiful and colorful but lacking the weight and depth that the rugged Hemingway, the Cézanne, possessed. As Hemingway ascended in fame and self-confidence, Fitzgerald declined, as if their mutual gravitational fields gradually pushed them farther apart on opposite paths.

Fitzgerald, designated by scholars as Hemingway's Dorian Gray,[46] was certainly rock-bottom when he attempted suicide. He was alone and drunk in Asheville while Zelda was hospitalized at Highlands Hospital just after a stay at Sheppard-Pratt. Scott was also recovering from a dislocated shoulder he had sustained diving from a fifteen-foot springboard into a shallow pool eight weeks earlier. He had just read the front-page article about himself in the New York Post: "The poet-prophet of the postwar neurotics observed his fortieth birthday yesterday in his bedroom in the Grove Park Inn here. He spent the day as he spends all his days—trying to come back from the other side of Paradise, the hell of despondency in which he has writhed for the past couple of years." The interviewer also described his "jittery jumping off and onto his bed, his restless pacing, his trembling hands, his twitching face with its pitiful expression of a cruelly beaten child . . . his frequent trips to a highboy, in a drawer of which lay a bottle. Each time he poured a drink into the measuring glass beside his table, he would look appealingly at the nurse and ask, 'Just one ounce?'"[47]

After reading these words, he overdosed on a phial of morphine, but the contents were mostly thrown up. The reason that the Grove Park Inn had ordered him to have a nurse in attendance if he wished to stay there was related an earlier clumsy attempt, which involved discharging a firearm in his rooms. Thus, even when he attempted suicide, Fitzgerald's efforts were weak and ineffectual when contrasted with Hemingway's.

Like many who contemplate suicide, Fitzgerald was deterred by considering his child, his daughter, Scottie: "seeing her," he wrote to his St. Paul friend, Oscar Kalman, "you will see how much I still have to live for, in spite of a year in a slough of despond."[48] And he was at least considering Ernest's version of harsh reality-based therapy: "There has been some question in my mind whether I should ever have written the Esquire articles. Ernest Hemingway wrote me an irritable letter in which he bawled me out for having been so public about what were essentially private affairs and should be written about in fiction or not at all."[49]

He left the Grove Park in December 1936 to lodge in a top-floor room at the Oak Hall Hotel, in Tryon, North Carolina, about forty-five miles southeast of Asheville. He had achieved sobriety for stretches of time in the winter and spring of 1935 in Tryon, and with the help of a local doctor he managed to stay sober again, indulging instead on milkshakes and coffee at the local drug store. It was during this period of recovery, when his agent was arranging his $1,000-a-week MGM contract, that he learned of the death of Gerald and Sara Murphy's son, after they had already lost their only other son to tuberculosis. Scott sent the couple one of the most touching letters ever penned:

> Dearest Gerald and Sara:
>
> The telegram came today and the whole afternoon was so sad with thoughts of you and the past and the happy times we had once. Another link binding you to life is broken and with such insensate cruelty that [it] is hard to say which of the two blows was conceived with more malice. I can see the silence in which you hover now after this seven years of struggle and it would take words like Lincoln's in his letter to the mother who had lost four sons in the war to write you anything fitting at the moment. The sympathy you will get will be what you have had from each other already and for a long, long time you will be inconsolable.
>
> But I can see another generation growing up around Honoria [their daughter] and an eventual peace somewhere, an occasional port of call as we all sail deathward. Fate can't have any more arrows in its quiver for you that will wound like these. Who was it said that it was astounding how the deepest griefs can change in time to a sort of joy? The golden bowl is broken indeed, but it *was* golden; nothing can ever take those boys away from you now.[50]

When a parent's worst nightmare had come true and no words could really change things, Scott had found words that could at least help. He had lived Zelda's psychosis with her, and he had emerged, at least temporarily, from his depression and alcoholism with wisdom and empathy. Yet, for Hemingway, the stigmas of psychosis and depression were not only a barrier to treatment; they actually served to preclude what few approaches might have been helpful. The demise of friends, the psychology of denial, and the dementia itself, which served to impair his judgment— all conspired within his mind. Depression was obvious, his dementia was unsuspected, but psychosis, his detachment from reality, was the white elephant in the room, and another diagnosis would have to serve as an excuse for hospital care—anything but "crazy."

Mayo

Chapter 7

Hemingway's physician in Idaho was fifteen years his junior and humbly described himself as "just a country doctor." Though it was obvious to everyone that his patient needed immediate help, Dr. Saviers felt the condition was "so far out of my field that I cannot even diagnosis it."[1] Saviers was underestimating himself. Though he had no local behavioral health facility or even a psychiatrist to consult, like many country doctors he displayed wisdom and compassion in dealing with his patient, and even if he did not have the psychiatric vocabulary necessary for a diagnosis, he could still describe Hemingway's symptoms: Ernest was anxious, depressed, obsessed with delusional fears; his moods were erratic, and his personality had changed. Routine conversations revealed a decline in his cognitive skills, and Saviers also came to believe that his writing had deteriorated to standards well below his abilities and stature. Surely the doctor had seen other patients who suffered dementias and displayed many of the same symptoms. But it is also true that he and Ernest were close, and it must have been distracting and painful to watch his friend decline.

A. E. Hotchner was another close friend, as well as business partner, sometime editor, frequent travel partner, and sometime errand boy. He had met Hemingway in the spring of 1948, over Papa Dobles at the Floridita, and was instantly trusted; in fact, he was always a confidant, even during Hemingway's most extreme periods of paranoia. Hotchner described Hemingway's clinical picture to a respected New York psychiatrist, who recommended the Menninger Clinic in Kansas, but he and Mary understood that an admission to a facility known solely for psychiatric care had to be rejected—there was the issue of publicity, but, besides that, Hemingway would never agree to it.[2] When he did agree to enter Rochester's Mayo Clinic in November 1960, he was told and believed that it was to address only his elevated blood pressure (which had risen to 220/125).

It is hard to be critical of this action; like many patients with psychosis, Hemingway needed treatment but refused it. He also needed privacy to recover, but his celebrity status would make this a challenge anywhere. At every turn, it seems that Mary was doing the best that she could.

Fifty years before Ernest's admission, his father had walked into that same clinic for a refresher course and sent a postcard to his then eleven-year-old son: "It will be only a few years before you and Papa will be visiting clinics together."[3] Standing in the same wards five decades earlier, Dr. Ed Hemingway was dreaming of his handsome little boy's future medical career.

It is widely thought that Hemingway's alias while hospitalized, "George Saviers," was assigned to protect his identity, and even his psychiatrist at Mayo believed the alias was given at the clinic's directive. However, the admissions process was so tedious that it agitated Hemingway. Dr. Saviers, who had accompanied him en route on Larry Johnson's single-engine Piper to Rochester, noted how restless Hemingway was becoming. They had come too far and too close to lose the patient now over paperwork, so Saviers filled out the paperwork in his own name simply to expedite matters.

On his fourth hospital day, Ernest sat in his room and wrote a letter "TO WHOM IT MAY CONCERN, My wife Mary at no time believed or considered that I had ever committed any illegal act of any kind. She had no guilty knowledge of any of my finances nor relations with anyone and was assured by Dr. George Saviers that I was suffering from high blood pressure of a dangerous kind and degree and that she was being booked [at the Kahler Hotel, Rochester] under his name to avoid being bothered by the press. She knew nothing of any misdeeds nor illegal acts and had only the sketchiest outline of my finances and only helped me in preparing my [tax] returns on material I furnished her. . . . She was never an accomplice nor in any sense a fugitive and only followed the advice of a doctor and friend [Saviers] that she trusted."[4]

So entrenched was his paranoia that despite the extensive medical evaluations and the writing duties that awaited him at home, his focus was solely on exonerating his wife, Mary, whom he believed would "take the rap" with him for the numerous fictional crimes that continued to torment him. His addition that she had "no guilty knowledge of any of my finances *nor relations with anyone*" indicate he still had fears of being charged with "indecent liberty."

The internist who cared for Hemingway, Dr. Hugh Butt, ran a series of tests and diagnosed him with mild diabetes. As his weight fluctuated, his blood glucose had likely been at various times prediabetic or diabetic over the previous decade, but this was his first official diagnosis of the condition. Dr. Butt was able to palpate the left lobe of his enlarged liver. Though most associate alcoholism with the development of cirrhosis, actually fewer than 15 percent of alcoholics will develop this complication. More common is a "fatty" and enlarged liver. Over time, scar tissue may accumulate and lead to cirrhosis, and the liver will shrink in size. Hemingway could have developed cirrhosis to a minor extent, but at this stage it was a "fatty liver" from alcohol intake (and also from being overweight) that caused the enlargement.

His internist was also concerned over blood pressure readings as high as 220/150, but he advised it was likely that anxiety was pushing Hemingway's pressure to these dangerous levels. The doctor wisely discontinued his reserpine, a possible contributor to depression. Reserpine was a widely prescribed antihypertensive agent at the time, but up to 20 percent of patients reported depression as a side effect. The drug acts in the brain to lower stores of serotonin and norepinephrine, chemicals needed in adequate supply to maintain a normal mood state. The patients at highest risk were those who already had a history of depression prior to reserpine therapy, such as Hemingway.

It has been theorized that Hemingway was suffering from a specific metabolic disorder, hemochromatosis, that accounted for all of his symptoms, physical and psychiatric. It has further been suggested that he inherited it from his father, a fellow sufferer.[5] This illness is essentially a disease of iron storage; iron itself is deposited in the liver and various other tissues, leading to numerous clinical signs and symptoms: liver enlargement, excessive skin pigmentation, diabetes, possibly even heart failure, and, of course, depression. Dr. Butt did suspect this as a possibility but advised against a liver biopsy. Though a tissue sample proves or disproves the diagnosis of hemochromatosis definitively, liver biopsies, particularly in 1960, carried a risk of hemorrhage, possibly a fatal risk and one that outweighed curiosity. In addition, a simple serum iron measurement would suffice. Cecil's *Textbook of Medicine*, the standard reference in 1959 and 1960, elaborated that "An elevated serum iron and saturation of the iron-binding capacity of the serum are the most useful special laboratory findings."[6]

The standard battery of laboratory work at Mayo while Hemingway was there would have included an iron level. Symptoms of hemochromatosis look like those of any number of psychiatric and medical illnesses, and it was briefly considered at Mayo because it was indeed a convenient "fit" for the patient's cluster of symptoms. But it was easily rejected either because a serum iron test was normal or because he lacked many of the hallmark clinical findings and because his clinical picture so obviously suggested something else.

The "something else" was dementia with associated depression and psychosis. However, in the eyes of his doctors, Hemingway was experiencing severe depression with psychotic features. And antidepressants *were* available at the time, as the first antidepressant, imipramine, was introduced in 1957, and in 1961 amitriptyline would also become widely used. There were antipsychotic medications as well; chlorpromazine was available by 1955. But there was as yet very little clinical experience with these agents, and their use was not yet standard therapy. Furthermore, the side effects associated with their use would have been problematic—a patient treated with early antidepressants (termed "tricyclics" because of their three-ringed chemical structures) and early antipsychotics might experience sedation, short-term memory problems, dry mouth, blurry vision, constipation, a drop in blood pressure, and sexual side effects, such as a decrease in libido or an inability to perform in the bedroom. Any degree of memory trouble would most likely have further distressed Hemingway, already aware of his cognitive limitations and ongoing decline. Like many depressed patients, he already lacked a libido, and he had struggled with intermittent bouts of impotence from at least his forties. Further difficulties would no doubt have led to more depression. There are many patients who take these medications alone or in combination without significant side effects, and some have no side effects at all, but more senior patients and those with organic brain disease, like Hemingway's CTE, are at higher risk for all of the side effects, particularly for memory and concentration difficulties.

The main error in Hemingway's case was not the failure to use newly synthesized antidepressants and antipsychotics but the failure to accurately diagnosis his condition. Perhaps it was his celebrity status that clouded the clinical judgment of his doctors, or perhaps it was his extensive worldly knowledge and genius that made the diagnosis of dementia unthinkable—but his brain was dementing, and series of routine memory tests, though they would not have fully proved his diagnosis, would at least have gotten the clinicians into the right ballpark. Yes, he was visibly depressed, he was tormented by various paranoid delusions, and he was indeed suicidal, but these were all symptoms of an overarching illness— "dementia, mixed etiology."

The standard treatment of a patient understood to have a severe psychotic depression in 1960 was electroconvulsive therapy. In fact, it is still a standard therapy today. Perhaps his clinicians were not oblivious to his symptoms of dementia but assumed that his cognitive issues—memory

deficits, disinhibition, paranoia, and personality changes—were all secondary to the depression. In fact, many patients with depression have
memory difficulties and look as if they have dementia. The term "pseudo-
dementia" has entered the medical literature and it is defined as just
that—symptoms of dementia that are due to depression, not Alzheimer's
or some other type of dementia. But patients with pseudo-dementia often
display apathy and don't even attempt to answer memory and concentration tasks. They often just say "I don't know" when asked elements
of mental status exams, and they appear as if it is too much of an effort
to even cooperate with a medical evaluation. By contrast, a patient with
dementia will usually try but simply not perform well on the exams and
tasks. Given their assumptions, it is understandable, then, that Hemingway's doctors expected a recovery in all of the domains affected by his
illness after his course of shock therapy, the fail-safe cure for depression
(usually at a 90 percent cure rate in the 1950s and 1960s).

Thus, he was administered ECT, each treatment consisting of an
electrical impulse applied at his temples, causing a generalized seizure.
The treatments were most likely given on a Monday-Wednesday-Friday
schedule. The most current textbook of the day (1960) described "Electric
Shock Treatment of Psychiatric Therapy" as follows: "The usual treatment involves the administration of 100 to 160 volts of alternating current
to the patient, between bitemporal electrodes, for a period of 0.1 to 0.6
of a second. Within five seconds, the patient has a convulsive seizure—
unresponsiveness and sudden generalized tonus, succeeded by forty seconds of clonus—which is followed by thirty to ninety minutes of confusion
and amnesia. Several preparatory measures are customary: a position of
mild dorsal hyperextension, gentle restriction of movement and a rubber
mouth gag between the teeth; inhalation of 90 per cent oxygen before and
after treatment is sometimes used. Muscular relaxants, such as succinylcholine, and appropriate anesthetics will lessen the danger of injury. . . .
Depressive reactions in middle or late life and manic depressive reactions
remain the primary indications for ECT. Ninety percent of these reactions can be interrupted with six to ten treatments, administered two to
three times per week."[7]

Hemingway is believed to have received fifteen such treatments, after which he was noticeably different but not cured. He was deemed safe
for release on January 22, 1961, and once again climbed into Johnson's
plane for the trip home to Ketchum. Things did seem much better at first,
though he was more silent and not up for company, canceling his usual
parties around the Friday-night fights on TV. He tried to work but found
himself mostly just shuffling papers. He and Mary began walking up to

four miles a day for exercise, and he ordered more than thirty new books from the Scribner's Bookstore, including Shirer's *The Rise and Fall of the Third Reich* and a new biography of Ezra Pound by Charles Norman. At this point in his life, Hemingway would find himself listed in the indexes of books on other literary giants, and few know this odd sensation of realizing one's immortality, of course, another way of realizing one's mortality. If he thumbed to page 257 of the Ezra Pound biography, he'd find a lovely passage about his youth, which must have stirred some enthusiasm for the sketchbook of his Paris years: "Hemingway was often to be found in the *pavillion* in the courtyard. 'A big young man with intent eyes and a toothbrush mustache was there when I arrived,' wrote Malcolm Cowley, 'and Pound introduced him as Ernest Hemingway; I said that I had heard about him. Hemingway gave a slow Mid-western grin. He was then working for the International News Service, but there were rumors that he had stories in manuscript and that Pound had spoken of them as being something new in American literature. He didn't talk about the stories that afternoon; he listened as if with his eyes while Pound discussed the literary world. Very soon he rose, made a date with Pound for tennis the following day and went out the door, walking on the balls of his feet like a boxer."[8]

Back home, a pattern settled in—he always woke before Mary, made breakfast, and went to his study to work on the Paris sketches and the bullfighting book, but nothing was progressing. He struggled with titles for the Paris book and wrote a list of options that were uncharacteristically terrible, such as *It Is Different in the Ring*, *The Part Nobody Knows*, *To Hope and Write Well*, *Good Nails Are Made of Iron*, *To Bite on the Nail*, and *The Early Eye and the Ear*.[9] He was fully aware of his difficulties, writing to his editor "am . . . also working on title. This is very difficult. (Have my usual long list—something wrong with all of them but am working toward it—Paris has been used so often it blights anything.) . . . All the truth and magic in but we need a better title than *The Paris Stories*." He even lists his additional stressors as "Cuba situation—lack of library to work from—etc."

He further asked Harry Brague, his last editor at Scribner's, to send him the King James Bible and the *Oxford Book of English Verse*, his longtime favorite sources for titles. He also volunteered that "Drs fixed my allowed alcohol intake as 1 liter of claret a day." And when discussing his writing: "This is all being done under difficulty but it is being done."[10]

It was no doubt a further setback when on April 15 he heard the news of the Bay of Pigs fiasco. The CIA had hoped to spark a Cuban uprising by training a small force to storm the island (the Bay of Pigs, or Bahía de Cochinos, is roughly one hundred miles southeast of the Finca). Despite the small number of CIA-trained Cuban exiles who landed, it still took Castro's forces three days to put down the attempt. Hemingway was already worried he would never see his Cuba home, his paintings, or his boat again, and now he must have been sure of it. His "Africa Journal" and two other manuscripts that would one day surface as posthumously published works were sitting in a Cuban bank vault and were also presumed lost.

Three days after the Bay of Pigs, he wrote to Charles Scribner Jr., stating that the Paris sketches should *not* be published: there was no ending, and the manuscript was cruel and unfair to Pauline, to Hadley, and—in a spark of honesty—to Scott Fitzgerald. There would be libel suits (though Fitzgerald had been twenty-one years in the grave), and if it had to be published, it would be labeled as fiction, and Scribner's would bear the burden of the legal action that was sure to follow.[11]

During the three months between admissions, he grew more and more abusive to Mary, driven to berating her because of his paranoia, which never really responded to the ECT. She had "neglected him" while he was in hospital, she was spending too much money, "not helping him find someplace safe from taxes," and she was even guilty of enjoying TV while they were in "so much danger." After trees had fallen across the Big Wood River behind their home, Ernest made the peculiar militaristic comment that their "defenses had been breached." Mary was clearly frayed, and it didn't help that she suffered a scalp laceration after a fall down the stairs in early April.

On April 21, a Friday morning, she came downstairs and found Ernest holding a shotgun and two shells, as well as a suicide note he planned to leave for her. Mary patiently talked to him, about his "courage, his bravery, faith and love," anything to stall for time. Dr. Saviers would be there, she hoped he was already on the way—Ernest was due for his routine blood pressure check, which was usually part of an extended morning visit by the doctor. It was a tense hour that required all she had emotionally, but Mary succeeded. Papa was alive. Saviers quickly grasped the situation and talked Ernest into a Sun Valley hospital stay, where he received sedatives. It was clear that he needed another psychiatric stay, but rough weather made the flight to Rochester impossible. A general hospital admission in Sun Valley would simply have to do to keep him safe for the time being. After sedatives and bed-rest there, he seemed better by April 24 and even convinced Saviers that the chores were mounting at home and he needed to tend to them. Mary simply needed him back there. But, taking no chances, Saviers sent a nurse, Joan Higgon, as well as Hemingway's friend Don Anderson, along at discharge just to be on the safe side.

Once in the driveway, Hemingway rushed into his home and went straight to the living room. Don wisely followed him and found Ernest shoving shells into his shotgun; he even managed to close the breech. Anderson was able grab his large friend from behind, pinning his arms against his body, and somehow found the gun's opening lever with his thumb. Joan quickly removed the shells. They were then able to then get Ernest back into the car and speed off to another hospital admission. By the next day a flight was possible as there was a break in the bad weather, and once again he boarded Johnson's plane. Saviers was joined by Anderson for this trip. While the plane refueled in Rapid City, it has been reported that Ernest left the plane to "stretch his legs" but was soon rummaging through cars and the tool chests in the airport hangars "looking for a gun" and that he even attempted to walk into the whirling propeller of another plane. When he was about thirty feet away and heading toward the props, he was saved when the alert pilot sensed what was happening and quickly cut the engine.[12]

Though the propeller story has been repeated as fact in each significant biography, Dr. Saviers, who was at his side the entire trip, disputed it: according to Tillie Arnold, "He said he and Papa were standing together, just watching the airplane like any spectator would do, and that he had no sense that Papa was ready to run into either of the rotating blades."[13] With or without this episode, Hemingway was still suicidal and needed treatment. And once again he received the wrong type.

His second and final stay at Mayo lasted two months, April 25 through June 26. While there, he learned that George Savier's nine-year-old son had been diagnosed with viral endocarditis and was also hospitalized. Hemingway was still receiving his shock treatments, but he managed to send a letter to the doctor, one of the last pieces of writing he ever penned:

To FREDERICK G. SAVIERS, Rochester, 15 June 1961
Dear Fritz:

I was terribly sorry to hear this morning in a note from your father that you were laid up in Denver for a few days more and speed off this note to tell you how much I hope you'll be feeling better.

It has been very hot and muggy here in Rochester but the last two days it has turned cool and lovely with the nights wonderful for sleeping. The country is beautiful around here and I've had a chance to see some wonderful country along the Mississippi where they used to drive the logs in the old lumbering days and the trails where the pioneers came north. Saw some good bass jump in the river. I never knew anything about the upper Mississippi before and it is really a very beautiful country and there are plenty of pheasants and ducks in the fall.

But not as many as in Idaho and I hope we'll both be back there shortly and can joke about our hospital experiences together.

Best always to you, old timer from your good friend who misses you very much.

(Mister) Papa

Best to all the family. Am feeling fine and very cheerful about things in general and hope to see you all soon."[14]

Though Fritz survived this bout of endocarditis, he died six years later, in 1967.

The Body Electric

Chapter 8

Michael Reynolds's classic biography of Hemingway uses the same Whitman reference as the title of this chapter for his chapter describing Hemingway's courses of electroshock therapy. The body is indeed an electric system, including the brain. The very tissue of the brain is a system of chemically charged networks, capable of sending and receiving impulses that in turn release chemical messengers to attach to specific receptors and signal other messengers and reactions inside the cells. But that's just the tip of the iceberg. Our brain cells construct an infinitely complex and interwoven network, with influences as direct as our senses and as vague as a stray and random memory. We can hear the music of a symphony and visualize infinite imagery in our minds.

The realization of these facts transcends the cold science of membrane and neurotransmitter. The capacity for abstracting Whitman's "I sing the body electric" to the title of an electric-based medical therapy for another great writer, all the while wondering whether a reference is necessary or whether "fair use" guidelines apply, fits into no single brain pathway but an unchartable array of instantaneous activity. The more we know, the less we know. But what is clear enough is that the mind's infinitely complex design and activity argue for our transcendental nature.

When electrical abnormalities occur in the brain, they may take the clinical form of seizures. These electrical discharges disrupt the delicate balance of electrical charges across membranes and cause a group of neurons to begin firing off in a nonstop manner. They can be either localized to certain parts of the brain or generalized, spreading to many areas. The exact bodily manifestation of the seizure depends on where in the brain the abnormal flooding of electrical impulse begins and whether and where the impulses spread. Temporal lobe seizures involve mood and behavior symptoms (even mimicking bipolar illness in some patients), while generalized or "grand mal" seizures involve a tonic phase (stiffness) followed by a clonic (shaking) period that involves numerous muscle groups. Patients may or may not lose consciousness, and they may even have various neurological symptoms that last for hours or days after the seizure has ended. These transient symptoms may be as severe as amnesia or paralysis or as minor as numbness or tingling. Yet "controlled" seizures, those we induce, can be therapeutic and even curative for certain conditions.

Electroconvulsive therapy, or ECT, developed like many medical therapies, out of sheer observation: it was noted that schizophrenics who also suffered from epilepsy were much less likely to be psychotic or depressed than those who were seizure free. This, along with the pathological finding that schizophrenics had fewer glia cells, cells that support and supply neurons, while epileptic brains had an abundance of them, argued for seizure induction as a form of therapy. The Hungarian physician Ladislas Meduna was using chemicals to induce seizures by 1934 (first camphor-in-oil injected into muscle, then Metrazol intravenously), and he reported a series of successes in treating schizophrenics. His first patient was catatonic, a condition that was often fatal at the time, but Meduna brought the patient out of the frozen state with his new seizure therapy. After his first publication, in 1935, he was visited by doctors from Europe and the United States who sought to learn about his advances, but he was repeatedly annoyed by the cost of having to entertain them at his home (but he still shared his ideas).

The problems associated with seizures are obvious—bone fractures (2 percent), dislocated joints (17 percent), and compression fractures of the spine (a staggering 50 percent rate) were all observed early on with these chemically induced seizures, but by 1940 injections of muscle relaxants prior to the treatments had eliminated most of these orthopedic problems. In 1938, two Italian physicians introduced electricity as the means of seizure induction, which proved far superior and more predictable than chemical induction. A version of this procedure has lasted and has continually evolved over subsequent decades.

There are several theories as to why ECT should work for depression or psychosis, but none are conclusive. In fact, much of the evidence for what ECT accomplishes on the molecular level is contradictory and counterintuitive when we compare it to what we know about other therapies for depression and, in particular, how antidepressants work. Early theories were more true to our Freudian past than to our neurotransmitter future, postulating that administering ECT was in reality a form of punishment, which then freed the patient of guilt—a guilt that was the root cause of the depression. ECT was thus a psychotherapeutic cure. But the theory presupposes that all sufferers are truly guilty in some way or at least perceive themselves, consciously or unconsciously, as deserving punishment. Studies of "sham ECT," in which all of the procedures of ECT are applied, including IV sedation, except the electrical impulse and seizure itself, do not benefit patients in any way.

The images and understanding most people have of the ECT procedure is highly negative, no doubt the result of a conflation of Hollywood depictions and organized efforts to publicly discredit the treatment. Most readers will recall the scene from *One Flew over the Cuckoo's Nest* in which Jack Nicholson's character is administered ECT as a punitive measure. When he emerges after a lobotomy, it is unclear to most viewers that this was a completely separate procedure, and many assume that the ECT created the zombie-like and permanent changes. (Lobotomy is a surgical procedure that disconnects the frontal lobe pathways from the rest of the brain. Though administered exclusively to psychiatric patients, it was developed by a Portuguese neurologist, and in the United States it was actively promoted by a neurologist, not a psychiatrist. The psychiatric community was instrumental in ending its use, which, thanks to these efforts, was minimal by the time the book *One Flew over the Cuckoo's Nest* was published, in 1962.)

In the film *A Beautiful Mind*, the main character undergoes insulin coma therapy but is also shown as having a seizure shortly after his insulin infusion. Seizures did occur in roughly 20 percent of patients receiving insulin coma, but viewers of the scene may be confused as to which therapy John Nash (played by Russell Crowe) received. These are difficult images to see and recall, yet the procedure of ECT in Hemingway's day had been refined to the approximate version that remains in use today. It was humanely administered and was lifesaving for many patients, such as those who were catatonic or psychotically depressed.

In 1960 and 1961, Hemingway's ECT treatment involved his leaving his private room in a hospital gown and being taken to a special procedure suite, where he lay on a gurney. He was probably quite frightened, fearing it was all an FBI plot of some sort and likely forcing a joke or two to counter his anxieties. An intravenous line was started in his arm, and amobarbital flowed into his veins. Within a few seconds he was asleep. A blood pressure cuff tightened around one ankle, and another intravenous infusion of succinylcholine paralyzed his muscles. The rubber bite-guard was placed in his mouth, and a conductive gel was rubbed in circles over his temples. A rubber strap was placed around his head, holding two metal electrodes, one over each temple, in place. The ECT machine was set at a high enough current level to induce a seizure. Though Hemingway was paralyzed, direct current through the temporal muscles would cause his jaw to clinch but the bite-guard prevented any injury.

Men require more electricity than women for a successful treatment, because of the thickness of the male skull, which acts as a resistor to the electric impulse. In both sexes, the skull is a very effective barrier—only about 5 percent of the electricity administered actually enters the brain; most of the current arcs from one electrode to another, so that 95 percent of the electrical impulse arches over the head, not *through* the brain. In fact, the amount of electricity needed for effective therapy is surprisingly minimal—enough to light a 60-watt bulb for merely one second. Hemingway likely received fifteen treatments during his first Mayo admission and ten more during his second.

Later, it was discovered that sending the electrical impulse through just the right side of the brain (or the left side in the patients who are left-handed) resulted in less confusion and fewer memory complaints than the bilateral approach. The unilateral technique spares the language center from the electrical stress (since most people are right-handed, their language center is on the left side of the brain). In 1963, clinicians began to debate whether one-sided, or "unilateral-ECT" was as effective as bilateral, and only recently has the issue been clarified. Unilateral is indeed as effective, provided the seizure duration it induces is adequate. Unilateral was first used in 1949, but in Hemingway's day, bilateral was the standard method. (Of course, this method would have accentuated his memory and cognitive side effects post-ECT, given the underlying vulnerabilities of CTE.) The seizure was timed and monitored by the shaking of his foot, as the blood pressure cuff had prevented the muscle relaxant (succinylcholine) from reaching this part of his body.

When he woke, forty-five minutes later, his mouth was dry and his vision was blurry. His head felt clouded. He wanted to get up, he wanted to speak, but his body wouldn't do what his brain wanted it to. It was like trying to rouse himself from the dirt in Italy all those years ago—his head felt heavy, his body was numb and not moving, the noise came in waves— these were the minutes he would never remember, when he experienced the world as a blur, the drunken disconnect between mind and everything else, the mind adrift and helpless, much the way his creation, Frederic Henry, described what happened after an explosive blast: "there was a flash . . . as when a blast-furnace is swung open, and a roar that started white and went red and on and on in a rushing wind. I tried to breathe but my breath would not come and I felt myself rush bodily out of myself."[1]

Hemingway was "postictal," the medical term for the state of amnesia and confusion after a seizure. It gradually clears, but for Hemingway it would clear more slowly and never fully. ECT has been universally blamed for *erasing* Hemingway's memory and thus ruining his craft. ECT's seizure induction does not erase memory, but it does temporarily disrupt the circuitry that allows the storage and retrieval of memories. Patients do not recall the events directly before or after the treatment, but objective memory testing usually shows improvement after ECT as the patient is no longer depressed or psychotic. But Hemingway was suffering from a dementia. His neuronal pathways, the bridges of connection in his mind, were rickety and collapsing, and the ECT was the storm that covered them with flood waters. ECT did not erase his long-term memory, but the procedure itself was a biological stress that his brain could not handle, and that stress accelerated his dementia's progression—as a result not of the *mechanism* of ECT but rather of the stress on his vulnerable system. (A hospitalization for a hip replacement would have yielded similar cognitive results.)

Once the first round of procedures was complete, Hemingway himself asked "Well, what is the sense of ruining my head and erasing my memory, which is my capital, and putting me out of business? It was a brilliant cure but we lost the patient." To Hotchner he would elaborate: "I called the local authorities to turn myself in but they didn't know about the rap."[2] This indicates that his paranoid delusions remained intact despite the intense treatments and is also an indication that his delusions were driven not by depression but by the process of dementia (as depressive delusions resolve with ECT, even with comorbid dementia). And one of his greatest fears was the loss of his ability to work and provide, particularly since he was overly concerned, indeed, delusional, about his financial situation. Just as Zelda's psychosis had put Scott "out of business," his doctors had done the same for him.

At this time he was struggling to complete and even to title *A Moveable Feast*. And the ECT was so problematic precisely because of his undiagnosed and underlying illness. At that time, his doctors expected that the ECT would cure depression and the associated delusions, particularly since ECT is most effective in the most severe cases. It is also the treatment of choice for catatonia, when the patient is mute and literally frozen, unable to speak or move. ECT is life-saving in such cases. The common statistic in 1960 was that ECT yielded a "90 percent cure rate." But Hemingway's primary illness was dementia. He suffered not only more severe memory disruption with ECT but more postictal confusion, both serving to convince him he was "out of business."

A review of the medical literature, including very recent studies, indicates that, on the whole, dementia patients can receive and benefit from

ECT and that, despite their being at risk for more complications than other patients, the majority do achieve the desired cure of their depression. But these studies are generally done with Alzheimer's patients. Hemingway's dementia had multiple causes: alcoholism, vascular injury, and concussive or traumatic brain injury.

Hemingway's mother suffered just such a stressful event in her seventy-ninth year that seemed to turn her mild dementia into a severe disability. The Hemingway scholar Bernice Kert described the sequence of events as follows:

> A head injury sustained at Oak Pak Hospital when an attendant mishandled her wheelchair and caused it to tip over had left Grace's memory severely impaired, and then senile dementia set in. Sunny took her into her own house in Memphis for the last months that she lived. "It was heartbreaking," recalled Sunny. ". . . She would hide from me like a child. . . ." When the family doctor tried to prompt Grace to recognize her daughter, she referred to Sunny as a lovely lady who was taking care of her. On the night that she was hospitalized for the last time, she sat at the piano and played several classical pieces with great gusto. A few weeks later she died in a Memphis hospital.[3]

Hemingway would have most likely been one of the 90 percent who responded well if his diagnosis had been only psychotic depression. His son Patrick received ECT in 1947 (unlike his father, he received no anesthesia or muscle relaxants before the electric shock was administered), and his son Gregory would receive many more treatments throughout his tormented life; in fact, Hemingway even wrote to Gregory asking him to agree to the treatments that had benefited Patrick so much, which he hoped would free Gregory of his intense suicidality. But Ernest's brain at this point was not capable of receiving the treatments and recovering, only deteriorating. (When Faulkner received ECT for his depression, he did recover, but the treatment induced a postictal state of childlike regression for an unusually long period of time. Faulkner's alcoholism was also well known, but his ECT was administered when he was slightly younger than Hemingway was when he received treatment; Faulkner was in the exact middle of his fiftieth decade, and though he had some risk factors for dementia, it never fully manifested.)

So why did the treatments continue? Why continue to administer a treatment to Hemingway that was failing? One reason is simply the unpredictable course of ECT: often, a patient requires more than the standard number of treatments to recover. Some patients need the recommended amount of antidepressant medication, and some need three times as much, and only that individual experiment determines the answer for that patient. For the majority of patients, administering more treatments proves to be the correct course of action. Those who administer ECT are well aware of cases that responded only after the eighteenth or nineteenth treatment rather than the usual four to eight sessions. Some researchers argue that response is a function of "cumulative seizure time," that is, keeping track of the length of seizures during the treatments until a threshold is reached that leads to a cure.

And Hemingway's case was challenging to his doctors in another way. Treating celebrities requires that physicians be mindful of appropriate boundaries, that they not allow their medical judgment to be compromised by this distraction or by narcissistic demands. Hemingway was not exactly treated like a celebrity but rather as a friend. He dined with Dr. Butt and family on several occasions, and he even shared Christmas Eve dinner with them. The patient also went target shooting with Dr. Butt and his son in an old quarry, shattering wine bottles and clay pigeons (an impressive twenty-seven in a row). Hemingway elaborated in a letter to his editor that he "dined last night with my Dr [at his] house" and they shared French wines—Muscadet, Haut-Brion, and Sancerre—"so things are perking up."[4] His physician was not only one of the best clinicians of his day; he was also a wine expert, and at Christmas time he was known for gifting cases. He allowed Hemingway two glasses of wine per night while hospitalized. We can only speculate about the conversations between doctor and patient that led to that decision, but he may have concluded that it was unrealistic to expect Ernest to agree to detox, go to AA meetings, and never drink again. Perhaps he didn't see the alcoholism as a problem at all. Either way, he couldn't let his patient go into alcohol withdrawal. And when Ernest reported that his libido had improved, Mary was summoned for a forced rendezvous. His doctors obviously understood the importance of his libido to his sense of self, but, not surprisingly, the night was less successful than hoped. The hospital ward was no substitute for the Paris Ritz.

His primary psychiatrist, Dr. Howard Rome, maintained strict confidentiality after Hemingway's death and for the rest of his life would indicate his code of silence by placing his index finger to his lips when asked by anyone to comment on his famous case. During Hemingway's treatment, he was well aware of his patient's delusions and tried to dispel his fears of FBI surveillance by meeting with the nearest agent. According to a memo dated January 13, 1961, in the FBI file from the Minneapolis agent to the Director:

ERNEST HEMINGWAY, the author, has been a patient at the Mayo Clinic, Rochester, Minnesota, and is presumably at St. Mary's in that city. He has been at the Clinic for several weeks, and is described as a problem. He is seriously ill, both physically and mentally, and at one time the doctors were considering giving him electro-shock therapy treatments.

[At the request of Dr. Rome, psychiatrist of the] Mayo Clinic, advised to eliminate publicity and contacts by newsmen, the clinic had suggested that Mr. HEMINGWAY register under the alias GEORGE SEVIER. [Dr. Rome] stated that Mr. HEMINGWAY is now worried about his registering under an assumed name, and is concerned about an FBI investigation. [Rome] stated that inasmuch as this worry was interfering with his treatments of Mr. HEMINGWAY, he desired authorization to tell HEMINGWAY that the FBI was not concerned with his registering under an assumed name. [Dr. Rome] was advised that there was no such objection.[5]

Dr. Rome has been universally criticized for his efforts in this vein, and he did indeed unwittingly contribute to Hemingway's FBI file. But the file's entry prior to this memo was photocopy of a newspaper article from 1958, titled "Hemingway's Suit," describing his legal attempt to block *Esquire* from "republishing some of his old stories about the Spanish Civil War"—a trivial entry, and not at all the focus of his delusions. In retrospect, Dr. Rome's gesture was compassionate. He understood that his investigation into the matter and his medical authority might reassure his tormented patient, and he sought the FBI's approval. He was confronting delusion with reality. But his patient was so deep in the world of unrealistic rumination that the very name he was using as an alias was somehow a source of crime and FBI concern. When Dr. Rome's reassurances fell on deaf and delusional ears, it was all up to the ECT.

After his second round, thought to be ten treatments, which was the usual schedule, he was at least aware of how he needed to present himself in order to obtain a discharge, even if still paranoid, depressed, and harboring a self-destructive desire. Hemingway was deceiving his doctors for a speedy release and would prove to still be delusional at the time, thinking one of the interns was really an FBI agent sent to the ward just to spy on him. He had played the game, learning what was expected of him for a hospital discharge and acting the part perfectly when he was really in no shape for release. Mary described him as sitting in his psychiatrist's office "grinning like a Cheshire cat," awaiting his dismissal, all the while knowing he had conned the doctors, knowing it would be disastrous, and feeling helpless.[6]

Mary had been in the same situation only six months before—on Christmas Eve 1960, when she sat weeping in her hotel room as her husband was being treated the first time at Mayo. She pulled herself together long enough to write in her journal that Ernest seemed "almost as disturbed, disjointed mentally as he was when we came here. . . . He no longer insists that an FBI agent is hidden in the bathroom with a tape recorder. . . . He still says . . . that he feels terrible . . . mumbles about breaking the immigration law (he has some unspoken guilt about Val). He is convinced that the Ketchum house will be seized for non-payment or something . . . still feels penniless . . . still waits for the FBI to pick him up." Despite the severity of his illness and Mary's distress, the pathological ballet between them was still intact. He was delusional and harboring "unspoken guilt about Val," and six days later, the first of the New Year's resolutions Mary penned in her journal was "I will not worry or fret or brood about other women in love with Papa."[7]

And just before his last discharge, she must have been as much distressed as incredulous. He was better only at acting the part of a recovered patient. He made the trip home uneventfully but never settled into his previous routine. He visited Fritz Saviers as he had hoped to, and Fritz did survive the bout of endocarditis. Later that night he dined on rare New York strip at the "Christy" restaurant with Mary as they sat in his favorite corner booth. They drank Châteauneuf du Pape. Once home, he and Mary sang verses from a favorite Italian song, "Tutti mi chiamano bionda" ("Everybody calls me blonde") as they readied for bed, and Ernest joined in on the refrain of "porto i capelli neri" ("I wear my hair black.").[8] She noticed nothing unusual when she got out of bed at 6 a.m. for a glass of water.

That morning, July 2, 1961, Ernest woke just before sunrise and put on his slippers, then his red bathrobe, dubbed the "Emperor's robe," that Mary had sewn for him years ago in Italy. He had suffered from insomnia for most of his adult life, and that night was no different. He was still tormented by the fear of surveillance and by imagined financial woes and often had the typical insomnia of one who indulges in too much alcohol—sleepiness at the start of the night and restlessness thereafter. However, during this night, as he drifted in and out of sleep not deep enough for dreams, his mind did settle into a place of strange clarity and resolve. He considered his wife that morning, but only to the extent of not waking her as he quietly walked past her bedroom and headed downstairs.

He then went directly to the windowsill in the kitchen where he knew he would find the keys he needed. He then made his way to a storeroom in the basement where his guns were locked up to prevent exactly what was to happen in about thirty seconds. His favorite shotgun was a 12-gauge, W. & C. Scott Monte Carlo B. He loaded the shells, snapped the barrels in place, and headed back upstairs and into the foyer. All of his vulnerabilities coalesced in one final instant.

It was less than forty-eight hours since he had arrived home after his release from the Mayo Clinic and his second round of ECT. Mary woke again, this time to what she surmised was Ernest slamming his dresser drawers shut.

The shotgun Hemingway used to end his life was retrieved by his friend Chuck Atkinson, who took it to a local welding shop owned by Elvin Brooks. Chuck had already busted the stock off, out of frustration and anger, and Brooks cut the gun into three pieces. They were so concerned about souvenir hunters that the pieces were buried in a secret location that Brooks's son believes will never be discovered because of subsequent construction in the area.[9] Only the trigger remains above ground. Unlike his rehearsal of this moment years earlier in Cuba, Hemingway is believed to have placed the barrels to his forehead, not at the roof of his mouth. Carlos Baker's interview notes of Dr. Scott Earle, present at the death scene, noted the base of the skull was intact.[10]

Of course, once a patient has fully decided to take his own life, the doctor becomes the enemy. The paradigm shifts, and the patient is no longer working with the doctor for a cure but works solely to defeat our efforts. Dr. Rome was not incompetent; he was simply treating someone who did not want treatment. Four months after he learned the fate of his most famous patient, he wrote to Mary: "I think I can appreciate what this has meant to you; the whole ghastly, horrible realization of its finality. And all of the endless echoes of why, why, why, why. And the totally unsatisfying answers. This kind of a violent end for a man who we knew to possess the essence of gentleness is an unacceptable paradox. It seems to me that these are some of the reasons why the ceaseless effort to make sense of things which seem not to fit. In my judgment he had recovered sufficiently from his depression to warrant the recommendation I made that he leave the hospital. You accepted this in good faith. I was wrong about the risk and the loss is irreparable for you and me and many others." His final wish for Mary was that "these answers to your questions help you find composure in your head if not your heart."[11]

In the days that followed Hemingway's death, Mary would indeed display composure of the head and hide what pain her heart may have felt. And though suicides may be predictable, this does not mean they are preventable. As much as a suicide can be predicted, Hemingway's was more predictable than most. Yet, before this publication, he had never received a fully accurate diagnosis.

Working Man

Chapter 9

As Hemingway's brain demented over his last decade, at what appeared to be an exponential rate toward the end, the very act of creative writing became a struggle. His lifelong therapy became instead a primary source of depression because of the loss of his capacities and the subsequent fear that he could no longer make a living. As discussed, his difficulty with memory and his mental decline were accentuated by the stress of ECT itself, and, Hemingway believed, to an irreversible degree. The physiological stress of the treatments was too much for his compromised brain cells, pushing his cognitive abilities into an inexorable decline, all the while an acute self-awareness fueled his torment. After his second discharge from Mayo, there would be no recovery, and Hemingway knew it. He believed his memory had been "tampered with," much as he sensed after his plane crashes, when it was a challenge just to remember and then to write about the Africa safari he had just taken. Given enough weeks, his memory would have recovered to some extent, but never fully.

It is often challenging to accurately diagnose dementia in patients with very high IQs or in those who display great talents. Any mental illness that occurs in such an individual is bound to be atypical in presentation as is evident from Friedrich Nietzsche's last decade of institutionalization, psychosis, and even mutism. However, in some cases of dementia, artistic ability may be preserved despite the deterioration of pathways for memory, processing, and cognition. Hemingway's own mother could still play the piano despite her dementia late in life. Learned musical skills, like other learned behavior, rely on the pathways of the basal ganglia, which control movements long committed to the *physical* memory. Her piano skills did not emanate from higher cortical structures that were deteriorating above the basal ganglia. An example of artistic ability and, arguably, creative enhancement in the face of progressive dementia is that of Hemingway's contemporary, Willem de Kooning.

De Kooning, born in a working-class district of North Rotterdam in 1904, is considered one of the greatest artists of the twentieth century. Because his clinical course was so similar to Hemingway's and because he too produced brilliant art until his death, it is worth discussing his mental decline in detail.

De Kooning began his career as an expert draftsman, but once he immigrated to America, his ultrarealistic approach began to evolve into a unique style of abstract expressionism. By the 1950s he and Jackson Pollock were in a league of their own. He called Jackson "The leader . . . the painting cowboy . . . the first to get recognition."[1] Their very names remain synonymous with the Abstract Expressionist movement they had popularized. But, for de Kooning as for Pollock, alcoholism took its toll, although not through a deadly car crash like the one that took Pollock's life at the age of forty-four, along with the life of one of his two passengers. Rather, de Kooning's drinking would contribute to the insidious and premature death of brain cells. At times his alcoholism was incapacitating and life-threatening. Though he did go through detox and even attended AA meetings, he would never stay clean for long. To complicate matters, as in Hemingway's case, prescription sedatives mixed with alcohol would cause further impairment. His biographers noted: "The sound of an ambulance wailing down Woodbine Drive [his street] to collect him became almost routine."[2]

De Kooning's dementia was also caused by multiple factors or had a "mixed etiology." Alcohol was one component, but at one point de Kooning was diagnosed with vascular dementia (at the time termed to "multi-infarct dementia") from a series of small strokes (common in smokers like de Kooning). In addition, his doctor suspected Alzheimer's as well (as the majority of patients with vascular dementia also have Alzheimer's findings at autopsy).[3] His clinical picture of dementia was very similar to Hemingway's, with two exceptions: de Kooning's vascular component would have been greater because of his smoking, and Hemingway had accumulated further damage and symptoms from his numerous concussions.

And de Kooning would also develop paranoia. During a trip abroad (to the Stedelijk Museum in Amsterdam) in the early 1980s, he feared he'd be deported upon returning to the United States.[4] Though at first he was indeed an illegal immigrant, he was now unaware that he had long been a U.S. citizen. By 1984 he failed to recognize those familiar to him and spoke very little. An existence of confusion was punctuated by brief moments and at times even extended periods of lucidity when he could carry on a conversation. He suffered from long stretches of mutism, his days and nights were scrambled (indicating a circadian rhythm disruption), and hallucinations developed and worsened. Eventually he required full-time attendants. Still, through the 1980s, his art flourished. In fact, the only time he was in complete control and seemed free of his impairments and disruptive symptoms was when he was at the easel. His production as measured by the sheer number of completed canvases during this period was the greatest of his life. With a term reminiscent of Andy Warhol's career, de Kooning was described as "a factory," completing fifty-four paintings in 1983 and fifty-one in 1984; in 1985, his most productive year ever, he completed sixty-three paintings.[5]

Historically, de Kooning had great difficulty finishing a picture. Somehow, his dementia erased this ill-defined anxiety, and he no longer agonized for days over his works—they flowed. Only during those periods early in the decade when he simply could not work due to injury or illness did his idle mind revert to its deteriorated state—the familiar and therapeutic "action painting" was not there to temporarily crowd out his confusion, agitation, and psychosis.

The late works are sparse, the canvases are more blank than painted, and nearly all of them were composed with just primary colors. When his wife and assistants placed colors other than red, yellow, and blue at his disposal, he ignored their efforts and remained in complete control of his palette. The late works are ethereal and pleasing, and, like Hemingway's work, their simplicity is deceptive. They are, however, somewhat uneven in quality, which is fully understandable given that patients with dementia usually have highly variable days. But overall they are more than competent. Even at the time of production, the canvases were deservedly very expensive, bringing $300,000 to $350,000 each, and today they sell for millions in galleries and at auction.

For de Kooning, the complex motor actions of painting, the brush that moves by instinct and feel, was at this point (probably as always) guided by a subconscious drive. The technical skill and his understandings of color and composition had long been second nature to him. De Kooning's art could flow from him as long as he could hold the brush. And, with regard to content, those who understand Abstract Expressionism know it's useless and inappropriate to analyze the works in terms of "what they mean" or "what they look like."

But Hemingway's critics would give him no such pass on his "meaning." And his skills would not be enhanced as his illness progressed: his art required a poet's attention to every word, an intact memory, and processing power—the very cortical activities that were in a state of decline over his last decade. The very tools he needed to write with were defective. But, like an abstract painter, Hemingway understood the subconscious underpinnings of his work. He deliberately did not reflect on what he was writing between stints with the notebook or at the typewriter: "That way my subconscious would be working on it and at the same time I would be listening to other people and noticing everything."[6] And when his art flowed for him, the story would write itself. Toward the end of his life, his psyche still held mythical and spiritual allusion and great insights, yet at some point they had become unexpressible and were trapped forever.

The fiction he completed and struggled to complete over his last decade can now be examined in the context of his changing mental state. But, as seems always the case with Hemingway, he leaves us with a paradox: the writing's technical decline and other signs of dementia, such as disinhibition, are present in the face of preserved or even enhanced capacity for abstraction. This capacity is one of the few mental activities to actually improve as a person ages, even when judgment and insight become impaired. This can be particularly challenging clinically, as demented people may demonstrate horrendous judgment in their activities, finances, and relationships, yet articulate elaborate justifications for those actions, leaving those who are concerned for them quite puzzled. Much of Hemingway's behavior left friends in such a state, yet all the while, when busy at his profession, he was still leaving buried treasure for endless Ph.D. dissertations. The later works, particularly the posthumous ones, deserve three complimentary examinations: technical, interpersonal, and symbolic.

Because Hemingway had earned literary success, both critical and popular, at such a young age, it is understandable that many assume he was a prodigy. But true to his blue-collar image, he was always a working man. It is often the case that it's much harder for the prodigy in adulthood. He faces the realization that his work is no longer special just because of his age, and he is competing against artists who have formally studied their discipline and whose product evolved through the failures of thousands of crossed-out words and hundreds of painted-over canvases. It would have been better if Hemingway had had to earn his success the traditional way and if he had received more than his share of rejection letters early on. But his timing in Paris was so fortunate as to qualify as divine intervention. He was able to learn his craft while surrounded by some of the greatest literary minds of the twentieth century. He was accepted into their circle before he had ever published, and though many in the group may have believed him to be gifted, he was still spending his afternoons in cafés, drinking rum St. James, and trying to get it right.

Hemingway declined college and sought on-the-job training. World War I was more educational than he would appreciate at the time, as was his early newspaper work. Once he arrived in Paris, Ezra Pound directed his reading list and editorialized on past and present greats, Sylvia Beach provided the books, and newspaper editors helped create his unique style. Pete Wellington was Hemingway's boss at the Kansas City *Star*. In a 1940 interview, Hemingway remarked that he could "never say properly how grateful I am to have worked under him." Wellington urged him (in his typical harsh manner) to avoid clichés and slang, to write in short sentences, and to strive always for a plainness of expression.[7] And Hemingway borrowed thematically from the great minds around him: Frederic Henry is the embodiment of T. S. Eliot's "Hollow Man," and recent criticism argues that Hemingway shared essentially the same philosophical and spiritual themes as Joyce. It was the perfect formula for America's own modernist, forever in the rough.

Still, the trajectory was not always upwards. His masterpieces were usually followed by critical disasters—*In Our Time* by *Torrents of Spring; A Farewell to Arms* by *To Have and Have Not,* and *Green Hills of Africa* before the success of *For Whom the Bell Tolls.* The work that seems to divide the critics down the middle with regard to literary merit is his 1950 novel *Across the River and into the Trees.* It would be one of the last complete works while the dementing process was still prodromal, or in a preliminary phase.

The title *Across the River and into the Trees* was derived from the last words of Stonewall Jackson, who was wounded in the right hand and left arm in a flurry of friendly fire just after nightfall at Chancellorsville. His left arm was amputated, but he also developed pneumonia. A few moments before his death, in a delirious states, he called out orders, paused, and then, smiling, said, "Let us cross over the river and rest under the shade of the trees." Hemingway's intent was for us to see Cantwell, as some scholars have, as an avatar of Jackson[8] rather than himself.

The book was generally panned by critics after its release, and only recently has it found some favor among them. Aside from the Adriana-Renata story (like Ernest, the Colonel would address Renata as "Daughter" throughout the short text), the less sexy question is how competent and original was it? In his notes from the Paris years, Ernest instructed himself on "Imitating everybody, living and dead, relying on the fact that if you imitate someone obscure enough it will be considered original. Education consists in finding sources obscure enough to imitate so that they will be perfectly safe."[9] The obvious comparison is to Thomas Mann's *Death in Venice,* and though Hemingway did not own a translation of this 1912 work until after 1956, he surely saw it translated for the March 1924 edition of *The Dial* during his Paris years. In fact, it becomes obvious he had read it when one researches his use of the phrase "grace under pressure."

The phrase was forever linked to Ernest when he was quoted in Dorothy Parker's profile, "The Artist's Reward," in the November 30, 1929, edition of *The New Yorker* ("Exactly what do you mean by 'guts'?" Hemingway replied: "I mean, grace under pressure.").[10] And his April 24, 1926, letter to Scott Fitzgerald references a conversation Ernest had had with Gerald Murphy about bullfighting: "Was not referring to guts but to something else. Grace under pressure."[11] But this unique Hemingwayesque phrase was coined by Mann for his classic and appeared not only in the *Dial* in 1924 but in the English-language version *Death in Venice and Other Stories,* of 1925. Perhaps there is no better example of Hemingway following his own advice, imitating everybody. But still, a more likely inspiration was closer to home by the early 1950s.

His third wife, Martha Gellhorn, an accomplished war correspondent, wrote the novel *The Wine of Astonishment* (later republished as *Point of No Return*). This work is strikingly similar in structure and plot to *Across the River,* which at the time of publication was Hemingway's first book after ten years. He was very aware of Martha's 1948 novel at the time he finally broke his writing hiatus. What he was told specifically by Charles Scribner in 1947 was that Martha "had written a novel about the war, and both Max [Perkins] and Wallace Meyer thought that the first two thirds of it were extremely good. It told of an American colonel who toured around the warfront with his chauffer and had love affairs, drinking bouts and the usual sort of thing, all of which they said was very effectively done and very masculine."[12] (The final third, which neither editor cared for, described the horrors of the death camps.)

Hemingway kept up through Scribner not only with Martha's literary career after they divorced but also with her personal affairs—at times obsessively. He asked about her in one letter that also informed Scribner that his new housemaid was named Martha. Ernest said it was pleasure to give her orders. And so, with his third wife on his mind, Ernest began work on *his* World War II novel in 1948, inspired by the Venice trip that began in December of that year, when he first met Adriana.

Like Gellhorn's Colonel Smithers, Cantwell relies on interior monologue to fill the narrative and reflect on the war. No previous criticism of *Across the River* has addressed its originality, just its quality, with critics wondering if it would have been worthy of publication without Hemingway's name on it and observing that a work that consists largely of reflection and inner dialogue, which is by definition stream of consciousness, could just as easily be the result of a rambling pen. Even Adriana, the muse herself, was not impressed with the book, particularly the character she had inspired, telling Ernest, "The girl is boring. How could your colonel love a girl who is so boring? A girl like that does not exist, if she is lovely and from a good family and goes to Mass every morning. Such a girl would not drink all day like a sponge and be in bed at the hotel."[13]

Hemingway's defense of *Across the River* was "they can say anything about nothing happening in *Across the River*, but all that happens is the defense of the lower Piave, the breakthrough in Normandy, the taking of Paris and the destruction of the 22nd Inf. Reg. in Hürtgen forest plus a man who loves a girl and dies."[14] At least that was his intent, however less successfully he achieved it than *The Wine of Astonishment*. With events such as the Normandy breakthrough, perhaps a character's recollection and a narrator's description would both be inadequate. And once again, there is no hiding the autobiographical aspects of Hemingway's short novel—Cantwell is separated from his ambitious wife, a former war correspondent. At the time, Martha was also publishing with Scribner's, and she threatened to leave the firm if Ernest did not delete the defamatory passages that so obviously referenced her in his novel.[15]

More recent criticism of *Across the River* makes the Stonewall Jackson connection more obvious, describing a man whose health is actively failing and who is trying very self-consciously through his inner dialogue to gain control or at least to understand his life as it slips away, even in his last moments. In the autobiographical sense, Hemingway had once again seen himself in the crystal ball.

The Garden of Eden was begun a bit earlier, in 1946, but it split away from his *Islands in the Stream* text as a separate work around the spring of 1948.[16] Hemingway continued to work on the *Garden* manuscript intermittently for rest of his life. Some themes were genuine departures, while others were well known—the young protagonist writer, David, struggling to write a book on African hunting, is familiar enough, but his bisexual wife, Catherine, and the love triangle with another woman, Marita, were quite experimental for the time. The sexually charged text may indicate some lack of inhibition, but it is difficult to draw any conclusions about Hemingway's skills as a writer from the published text, as he never felt it ready for publication. Still, it would become the second posthumously released novel, in 1986.

The original manuscript at the Hemingway Archives is 200,000 words, arranged as forty-eight chapters, yet it would be edited down to 70,000 words in thirty chapters by Scribner's. Much like in his rambling

Islands in the Stream and in *The Dangerous Summer* he could never stop expanding; the repetitiveness and unwieldy expansion of *Garden* indicate progressive memory impairment. His signature economy of style was gone, as he was unable to fully remember what he had written before and therefore what to cut out. As his last decade progressed, he forged ahead on these last works, repeating himself. Only when his cognitive skills declined to another threshold, making the act of writing much harder, did the old style return by default in *Moveable Feast*.

What was deleted by the editors of *Garden* included a second love triangle, involving a painter, his wife, and her male lover, as well as a chapter labeled "provisional ending." The work has been compared to Fitzgerald's *Tender Is the Night*, as well as to Fitzgerald's personal life—in both circumstances, the writer is forced to choose between pursuing his career and caring for his mentally ill wife. Critics have noted how unstable Hemingway's Catherine is and have assigned various psychiatric labels; the character best fits the definition of a borderline personality, someone with intense inappropriate anger, fear of rejection and abandonment, intense and unstable relationships, self-destructive behaviors, and gender identity issues. Like Catherine, a borderline may even experience psychotic symptoms at times. It is important to note that when critics compare this character to Pauline, Hemingway's second wife, it is only in terms of her sequence in the writer's love life and of her general look and haircut; there is no evidence that Hemingway was assigning such severe psychopathology to Pauline or that Pauline would be diagnosed as such.

Still, each character in *Garden* can be identified as an echo of someone in Hemingway's past or current circle—Mary, of course, being "Marita" (little Mary). And critics have suggested that Pauline's sister was perhaps in part an inspiration for Catherine, as Virginia (Jinny) Pfeiffer was close to Hemingway prior to Pauline's death. Again, there is no evidence of such psychopathology in Jinny, but Hemingway admired her and claimed she had "as much talent or more for writing than I have." Her sexuality intrigued Ernest as well. Patrick Hemingway was quoted as saying that "Aunt Jinny was lesbian and she was quite keen on getting my mother to be homosexual as well. . . . There was always this undercurrent with Jinny."[17] But it was most certainly Ernest's intimacy with Mary and Pauline at the time that inspired the most risqué parts of his *Garden*. And he was reliving his 1926 personal Garden of Eden as well.

Hadley told her first biographer that during their Paris days Pauline liked to crawl into bed with Ernest and her at Schruns and also when the three of them vacationed together at Juan-les-Pins.[18] After Ernest had left for New York to secure a contract with Scribner's and Pauline was back in

Paris, she wrote to Hadley, "Oh, my soul, I wish I woz in Schruns. I miss you two men. How I miss you two men!" The interpretation is obvious enough, but Pauline could also be reminding her rival for Ernest that she was the smaller, younger, prettier, and more feminine of the pair.

Schruns is a small town in western Austria where Ernest and Hadley had taken skiing vacations, and Juan-les-Pins is a town on the French Riviera where Scott and Zelda had rented the Villa Paquita. To allow Hadley and Ernest to stay on at Paquita from June 1920 until they returned to the United States, the Fitzgeralds moved to another cottage, the Villa St. Louis. Scott brought along a manuscript of *The Sun Also Rises* to review. Thus, these weeks, during which Ernest, Hadley, and Pauline enjoyed one another's company in the same bed, occurred *after* Ernest and Pauline were already intimate. One researcher noted that Ernest and Hadley were both large individuals, and beds at the time were generally twin size unless custom made.

However Hemingway may have defined love as a young man, he believed himself to be in love with both Hadley and Pauline at the time and wrote to his father in 1926, that it was "pure hell to be in love with two women at once." The wise doctor quickly dismissed his son's dilemma as "nonsense."[19] As a much older man, he wrote clearly enough in *A Moveable Feast* that he loved both women at the time, and it is also clear from the text that, more than thirty years later, he still loved Hadley and could not forgive himself for the way he left her. To assuage this guilt, he portrayed himself as a distracted, hardworking, and innocent victim of the feminine forces swirling around him rather than as an active participant in the affair.

And two decades on, while writing *Garden*, Ernest would again enjoy two familiar partners at once. In 1947 he wrote to his World War II friend, Buck Lanham, of his and Mary's rejuvenated love life during the time Pauline was visiting in Cuba. She had arrived to help Patrick recover from what at first was postconcussive symptoms after a car wreck; as the week drew on, his headache worsened, and he developed a fever. It was probably unrelated to the accident, as he had developed some infectious process, but, with Mary dealing with family matters in Chicago, Pauline was a welcome sight at the Finca.[20]

When Mary returned, she and Pauline got on well and became close. Ernest's code words for his new love life in letters to Charles Scribner and Buck Lanham were "the happiness of the Garden that a man must lose." He singled out Martha as the only one of his wives not to play along: "she could never depict happiness truly; the happiness of the Garden that you must lose."[21] He also urged Lanham to "KEEP ALL THIS UNDER YOUR HAT

TOO." Pauline wrote to Ernest and Mary in 1948 as "Dear Men," her greeting from twenty-three years earlier. She began collaborating with Mary on the plans for his "white tower" at Finca in the summer of 1947, and they visited each other frequently in the few remaining years of Pauline's life (Mary even traveled to California). And Ernest was furious when he learned that Pauline had met with Martha in Italy without his knowledge in 1949, and in *his* beloved Venice.[22]

The alternative ending to *Garden* portrays a couple on a beach, and it's David and Catherine, not David and Marita as expected. Catherine has been released from a Swiss asylum, and, true to her pathology of borderline personality, she asks David to agree to a suicide pact if she decompensates again. The text, as left by Hemingway, is repetitive and less coherent than any finished product he would have ever approved. Still, *Garden* was very risqué for the time, and Hemingway was ever attentive to his hair fetish in the text. The boldness of the work is undeniable. *Garden of Eden* was begun nine years before the 1955 publication of *Lolita*. Hemingway later purchased the 1958 U.S. edition.

The writer he created, David Bourne, is focused on recollecting his experiences hunting an elephant in East Africa with his father. To his credit, Hemingway always considered killing elephants taboo. He never hunted them, and on his last safari he was far more interested in watching elephants and other animals than in killing them. In his "Africa Journal," he had elaborated: "In the night I thought about the elephant . . . and about the long time he had lived with so many people against him and seeking to kill him for his two wonderful teeth that were now only a great disadvantage to him and a deadly load for him to carry." An analyst would substitute Ernest for the elephant and "persona" for the tusks.

In the night, Hemingway continued to reflect on the old elephant: "I knew that old bulls were driven out of the herds long before they were impotent but I did not know why some were still loved after they had gone by themselves and why others were not."[23]

Islands in the Stream, True at First Light, and *A Moveable Feast* all suffered similar fates—so heavily edited as to compromise the author's intent. Thus, in their commercial forms they are incapable of fully reflecting the state of their author's skills. When Valerie Danby-Smith (later Valerie Hemingway) arrived in Cuba after Hemingway's death to sort his papers, she discovered that the manuscripts "were not even close to meeting Hemingway's exacting publishing standards." And eventually "They were, to a certain extent, reconstructed by editors specifically chosen to shape the working drafts into coherent, saleable novels of reasonable length." The pages were "rambling, sometimes incoherent."[24] What was published as *Islands*, even after editing, reads as a rambling sketch-book of ideas and autobiography in which, once again, simply changing the names serve as the author's weak attempt at concealing identities.

The 200,000-word manuscript of Hemingway's "Africa Journal" would have a complicated legal history and a legacy of controversy, but it was ultimately edited for Scribner's by his son Patrick. The original assign-ment for *Look* magazine was an article concerning the 1953–54 safari—and the magazine expected only 10,000 words. Patrick would cut at least 50 percent of his father's 200,000 words and described the result as fic-tion, although largely based on fact. It is unfair to judge another first draft or sketchbook as the finished work of a Nobel Prize winner. Hemingway was drinking heavily on the safari and reported difficulty remembering the trip once he was back in Cuba, no doubt the sequelae of his latest concussions and ongoing alcoholism and a profound harbinger. Patrick's *True at First Light* was published in 1999, and yet another version would come to print in 2005 with the title *Under Kilimanjaro*; this version was absurdly billed as "truer to the author's intent." Neither can be. The artist always leaves more in the scrap heap than on the canvas for public view-ing, and a writer's sketchbook is just that.

The highly acclaimed *Old Man and the Sea* would become required reading for thousands of schoolchildren and helped to confirm the Hem-ingway legacy after fifteen years of failure in the eyes of critics. His theme was common by now; in Santiago's words, "A man can be destroyed but not defeated." His struggle against the seen and unseen forces against him and his eventual loss were reminiscent of that inevitable fate that Harry Morgan had expressed in *To Have and Have Not*: that "a man alone ain't got no bloody . . . chance." Santiago's eventual triumph, however compro-mised, has been compared to Hemingway's mastery of his own craft, and thus, in this way, the novella is also a return to his writing basics. Much as the batter in a slump is told to focus on the fundamentals of stance, swing, and timing, Hemingway could also be viewed as returning to his fundamentals—the plainness of speech, a deceptively simple style, and naturalistic themes.

Though initially serialized in *Life* in 1952, the work was complete by mid-February 1951, fully ten years before Hemingway's death. It would be his last fully original novel in publication. It is so widely read and taught because it is so short and because its themes are easily elaborated. Rather than a metaphor for the mastery of the his art over a lifetime, perhaps it's a statement of the effort it took to keep a grasp on his skills, as Santiago struggles to hold his prize—finding it has been devoured all the same. And as a final insult and a perfect symbol for how Hemingway felt his work had been misjudged, Santiago's achievement is completely misunderstood (a waiter tries to explain to tourists that sharks have eaten the marlin, and they quickly conclude the skeleton is that of a shark).

Hemingway had conceived the story twelve years earlier and wrote to his editor of the projected narrative: an old commercial fisherman struggles with a swordfish for four days and nights, only to lose it to sharks as he pulls it alongside his skiff.[25] The literary critic Edmund Wilson believed *Old Man and the Sea* was "a good enough little story" that only appeared to be a masterpiece because it followed the disaster of *Across the River*. Dos Passos agreed and noted that he was "fascinated by the 'operation,'" by which he meant the timing and presentation of the work, not its substance. In fact, he "could hardly judge the story: it was like a magician's stunt—when he makes the girl float through the hoop, you don't notice whether she's pretty."[26]

The first published version of *A Moveable Feast* was edited by Hemingway to some extent; he corrected his handwritten pages and, later, the typed pages. Some of the retyped manuscript had revisions in his hand, but there was never any version he considered a finished product. Mary was largely responsible for "finishing" this project, and in the process his chapters were rearranged. This compromised Hemingway's main goal of the work. In his post–World War II years, he synthesized memory and writing in a consciously Proustian manner. The chapters built on each other thematically, and he understood their order to be critical to the progression and understanding of his books. Just as in 1950, when he feared that Hotchner's editing of *The Dangerous Summer* had destroyed its "Proustian effect,"[27] he expressed this exact concern regarding *A Moveable Feast*. Furthermore, when justifying the work as both fiction *and* memoir, he again recalled Proust: "All remembrance of things past is fiction."[28]

Because *A Moveable Feast* was his focus during the last three to four years of his life, at a time when his dementia was evident and progressing, even if never diagnosed, this text deserves special examination—not the widely known text, or the "Mary Hemingway version" but the manuscript at the Kennedy Library, that, fortunately, was made available, more or less in its raw form, by Ernest's son Patrick and his grandson Sean in 2009. The discussion in chapter 10 is based on this original manuscript—the one Hemingway could never finish and could never title because of his dementia. At the time of his death, his paranoia was so prominent that he insisted the work never be published at all.

A Moveable Feast

Chapter 10

Hemingway once remarked to A. E. Hotchner: "If you are lucky enough to have lived in Paris as a young man, then wherever you go for the rest of your life, it stays with you, for Paris is a moveable feast." Later that night, Hotchner wrote the words down, and years later he "gave them" to Mary as she searched for a title for the Paris memoirs.[1] As a young man in Paris, Hemingway was instructed in Roman Catholicism as preparation for his marriage to Pauline. The priest from her parish, Saint Sulpice, likely elaborated for Ernest that a moveable feast is a church feast day linked to the varying date of Easter.[2] Ernest had used the phrase "moveable feast" in two letters from 1950, as well as in his "Africa Journal" and in *Across the River*.[3] In a letter to Buck Lanham he told his friend, "Loneliness is a moveable feast" (September 27, 1950). And Colonel Cantwell informs a room-service waiter that "Happiness, as you know, is a moveable feast." (The waiter is equipped with "Campari bitters and a bottle of Gordon Gin.")

But Hemingway was very meticulous and thoughtful about titles and never derived them from causal remarks. His preferred source for choosing one was the King James Bible. Mary would take many other liberties with his manuscript, but at least this one seemed to fit perfectly.

Though Hemingway was working on other books as he wrote *A Moveable Feast*, both *The Garden of Eden* and *The Dangerous Summer*, he began *A Moveable Feast*, most likely by the spring of 1957. Yet he believed it incomplete and in fact unpublishable at the time of his death, four years later. He progressed with *A Moveable Feast* from July to December 1957, then worked on it alternately with the sexually charged *Garden of Eden* between January 1958 and March 1959, even carrying the manuscript to Spain and back. *The Dangerous Summer*, his bullfighting obsession, took all of his energies from May 1959 to October 1960, but he then devoted himself entirely to *Feast* from January 1961 until his suicide, in July.

Of course, there is no evidence he worked on the manuscript while hospitalized, and between hospitalizations he mostly shuffled papers, ordered the chapters, and ruminated about his inability to write. He was convinced that his skills would never return. At some point, his dementia progressed, and his cognitive skills declined below the threshold necessary for literary work of his caliber, and after ECT his skills were irretrievable.

Perhaps the manuscript we know as *A Moveable Feast* was thus "completed" just in time. Between his two hospitalizations (January to April 1961), he was laboring up to five hours a day on his Paris sketches but was incapable of real progress. "He was exhausted and found it almost impossible to write. In February he was unable to write a coherent sentence for a presentation volume for President Kennedy. He would often sit with his physician, George Saviers, tears coursing down his cheeks, complaining that he could no longer write."[4] The physiological stress of his ECT (not the mechanism of the ECT) had worsened his dementia—he could no longer access the creative genius that had served him for decades.

And Hemingway's handwritten and typed pages for *Feast*, under close examination, further confirm that dementia was his primary diagnosis by 1957. Still, his abstraction and capacity for description shine through, making it one of his most compelling efforts. A Hemingway autobiography, however embellished, still held great historical significance, and at the very least he could still seduce his reader with Lost Generation gossip.

When Hemingway completed a book, he felt physically and emotionally drained, and he acknowledged as he aged that writing was "more difficult all the time."[5] The only part that seemed to flow was the dialogue. He made very few revisions or corrections to the conversations; by contrast, his descriptive passages required extensive changes. His French was never completely fluent. During the 1920s, it was Hadley who spoke to most of the waiters and dealt with their landlords. Perhaps more telling than the technical decline evident in the numerous misspellings and misunderstandings of French words is his lack of insight, even apathy, regarding the numerous words that didn't look quite right.

The last sentence Hemingway ever wrote as a professional writer concerned *Feast*: "This book contains material from the *remises* of my memory and of my heart. Even if the one has been tampered with and the other does not exist."[6] "Remise," in the legal sense, means a formal release or the giving over of a claim. But Hemingway may have also been reminding us of a fencing term—a "remise" in this context is a thrust that hits the intended target after a first attempt has failed. He considered this book his final gift to Hadley and was attempting to do her justice the second time around. Sports metaphors were commonly used when he discussed his work. When Mary complained that the Paris sketches were hardly autobiographical, as she and many others had hoped, he explained that he was working by "remate," a jai alai term for a double-wall rebound.[7] And we do learn a great deal about the author through his dealings with others, although we already knew he could hold a grudge for a lifetime. The initial criticism of the work, that he had created a "feast of victims," was more than justified.

In *Feast*, Hemingway assumes the detached yet fully aware stance of one of his earliest protagonist, Jake Barnes. Like Jake, he is keenly observant and usually the only sober one in the gang. And throughout the text, Hemingway portrays himself as self-sacrificing and poor, skipping meals to provide for his family, a man with an eye for beautiful girls but still the loyal husband. He is a student of his craft, a humble writer who is striving to learn all he can from others. Hadley is portrayed as "blissfully in love with her husband, admiring the smallest of his decisions as if they were wonders of life."[8] Most of the others, particularly Scott Fitzgerald, are savaged.

Hemingway's judgment while writing *A Moveable Feast* had deteriorated, and he failed to understand that transparent and relentless self-glorification, particularly at the expense of others, could serve only to diminish his stature. Montale, the Italian poet and critic, believed that *A Moveable Feast* (as well as *Across the River*), demonstrated that Hemingway was at this point in his life "moving towards a costly decomposition altogether congenial to the childlike nature of a man who had not grown up, a man *manqué*."[9] Montale's insight can be reframed in terms of the "decomposition" of skills as a result of ongoing dementia and of a "childlike nature" (in written word and personal behavior) resulting from emotional regression, commonly seen in this illness. Without appreciating his diagnosis, it is understandable that Hemingway would be perceived as an artist who is incomplete and underdeveloped—a man "*manqué*."

As for his memory, Hemingway believed that it vanished progressively with each of his ECT sessions. His last written words justify his suicide: he is "out of business," his memory "does not exist." And he makes one last argument for Hadley's forgiveness—it wasn't his fault, his heart was "tampered with."

Despite the limitations caused by Hemingway's illness, Paris does come alive in the book. He captured its essence beautifully, and the descriptions of the specific paths he took, though fraught with spelling and geographic inaccuracies, are still lovely. Long-term memories, like one's ability for abstract thinking, are usually sustained until the later stages of illness, while short-term memory and processing decline first in dementia. The editing and basic wordsmith skills were just what he lacked, and they were provided by Mary and Harry Brague, his last editor at Scribner's. It was Mary who primarily revised the manuscript for more than two years prior to its publication: Ernest suicided on July 2, 1961, and Mary did not submit her final version of *A Moveable Feast* to Scribner's until July 27, 1963.

The work alternates wonderful imagery with striking vehemence. Consider how he handles Fitzgerald: "His talent was as natural as the pattern that was made by the dust on a butterfly's wings. At one time he understood it no more than the butterfly did and he did not know when it was brushed or marred. Later he became conscious of his damaged wings and their construction and he learned to think. He was flying again and I was lucky to meet him just after a good time in his writing if not a good one in his life." Curiously, the Mary Hemingway edition is less forgiving. She deletes the hopeful words "He was flying again" and adds that "[he] could not fly anymore because the love of flight was gone and he could only remember when it had been effortless."[10] Undercutting Scott would be unnecessary, as Ernest, in turn, was much harsher.

Scott is described as an obnoxious drunk, a whining hypochondriac, a bully to his inferiors, and the most annoying and miserable companion imaginable. It seems Hemingway's duty to rescue Scott from his drunken bumbling, such as when Scott relentlessly harasses fellow train travelers. And, of course, there are the infamous passages about Fitzgerald's "measurements" not being manly enough and about his inability to satisfy Zelda.

When Hemingway introduces Scott in the text, he leaves little doubt that his goal is to feminize him: "Scott was a man then who looked like a boy with a face between handsome and pretty. He had very fair wavy hair . . . and a delicate long-lipped Irish mouth that, on a girl, would have been the mouth of a beauty. His chin was well built and he had good ears and a handsome, almost beautiful, unmarked nose. This should not have added up to a pretty face, but that came from the coloring, the very fair hair and the mouth."[11] The internal rhyming of "very fair wavy hair" and "very fair hair" all hint at "fairy," and an "unmarked nose" would indicate, to Hemingway, a wimpy life—one without boxing.

Next he sets out to further humiliate and emasculate Fitzgerald. In the chapter "A Matter of Measurements," Scott confesses to Ernest that, according to Zelda, he is inadequately equipped to satisfy women. A trip to the men's room for an inspection, followed by Hemingway's judgment that Scott's equipment is "perfectly fine" and there is no cause for alarm, is no reassurance to Scott. They then trek to the Louvre to evaluate the statues, Scott clearly possessing every inch of marble he had examined himself. Hemingway also uses the sketch to attack Zelda for trying to ruin Scott's productivity. She is jealous of his talent, so she is simply trying to destroy it and put him out of business, he suggests.

Although Hemingway had related the same story of Scott's agonizing over his limited phallus in a letter almost a decade earlier and was generally true in *Feast* to that earlier account, other facts in the text about Fitzgerald don't hold up to historical scrutiny. The detail that Scott had never made love to a woman before Zelda is contradicted by his own account of seeing a prostitute while in college and by that of the actress Rosalinde Fuller, whose unpublished autobiography elaborated on her intimacy with Scott prior to his marriage to Zelda. Furthermore, the account of Ernest's initial meeting with Fitzgerald as Scott drank with a fellow Princeton man, the baseball star Duncan Chaplin, is also inventive, as Chaplin was not in Paris during 1925.[12]

Hemingway wrote to Maxwell Perkins in June 1925 that "Scott Fitzgerald is living here now and we see quite a lot of him. We had a great trip together driving his car up from Lyon through the Cote D'Or. I've read his Great Gatsby and think it is an absolutely first rate book."[13] When it comes to recalling the travel for *Feast*, Ernest first sets the scene with his high hopes: "I would have the company of an older and successful writer." But the trip is nothing short of a disaster; Scott is an inept, whining hypochondriac who basically requires babysitting.

The car they retrieve, a Renault, has no roof—it has been cut away. Zelda, we're told, "hated car tops." Even on a guys-only road trip, it seems Zelda's psychosis is inescapable. The pair are soaked in the rain during their drive home. Ernest then continues to feminize Scott in the text, loosely connecting him with a young girl losing her virginity. "I am not sure Scott had ever drunk wine from a bottle before and it was exciting to him . . . as a girl might be excited by going swimming for the first time without a bathing suit."[14] Yet Scott's comments in 1925 are in line with Hemingway's letter about their "great trip" together: "Hemingway and I . . . had a slick drive through Burgundy. He's a peach of a fellow and absolutely first-rate."[15]

With dementia comes regression, and at Hemingway's worst, much as in his "Africa Journal," he regressed to adolescent sexuality (his concern with measurements). And as he struggled with his manuscript, privately noting that his cognitive skills and memory were faltering, he also regressed to projection: "You could not be angry with Scott any more than you could be angry with someone who was crazy."[16]

Though three of Hemingway's short stories were first published in the *Transatlantic Review*, Hemingway vilified and insulted its editor. Ernest had even worked proofreading manuscripts for him in Paris, but his late-life assessment of Ford Madox Ford is one of the cruelest in *Feast*. Ford is described as a habitual liar with malodorous breath, in fact, "fouler than the spout of any whale." Ford's stench drives Hemingway to hold his breath when near him "in a closed room." If he *has* to visit with him, he prefers the open air.[17] In Hemingway's eyes, Ford Madox Ford, whose real name was Ford Hermann Hueffer,(he had changed it after World War I) is a phony, a liar, and drunkard. Legend has it there was a dispute over money that left Hemingway with enormous contempt for Ford, and once again, Hemingway proves he could get even, no matter how long it took.

And John Dos Passos is the "pilot fish," swimming along with the rich, scouting talent for the upper class. The metaphor is clear enough, but the language conjures up two unpleasant biological images: pilot fish feed on parasites, and labeling someone as a "fish" is usually a way of mocking facial features. Similarly in *Feast*, he describes Wyndham Lewis as having "a face that reminded me of a frog, not a bullfrog but just any frog, and Paris was too big a puddle for him."[18] This is probably the only assault in *Feast* that *is* justified, as Lewis had titled his 1934 essay on Hemingway "The Dumb Ox." The review is every bit as insulting and misinformed as his title suggests. Ernest was so outraged when he saw it that he smashed a vase of tulips at his beloved Shakespeare and Company. He insisted on paying Sylvia Beach 1,500 francs for the flowers, vase, and thirty-eight soaked books.[19] Though he probably went too far in describing Lewis as having the eyes of an "unsuccessful rapist," whatever that means, Ernest should be allowed some retaliation in *Feast* for the "dumb ox" insult, and one can easily see how Lewis reminded him of a frog.

But Dos Passos deserved no such treatment. Dos Passos is now the forgotten man of literary modernism. He was considered at one time America's Joyce, and his photo appeared on the cover of *Time* a year before the impressionistic painting of Hemingway deep-sea fishing graced it. The two men shared so much life together that Hemingway at one point even tried to fix Dos up with his sister Ursula (who found him unattractive, nervous, and "jumpy").[20] This was not a problem; Dos soon married Hemingway's longtime friend and former romantic interest Katy Smith.

During the Spanish Civil War, Dos became disillusioned after the kidnapping and execution of his friend Jose Robles. And he soon realized the "cause" that had brought them over there was simply proxy Stalinism with all its attendant horrors. He put the question directly to Hemingway: "what's the use of fighting a war for civil liberties, if you destroy civil liberties in the process?" Unable to face the two possible answers, that he had been duped or that he had been complicit, Hemingway regressed to attacking the messenger: "Civil liberties, *shit!* Are you *with* us or are you *against* us?"[21]

Further egged on by the unexplained dislike of his girlfriend at the time, Martha Gellhorn, of Dos, from that point forward Hemingway was solidly against his longtime friend. The couple even spread rumors of Dos's "cowardice" in Spain, which were certainly untrue. Dos put himself at great risk trying to track down his missing friend (who, unknown to Dos, had been executed by the time he arrived there). The worst of Dos's transgressions was the caricature of Ernest as an "Indian-like boy" with dirty fingernails in his 1951 novel, *Chosen Country*, but Ernest had long before assigned Dos to enemy status. And, sadly, once he broke off the friendship, he was never close to another artist in his league. Hemingway was surrounded thereafter only by sycophants and hangers-on.

And as a man nearing sixty, reflecting on his Paris days, he found that dementia accentuated both his aggression and his fears and forced his inventive recollection into the narrow, dead-end path of vengeance. But Hemingway could not savage Dos for sins he had not yet committed. So he reduced their Paris years together to the sole memory of Dos's sycophantic hobnobbing. Dos's evil deed from the 1920s was simply introducing Ernest to a circle of people richer than he was (that is, Pauline). Once again, Hemingway was the victim of events that eventually ruined his marriage, and Dos was the Iago.

Hemingway never shied away from satire, and he could be good-natured or cruel or both in one sentence. And he seemed to delight in sucker-punching acquaintances and friends. Characters in *The Sun Also Rises* read as a "who's who" of Hemingway's friends, enemies, perceived enemies, and casual acquaintances from his Paris years. Despite the fact that Harold Loeb, Dos Passos, and Sherwood Anderson all lobbied publisher Horace Liveright to accept *In Our Time*,[22] Hemingway seemed to write *The Sun Also Rises* with one goal in mind: "to tear that bastard Loeb apart."[23]

The Torrents of Spring was his right-handed lead punch at Sherwood Anderson, the notable who opened all doors to him before he had ever published a single word. Indeed, without Anderson, there might never have been a Hemingway. And agents from Scribner's told him flatly that his original manuscript of *To Have and Have Not* was too libelous to publish.

But what clinicians and family often observe in dementia is the exaggeration of preexisting traits—a naturally generous person when becoming demented often loses judgment and starts to give away their money and possessions; an instinctively assertive person may become violent. Exaggerated violence took the form of verbal attack and insult in *Feast*. The Paris sketches display the effects of disinhibition from dementia combined with Hemingway's fondness for assault. The passages range in brutality from blatant to more than blatant.

The least vehement but most prescient is likely the tenth sketch, "With Pascin at the Dome." It features Hemingway's encounter with Jules Pascin, a painter who had agreed to illustrate a book of Hemingway's "dirty poems,"[24] and his models at the time, two sisters. Pascin was a representational artist who generally worked in soft colors. He painted doll-like young ladies who all shared youthful faces—some shapely, most rather plump. The sisters at the Dome were plenty attractive; one enjoyed modeling her tight sweater for Hemingway at the table while needling the drunk Pascin. Hemingway was, by his description, cool and detached, taking it all in and never seduced or even tempted by the girl's game. Hemingway had portrayed himself as the ever loyal husband, although the "Madame Louisette" business card found among his Paris notebooks may argue otherwise.[25]

Pascin behaved like an abusive, sloppy drunk. Ernest ends the sketch by mentioning the painter's death but not elaborating on the details. But Jules is connected to Hemingway's circle of family and acquaintances who chose death at their own hands—Pascin was just forty-five, suiciding roughly five years after the encounter in *Feast* would have occurred. Hemingway's reflection on Pascin led him to conclude in the text that "the seeds of what we will do are in all of us."[26] Pascin's death outdid Hemingway's in terms of dramatics: he hung himself in his studio after first cutting his wrists and writing a message to a past lover on the wall with his blood. His will split his estate between his wife and his mistress.

The most controversial aspect of the making of *A Moveable Feast* was delved into by the Hemingway scholar Jacqueline Tavernier-Corbin, the foremost expert on the work; she believes that the famous Ritz Hotel trunks never existed. The story is legendary, almost magical—the long-lost trunks bring to life the Paris days for an author now ready to write his much-anticipated memoirs. But the weight of physical and psychological evidence indicates that the Ritz "discovery" was indeed a fantasy and in some sense a conspiracy.

There is first the impracticality of a trunk, which was either labeled as Hemingway's or somehow known to the staff of the hotel as obviously his property, being simply tucked away unnoticed until he arrived decades later (one need only consider how less than eager Paris hotel bellmen are to store and retrieve luggage when you are actually a paying guest with tip in hand). Hemingway had bragged that he had entered Paris with the very first troops during World War II and liberated the Travelers Club and the Ritz the first afternoon.[27] He and Mary stayed there as well, and he wrote to Patrick Hemingway from the Hürtgen Forest in November 1944, "Papa still staying at Ritz (joint we took) when back in town."[28] If trunks were waiting then, his presence was never a secret.

When Hemingway left Paris in 1930, he was already a public figure, and as his fame grew it would have been fairly easy to track his whereabouts with a letter or call to his publisher and then to ship his belongings to him. Furthermore, was it one trunk or two? Hotchner claims he was present at the very moment in Paris when "We opened the trunk and it was a treasure trove of manuscripts."[29] Yet Mary described the Ritz Hotel trunks as "two small, fabric-covered, rectangular boxes both opening at the seams (containing) blue—and yellow-covered penciled notebooks and sheaves of typed papers, ancient newspaper cuttings." Mary gave other details—the locks were rusted and were easily "pried open," and the contents also included "bad watercolors done by old friends, a few cracked and faded books, some musty sweat shirts and withered sandals. Ernest had not seen the stuff since 1927, when he packed it and left it at the hotel before going to Key West."[30] But Ernest left in March of 1928 for Key West. And if they were two "small" boxes, it is unlikely they contained paintings, sweatshirts, and sandals in addition to all the manuscripts later claimed by Mary and others.

But most damning is the evidence that when he did leave Paris, his possessions were scattered among four apartments, When he and Hadley separated, Ernest moved into Gerald Murphy's studio apartment in the rue Froidevaux, but he still kept the apartment he and Hadley had shared in the rue de Notre-Dame-des-Champs (until June 1927) and kept some of his belongings there. He and Pauline moved to their own apartment at 6 rue Férou, while Hadley moved to her new one at 35 rue de Fleurus. She wrote to him in 1926 about coming to get his "suitcases, etc. They are all piled up in the dining room."[31] It is clear that Hemingway had belongings in all four apartments, so why the need for a fifth place for storage?

Just like many others who have searched through the biographies and the many documents and letters at the Hemingway Library, I can find no evidence that Ernest and Pauline actually stayed at the Ritz, even after they had given up their apartment in the rue Férou. It seems highly unlikely he would store trunks at a hotel where he was not staying, no matter how many times he may have frequented the bar. When Tavernier-Courbin wrote to the Ritz management in 1980, she learned that the "books indicating items left for storage for the years 1926 and 1928 have been destroyed." The management also stated that "Old employees of the Ritz recall that Mr. Hemingway often left things at the hotel between trips but, no one remembers that he left anything for thirty years."[32]

Hemingway never used the word "trunk" as far as is documented and wrote only that "I found stuff here that has been in storage for 30 years. Good stuff for you and Mss. of The Undefeated, Fifty Grand, most of In Our Time and Men Without Women all holograph and Big Two Hearted River in the copybooks I used to write it in the café. Plenty stuff to make the trip worthwhile. Bough[t] some good Vuitton bags packed the stuff all day yest. . . . Some is pretty exciting to see again."[33]

The letter was to Lee Samuels, a figure in Hemingway's business dealings on a variety of levels. One was arranging for the sale of original Hemingway manuscripts. Thus, the letter Ernest sent was essentially a business proposal with an exciting context. The columnist Leonard Lyons reported in 1957 that the manuscript of *A Farewell to Arms* was among the famous Ritz finds; however, it was well known that Hemingway gave this manuscript to Pauline's uncle Gus Pfeiffer in 1930. It seems undeniable that the famous "Ritz Hotel trunks" were evocative rather than material.[34]

Mary was primarily responsible for crafting the legend of the Paris trunks after Ernest's death, as she understood the historical and financial aspects of her husband's memoirs. In her 1964 account, the Paris staff was threatening to send the trunks to the incinerator, but by the time she wrote her memoir, *How It Was*, in 1976, she "recalled" that the Ritz staff "made a speech to Ernest, its tone so formal they had obviously rehearsed it. It was now thirty years or more since monsieur had left with them two pieces of luggage, one rather small, one large, enjoining them to care for them well since they contained important papers. In their opinion it was now time to relieve them of the responsibility."[35] Ernest never mentioned such a dramatic speech. Clearly her recollection was more than inventive.

Ernest's psychological need for creating the myth of a "Paris trunk" is also clear. At the time he was writing *A Moveable Feast,* a time that Hemingway understood to be close to that of his death, he was seeking forgiveness from Hadley. Because of his fatalistic thinking, he believed he was moving ever more quickly toward his demise. We know also from his manuscript that Pauline was on his mind, but he chose to delete her section, as this was Hadley's book. Pauline had died in 1951, soon after Ernest argued with her by the phone over the arrest of their son Gregory, usually reported as involving a "drug incident" (in reality it was an arrest for cross-dressing).[36] She had flown from San Francisco to Los Angeles to check on her son and to get the full story. The next night, Ernest received her call from her sister's house in Los Angeles; it was midnight in Cuba. According to Pauline's sister, Jinny, the conversation started out calmly enough, but soon Pauline was "shouting into the phone and sobbing uncontrollably."[37]

Pauline had suffered from headaches and hypertensive episodes so severe that her systolic pressure reached 300. She did get some sleep after the heated call but woke at 1 A.M. with severe abdominal pain. She was taken to St. Vincent's Hospital and died on the operating table three hours later.

What was unknown to Ernest and even to the doctors who treated her was that Pauline had a rare abdominal tumor, a pheochromocytoma. This tumor is known to secrete adrenaline and to elevate blood pressure to dangerous levels. This was the cause of her intermittent headaches and hypertension over some months, and when the tumor released adrenaline in the night her blood pressure spiked. Pauline was under anesthesia when her tumor stopped pumping out adrenaline. Her pressure dropped precipitously, and, because of the effect of the anesthesia, it was impossible for her blood pressure to recover to normal levels. She died of shock while the surgeons searched for a bleeding vessel in her abdomen, which they presumed was the cause of her pain.

Jinny and Gregory both believed that Ernest's rant had elevated her blood pressure even further and killed Pauline. During their last visit, Gregory (with his wife, Jane, and infant daughter) minimized his arrest, stating it was "not really so bad." Ernest angrily shared that it was more than bad, asserting that it had killed his mother.[38] While departing, Gregory flatly told his father, "You killed my mother." They remained mutually repelled like two electrons for the rest of their lives. Ernest, in turn, blamed Gregory and his arrest for the death. In Ernest's depressed and ruminative mind of the late 1950s, he was no doubt a murderer.

But Ernest deleted the chapter in *A Moveable Feast* that included Pauline. The Paris book was about Hadley, and the central event that he came to mythologize from his years with her with was her loss of his first stories.

In early December 1922, Hadley had packed all of the manuscripts that she could find strewn about their Paris apartment, including the carbons, in a small valise and headed for the station to board an overnight train to meet her husband in Switzerland. At the Gare de Lyon, she handed the luggage to a porter, only to find the valise missing when she got to her compartment. She frantically searched all the other compartments with the conductor, but it was soon obvious the case had been stolen. When she met Ernest at Lausanne, she was sobbing so uncontrollably that she was unable to even tell him what was wrong.

Some biographies report that he left that very night and headed back to Paris to look for any left-behind manuscripts or carbons in the apartment, taking their lead from the text of *Feast* itself: "I was making good money then at journalism, and took the train to Paris. It was true alright and I remember what I did in the night after I let myself into the flat and found it was true." What exactly he recalls he did "in the night" was either a hint at scandal to add spice to his fictionalized memoir or his own confused recollection. All biographical evidence suggests he stayed in Lausanne with his wife. Two friends, Lincoln Steffens and Guy Hickok, were returning to Paris on the next train and asked about the lost case on his behalf when they reached the Gare de Lyon.[39] For Ernest and Hadley it was an enjoyable and eventful trip, with plenty of skiing on the slopes above Chamby, and the couple returned to Paris almost a month later, in mid-January, 1923. It appears that Ernest showed great sensitivity toward his wife at the time of the loss, and whatever anguish they shared was short lived. Perhaps he took Ezra Pound's advice that if a lost story's form was correct or right at first, he should be able to reconstruct it from memory. If that failed, the story lacked proper construction and would *never* be right.[40] Hadley had done him a favor, and later on he admitted as much: "was probably good for me to lose early work."[41]

Whether good for honing his craft or not, the subject of a writer's work being lost or destroyed would reappear in future manuscripts. David, the protagonist in *Garden of Eden*, would see his stories burned, and a deleted passage from *Islands in the Stream* equates lost manuscripts with the author's metaphorical castration; he sleeps with a pillow between his legs to ease the "recovery." His reflection on the lost case made the event seem more traumatic as the years advanced.

Finally, he was ready to offer his peace to Hadley, and creating the Paris trunk was the key. In a crossed-out passage from *Feast*, he wrote: "We had been *armored together* by two things. The first was the loss of everything I had written over a period of four years except for two stories and a few poems" (emphasis added).[42] He could never expect the Ritz "find" to be accepted as the same valise she had managed to lose in a Paris train station years ago, but at the basest level the return of lost manuscripts from the same period was more than his olive branch to Hadley: this time it was profitable. In 1922, she lost a pile of unedited stories no one would publish. The book that would become *A Moveable Feast* was listed on Scribner's forthcoming book list in 1960 and 1961—and was much anticipated.

Hemingway described the second thing that "armored" him to his wife in a beautifully romantic passage: "When we lived in Austria in the winter we would cut each other's hair and let it grow to the same length. One was dark and the other was dark red gold and in the dark in the night one would wake the other swinging the heavy dark or the heavy silken red gold across the others lips in the cold dark in the warmth of the bed. You could see your breath if there was moonlight." Ernest called Hadley the "heroine" of the book, who would understand "when you wrote fiction with her in it."[43] In his "Africa Journal," written in the 1950s, Hadley was "The wife I loved first and best."[44]

Finally, the mythical trunk served as a way of saving face for Hemingway, who had said that "It is only when you can no longer believe in your own exploits that you write your memoirs."[45] He had written himself into a corner, and the trunk(s) allowed for a glorious public escape.

He had also written himself into another bind: as his dementia exaggerated his spirit of aggression, his paranoia made him obsess about the consequences. He was sure that libel suits would follow *Feast*'s publication. And so he relied on his old insurance policy of insisting that his work be considered a "fictional" account. His original manuscripts include seven pages in which he worked on a possible preface, with the line "This book is fiction." written nine times, and there are at least three other phrasings to that effect. But this book used real names and described real places he had been. It was long anticipated and hyped, and his readers *wanted* biography.

Hemingway would have been very displeased with Mary's preface, which stated, "If the reader prefers, this book may be regarded as fiction." He wrote to Scribner's to withdraw it in April 1961, between his Mayo admissions, but Mary never posted the letter.

Alone

Chapter 11

Hemingway's funeral took place on July 5, 1961. He was buried just twelve miles from where Ezra Pound was born. It was an unusually hot morning; in fact, one of the altar boys fainted at the start of the service and had to be revived. At the conclusion, Mary was seen "almost running" out of the cemetery. "That son of a bitch! I'm just so damned mad that I had to get away!" she told Tillie Arnold, who caught up with her just before the cemetery gates.[1] Mary was angry with the priest for ignoring her wishes, but the sentiments she expressed obviously applied to the deceased as well. She had nursed him through it all the best that she could, dutifully accepting the abuse from his traumatic brain injuries, his alcoholism, and his narcissism. She had reassured him when he was paranoid, though it was futile, and once his dementia progressed no one could rescue him. She had averted disaster before, but this time there was no stopping him.

Perhaps she had already heard the grumblings that it was all her fault, leaving the keys he needed to access his guns in plain view, not seeking more competent treatment, not informing his children of how sick he really was. Now, the priest became the target of her years of pent-up anger. He had either flatly refused to honor her wishes or, more likely, just misunderstood them. Mary had asked that he read from First Ecclesiastes:

> What profit hath a man of all his labour which he taketh under
>   the sun?
> One generation passeth away, and another generation cometh:
>   but the earth abideth forever.
> The sun also ariseth, and the sun goeth down, and hasteth to his
>   place where he arose.

The wind goeth toward the south, and turneth about unto the
    north; it whirleth about continually, and the wind returneth
    again according to his circuits.
All the rivers run into the sea; yet the sea is not full; unto the
    place from whence the rivers come, thither they return again.
All things are full of labour; man cannot utter it: the eye is not
    satisfied with seeing, nor the ear filled with hearing.
The thing that hath been, it is that which shall be; and that which
    is done is that which shall be done: and there is no new thing
    under the sun.
Is there anything whereof it may be said, See, this is new? It hath
    been already of old time, which was before us.

Even now it seems the Bible was written solely as a tribute to Hemingway.

The priest had read only the first line from the Catholic Douay Bible, a quite different version, and Mary was also distressed at the extensive "Hail Marys," which she had expressly limited to eight. "The son of a bitch went on and on with the Hail Marys,"[2] she complained.

Perhaps she was more overwhelmed than she would admit: there was the estate, the Cuba home with its artwork and valuable manuscripts and papers, the arrival of family, and of course the publicity. She had done her best to control it during the moments that followed his death.

According to A. E. Hotchner's memoir, once Mary woke to the sound of the blast and discovered Ernest had suicided, she immediately contacted their friend Leonard Lyons, the well-known columnist. Lyons elaborated later: "The first thing she did was go to the phone and put in a call to my New York Apartment. She was told I was in Los Angeles, whereupon she put in a follow-up call to my Beverly Hills hotel and woke me up. 'Lennie,' she said very calmly, 'I'm calling you because Papa has killed himself.' After I recovered from the shock of her announcement, I asked her how it had happened. 'With a shotgun. Now, what I'd like you to do is this—arrange for a press conference at your hotel—make sure all the wire services are there—and tell them I have informed you that while Ernest was cleaning his shotgun this morning, in preparation for going on a shoot, it accidentally discharged and shot him in the head. Got that?' Only after she arranged all this with me did she phone Ernest's doctor and tell him what had happened."[3]

Such coolheaded instructions in the face of horror imply planning in advance. Of course, it was no secret her husband was suicidal. And she shouldn't be blamed for imagining her possible reaction and plans many days or months before the potential tragedy. Her desire to control the media is certainly understandable as well. Though the press was not as irresponsible and reckless as the current mainstream media, among her contemporaries in the press there have always been sensationalists who cared little for the humans they trampled to get headlines. However collected she was at the scene of the tragedy, she still found it necessary to spend the night in the hospital to recover from the shock, and, even if she was not particularly distraught that morning, no doubt it was best for her to spend the night elsewhere. Mary also had to pull herself together in order to make funeral arrangements and prepare for the numerous expected guests. And Ernest had certainly left a mess. Fortunately, George Brown (the New York boxing coach whose gymnasium Hemingway frequented) had driven him from Mayo and was staying in the guest house. He and a local man, Don Anderson, cleaned the foyer so well that Hemingway's sister Sunny remarked that there was no sign of the tragedy that had occurred, not even a stain (and Lloyd Arnold burned the recovered remains).[4]

Patrick Hemingway didn't find his father's suicide "as straightforward as it was supposed to be." He added, "I have no trouble with my grandfather's suicide, but my dad had been under what I would call prison restraint and I don't see how a person kept in a room with bars on the windows, never alone, could want to live. . . . Then they let him come home, but leave his arms and ammunition where he can get them when the only reason for keeping him behind bars was to keep him from killing himself. I believe it was criminal not to have taken the easy things away from him. . . . I don't believe the virtuous widow theory. . . . Neither I, nor any of my brothers were even consulted. But that's not all. There was a deliberate attempt to cut us out of our relationship with him. For example, he and I corresponded twice or three times a month after 1952. But all my letters have disappeared. Not one is in the Kennedy Library. That amazes me, especially when there are lots of letters from trivial people. The thing that is missing in accounts of their marriage is the brutality of their relationship. You asked me why I didn't see my dad? It wasn't pleasant to be around them. They just went after each other tooth and nail. I think he wanted to get rid of her."[5]

Patrick observed what many others had and what Mary had written to Charles Scribner about years earlier, in 1950: "he has destroyed what I used to think was an inexhaustible supply of devotion to him. He has been truculent, brutal, abusive and extremely childish. It has been more than a year since he actually hit me." She also observed, accurately, that "it looks like the disintegration of a personality to me." She elaborated in another section that "last spring in New York, after thorough examinations, I discovered definitively that my one remaining reproductive tube is congested and I can't have a baby. When I married Ernest I had no faint idea that this was or would be true. . . . He taunts me with this. And it may be one of the basic reasons for his behavior."[6]

It's no surprise, then, that while all of Hemingway's guns were locked in the storage room of his basement, he could see the keys sitting on the window ledge above the kitchen sink. Mary later justified this by writing that "no one had a right to deny a man access to his possessions." Perhaps knowing the statement is indefensible and frankly absurd when discussing a suicidal individual, she added, "I also assumed that Ernest would not remember the storeroom."[7] This, if true, was a very costly gamble. If Mary had gone to a psychoanalyst and puzzled why, why she had been so thoughtless as to leave the keys in plain sight, he would have stroked his beard and asked her to reflect on Papa's suffering and on her suffering and then remained silent. One of the cardinal rules of psychotherapy is that it doesn't always follow that just because the analyst has an insight, the patient is ready to hear it.

The theory that Mary had facilitated her husband's death was echoed by their mutual friend William Walton in his 1993 interview with the Hemingway scholar Rose Marie Burwell. Walton was close to the Hemingways and the Kennedys and served as chairman of the Commission of Fine Arts through both the Kennedy and Johnson administrations. According to Burwell, "When I said to Bill Walton in August 1993, 'Unconsciously, Mary wanted him to do it,' Walton replied 'Now that you have said it, I will say what I have never said before, but have known since Mary called me a few hours after Ernest's death: yes, she did.'" Burwell further observed that "For Mary Hemingway, as for the heroine of a Victorian novel, death had done the work of the divorce court; and I have no doubt that—exhausted and without help from Hemingway's family—she saw, but could not bear to admit, that his suicide was the only release for either of them. In the fall of 1959, Hemingway described Mary's determination to separate part of her life from his as a tactic aimed at driving him to suicide."[8]

A Catholic burial was symbolic in the sense that it would prove his death was *not* a suicide. Mary had told the *New York Times* that she felt certain this, "in some incredible way, was an accident." Part denial, part protection of her husband's reputation, this statement corroborates Lennie Lyon's account. But the official ruling on his death settled the issue as far as the priest was concerned—"the church accepted the ruling of the authorities that Hemingway had died of a self-inflicted gunshot wound in the head."[9] Furthermore, he had been excommunicated after his divorce from Pauline. Suicide and excommunication were both reasons for refusing him a High Mass, so a graveside service was the best compromise Mary could reach.

The Hemingway estate was valued at $1.4 million prior to any taxes, and there was of course the literary estate, including unpublished and incomplete manuscripts. His will, written in September 1955, stated that "I have intentionally omitted to provide for my children now living or for any that may be born after this will has been executed, as I repose complete confidence in my beloved wife Mary to provide for them according to written instructions I have given her."[10] But it appears that there were no such instructions left; if there were, they were no more generous than this one sentence. Of course Ernest knew that there was no particular closeness between Mary and any of his sons. His condition in 1955, at the time he wrote the will, was far from healthy. By early 1954 he had suffered the litany of injuries from the plane crashes and the concussions, and a list of his diagnoses from 1955 included nephritis (a kidney inflammation, probably from infection), as well as hepatitis (liver inflammation), and he was even bedridden for more than a month due to liver disease. He was well aware of his mortality, but he was also declining mentally.

The language in the will is certainly deliberate and had to be hurtful: "I have intentionally omitted to provide for my children." It is very curious that he includes the possibility that he may "have children born after this will has been executed." Was this delusional grandiosity or a last statement of sexual prowess—a part of the legend he wanted to maintain until death? It was, after all, that same year that he confided to Hotchner that "September I will have an African son. Before I left I gave a herd of goats to my bride's family. Most over-goated family in Africa. Feels good to have African son. Never regretted anything I ever did."[11] Perhaps he and Debba had consummated their relationship, or perhaps he wanted to lend more credibility to his boasting. (If Debba was in fact pregnant, which is unlikely, she had no way of knowing the child's sex in advance, never mind the fact she had no means of communicating with Hemingway.) A legal challenge might have revealed doubts about his capacities at the time the will was written, but such challenges are lengthy, expensive, stressful, and often very difficult to prove conclusively.

Mary wrote (in a 1976 letter) that the famous Joan Miró painting *The Farm* seemed to her "the most important of the various pictures and other things that Ernest left me in his will."[12] Excluding the literary estate, she was indeed right; however, its ownership at the time of his death was controversial. His son, Jack, felt he or at least his mother, Hadley, was entitled to keep the painting; Ernest had purchased it as a present for Hadley's thirty-fourth birthday. Hemingway, who said in the last year of his life that he always wrote better after viewing paintings, had his sights on this particular painting before Mirós looked like Mirós and certainly before they were collectible. Hemingway clearly recognized its significance and appreciated its folksy and harsh angular composition. It's a large painting (roughly four by five feet), painted in a transitional style for the artist—part surrealism and part cubism, on the way to his bold signature abstraction—and the work held great sentimental value as well.

Hadley and Ernest had attended the first Miró solo show at Galerie Pierre, in June 1925. While Hadley had her exhibition program autographed by the artist Max Ernst and by the writers André Bréton and Louis Aragon.[13] Ernest spotted the canvas he would describe as capturing the very essence of Spain: "It has in it all that you feel about Spain when you are there and all that you feel when you are away and cannot go there. . . . No one else has been able to paint these two very opposing things."[14] And typical of his usual spot-on assessments of any form of art: "No one could look at it and not know it had been painted by a great painter."

It was, however, already listed in the show's catalogue as belonging to Evan Shipman, a poet and friend of Hemingway's who wrote for *American Horse Breeder* magazine. Shipman had introduced the gallery's dealer to Miró, and in repayment the dealer had offered him any painting in the show, with the full price going directly to the artist, without a commission. Shipman chose *The Farm*, made a down payment, and, according to Hemingway's version of events nine years later, came to see him that very day.

Shipman noticed how disappointed Ernest was and understood immediately that he had hoped to own the painting as well. Shipman's biographer reports they flipped a coin, and Hemingway lost, but Shipman yielded to his friend's desire anyway.[15] Over the years and through subsequent retellings, the story evolved into the more romantic version that Hemingway elaborated in his letter nine years on. The day Shipman came to Ernest's apartment, he said, "Hem, you should have *The Farm*. I do not love anything as much as you care for that picture and you should have it.' . . . so we rolled dice [to decide] and I won and made the first payment."[16] In another version, Hemingway lost the roll of the dice just as he had lost the coin toss, but Shipman wanted the approval of the dashing young colleague more than the Miró, and he insisted that "Hem" buy it anyway. The roll-of-the-dice versions have become classic Lost Generation legend and too rich to compromise with accuracy.

Convincing his wife that it was a wise purchase was another issue—according to Hem, the cost was 5,000 francs, more than a month's worth of living expenses for the young couple. So Hemingway made it clear that he was thinking of her all along, that it was *her* gift. *The Farm* would hang in their Paris apartment, and Miró himself would inspect the chosen site, approving of its placement above the bed. The costly present was Hadley's by her November 9, 1925, birthday, but she would also get divorce papers on December 8, 1926. She demanded that the painting follow a truckload of furniture (and the Richardson family silver) to her new apartment after Ernest left her for Pauline. She specifically named it as *her* property at that time, and Hemingway complied. In another account, it wasn't in a truck but in a wheelbarrow Hemingway rented and wheeled himself from one apartment to the other, from rue Notre-Dame-des-Champs to rue de Fleurus.[17] Though Hadley remained stoic, Ernest would burst into tears when unpacking many of the sentimental items, fully consecrating his labor as an act of contrition. Yet when he and Pauline left Paris in 1931, the painting was among the items they had shipped to Key West. Though still officially Hadley's painting, Ernest had "borrowed" it.

Though he recalled its cost as 5,000 francs, documents reveal it was 3,500 francs, or $175 at 20 francs to the dollar, still a huge sum. He put 500 francs down with a promise to pay the remainder by October. He scrounged and borrowed and ultimately used some of Hadley's trust money to buy the painting, but it would prove to be their wisest investment.

When the painting was included in an exhibition at the Art Institute of Chicago in 1934, the owners were listed as "Mr. and Mrs. Paul Scott Mowrer, Chicago," as Hadley had remarried. But in January 1935 another show catalogue from the Pierre Matisse Gallery of Madison Avenue attributed *The Farm* to Ernest Hemingway's collection. According to two sources, Ernest had promised to return the painting within five years. But by January 1940 it was still in his possession, even if not true ownership. It hung in the dining room of his Key West home and eventually in his Cuban home. Though Castro rolled into Havana in January 1959, *The Farm* was saved from his regime's "appropriation" of the Hemingway property, as Ernest had lent it to New York's Museum of Modern Art. It was the political savvy of the MOMA staff that secured it for the 1959 exhibition "Joan Miró" and thus returned Hadley's painting to American soil (but still in Cuba were Hemingway's paintings by Paul Klee, Andre Masson, and the cubists Juan Gris and Georges Braque).

The Farm's value today is enhanced by the legend, the famous provenance, and its unique place in the Miró oeuvre. Miró began the work at his family's summer home in Mont-roig del Camp and then hauled the large canvas to Barcelona and on to Paris, where he completed it in his dilapidated, unheated, but tidy studio. He took it to several dealers, all of whom held it for a while and then requested he retrieve it. Picasso's dealer even advised him to cut the canvas into eight smaller pieces and sell them separately. To repay the loans that he used to buy the work, Hemingway stooped to delivering produce part time, according to one of his Paris friends, Gerald Murphy. The painting's value in the years just after his death, as determined by the settlement Jack Hemingway accepted from Mary to relinquish any claim on the painting, was $20,000.[18] Mary eventually hung it in her New York apartment, and she donated the painting to the National Gallery of Art in Washington in 1987.

The Cuba house was next on the agenda. Working with Kennedy's State Department, Mary was allowed to return to Finca, where Castro himself came to call. The house would become a museum, and Hemingway's beloved boat, the *Pilar*, was dry docked on the grounds. Two paintings could leave the island with her, as well as her jewelry, some twenty-five of his books, and his papers. She described the transaction as "handing over the house in exchange for those 40 pounds of precious papers."[19] However, according to Jeffrey Meyers's biography, she burned "many papers she was certain Hemingway would not want anyone to publish or to see."[20] This was according to Ernest's instructions and included "diary-like drafts of inferior fiction" and letters about Martha and illness in his family. (To some of us, this is akin to burning the Dead Sea Scrolls.) The remaining letters and manuscripts are now housed in the John F. Kennedy Presidential Library and Archives in Boston.

She wrote to Walton on August 1, 1961, "On Papa's typewriter" (using the stationery embossed with "Finca Vigia" at the top), "I doubt that Papa would be totally in favor of this arrangement for disposal of the Finca; but since we cannot haul this place out to sea and sink it, as I hope to do with *Pilar*, I think he would prefer this to any other arrangements we might make." No doubt he would have preferred that his beloved fishing and "sub-hunting" boat be scuttled, but his long time first mate Gregorio Fuentes feared what Castro would do in retaliation. The boat is now on the Finca grounds.[21]

The years Ernest and Mary shared were turbulent from the start. One cannot argue that she didn't know what she was in for. When they were new lovers just getting to know each other at the Ritz in Paris during their World War II days, he had slapped her across the face after she scolded him for behaving "horribly" the night before. His friends were all "drunks and slobs" who "threw up all over her bathroom."[22] He was "a big bully . . . a woman hitter . . . a fly-blown ego." After his scolding,

Hemingway transformed overnight to the contrite but naughty little boy, asking forgiveness and another chance to be good to the angry and disappointed mother. They played their parts flawlessly that day and adopted these comfortable but pathological roles for the rest of their lives. His behavior was not contrite for long; he soon took a photo of Mary and her second husband, dropped it into the toilet of her Ritz bathroom, and fired six rounds into the bowl. He shattered the plumbing and was again banished.[23]

Perhaps the allure of celebrity and financial security trumped any expectation of future verbal and physical abuse. One way of coping, of course, was to simply join in with Ernest. Mary Hemingway's drinking has generally been reported as problematic only in the years following Ernest's death; however, a waiter at their favorite Ketchum restaurant said, "I didn't care for Mary that much. It seemed like all she did was sit there and drink one martini after another. . . . Often she would only take two or three bites of her food while she got plastered on martinis."[24]

But when they met during their Paris days, perhaps she really did fall deeply in love despite his brutish behavior, and perhaps that's why she tried to protect his reputation by denying his suicide. Her sense of identity would always remain linked to Ernest—the header on her personal stationary would read "Mrs. Ernest Hemingway" for the rest of her life.

Mary's stoic denial would eventually fade to resignation. Below the olive-drab top of the *Look* magazine cover dated September 6, 1966, were the words "HEMINGWAY—His wife sets the record straight on her life with the great novelist." The bottom half shows Julie Andrews on a sailboat, showing off her perfect legs and giving us a faint smile. Mary agreed to the interview with the renowned and accomplished Italian journalist Oriana Fallaci, perhaps because of their shared histories as war correspondents (Mary reported from Europe during World War II, while Fallaci fought in Italy with a resistance unit despite her youth and later reported from Vietnam and other conflicted places around the globe). Perhaps it was because of Oriana's elegance and stature, or perhaps it was just time. Her second question to Mary was

> "You've just said something: 'that he killed himself there [Ketchum].' To my knowledge, it is the first time you've admitted Hemingway's suicide. Until now, and against all evidence, you've always maintained his death was accidental."
>
> "No, he shot himself. Shot himself. Just that. For a long time, I refused to admit it . . . it's true. I've never discussed it with a psychiatrist, but I suppose it had something to do with self-defense. . . .

I defended myself like that, by pretending it had been an accident. Admitting the truth would've snapped my nerves, split open my brain. But I soon realized it was stupid to go on pretending and believing it an accident.

"Yes, if Ernest thought that was the right thing to do, I must accept it. Without thinking of how lonely he left me, without crying with the regret that I wasn't able to stop him . . . we cannot judge the behavior of a sick and desperate man. In his condition, I too, would've ignored the sorrow I was about to inflict . . . would've ignored the idea of leaving him alone. . . . there is a kind of loneliness much worse than my present one: his. And writers are lonely persons, even when they love and are loved."

"You are very lonely, aren't you, Miss Mary?"

"Totally lonely . . . I never had any children of my own. How sad not to have been able to bring a miniature of Ernest into this world. I longed so much for a child, and so did he. In 1947, a year after we were married, I became pregnant. Ernest was so happy; he hoped it would be a girl. But the child was never born, we lost it during a trip to Wyoming. The greatest loss of my life, except the death of Ernest. Yes, I am all alone."

Mary concluded the interview by reiterating this state: alone with her loneliness.[25]

Modern Times

Chapter 12

If Ernest Hemingway walked into a modern clinic or hospital with his exact symptoms—anxiety, depression, and delusions, as well as an overall decline in his cognitive abilities—his evaluations and treatment would be very different from what he experienced in 1960 and 1961. One would hope for a vastly different outcome as well. This chapter is not a criticism of his care at Mayo; indeed, some of the measures taken deserve praise. Hemingway received state-of-the-art therapy while at Mayo, just for the wrong diagnosis. ECT would have been curative for a case of psychotic depression, not his mixed-etiology dementia with associated depressive and psychotic features.

There are many options now for patients with dementias, and some are natural therapies, such as vitamins, ketones, and amino acid based. There are even new and promising strategies that may *prevent* dementias. I hope the reader will find this departure enlightening, but it is not a guide for their own therapy, as that is always reserved for you and your personal physician.

Nothing in medical school prepares a doctor for the celebrity patient. Although there are plenty of opportunities to deal with demanding, difficult, or entitled patients, the real challenge for the doctor of the famous patient is not letting the person's very presence become a distraction. It is best to be singularly focused on the medical issues at hand. By the reports we have, there is every indication that Hemingway was a model patient. A retired Florida physician who was a medical student when Hemingway was at Mayo during the second admission recalled in an interview that Hemingway was still recognizable as the man on dust jackets, but he was much less robust. Though he was famous and conveyed such a stature, he was humble and deferential and spoke little on the ward. He was respectful and cordial to the student and others but overall reserved.

Dr. Rome had at least one luncheon with Hemingway and seemed more mindful of appropriate patient-physician boundaries than his internist, Dr. Butt, who shot skeet, dined, and drank with Hemingway. By today's standards, such recreational, nonclinical contact is generally off limits for the psychiatrist.

Hemingway's privacy would of course be respected, and it is still common to admit patients under aliases. Reporting that he was admitted for hypertension was the method chosen to maintain confidentiality. His doctors were correct to order a battery of tests—routine blood work, including a thyroid screen, B12 and folate levels, iron level, and physical exams. Today we would also order neuropsychological testing, an MRI scan of brain, and a PET scan as well. In all likelihood, on the basis of his symptoms, his MRI report would read "moderate atrophy and small-vessel ischemic changes." The atrophy would mean that there was some shrinkage of the brain, or a loss of brain volume. A small degree is normal with aging, but an exaggerated amount is common in dementia (and also in patients who are chronic drinkers). The small-vessel ischemic changes would be interpreted as small strokes over time, due to his long history of prediabetes and poorly controlled hypertension. None of these strokes by itself would result in major neurological findings, such as paralysis or weakness, but a diffuse collection of them would contribute to his dementia. This was the predominant component of de Kooning's mixed-etiology dementia due to chronic smoking. A functional MRI would detect changes in blood flow and neuronal activity from past concussions.

The PET scan would measure overall metabolism of the brain. By infusing glucose tagged with a radioactive tracer and then scanning for where in the brain that radioactivity is seen, we can see which cells are taking in glucose (energy) and utilizing it and which ones are not. In general, the darker areas on the scan indicate an accumulation of dead or dying cells. In Alzheimer's, some of the cells may be viable but unable to take in and utilize glucose, and these cells are essentially nonfunctional.

On the basis of his clinical history and symptoms, we would expect Hemingway's PET scan to demonstrate that all lobes of the brain were affected to some extent. If he had some component of Alzheimer's dementia, the temporal and parietal lobes would show the least glucose utilization (areas for memory and processing). No doubt, his PET scan would have some abnormalities, but this test is the most challenging to predict because of his several concussions. PET scanning is fairly new technology, and what limited data we have from boxers and NFL players show that multiple areas are affected, frontal and cerebellar areas in particular (but again, this is very preliminary).[1]

His neuropsychological testing would be somewhat difficult to predict as well with accuracy. This would involve some paper-and-pencil tests of memory and processing, and he would have to complete them in several sessions (just the hospital paperwork was a great source of anxiety). The testing is often confounded by the genius who outsmarts his own deficits to arrive at better-than-expected scores. Still, Hemingway would not be able to compensate for short-term memory deficits and might have difficulty with attentiveness and concentration. Some of these evaluations would also indicate his paranoia and depression, and, if a more extensive battery of testing was chosen, it might be possible to see whether reaction time and motor skills were compromised (although his bird-hunting skills seemed very much intact).

Hemingway would still demonstrate a capacity for and no doubt a gift for abstract thinking, which improves over time and deteriorates much later in dementia. But this capacity is a double-edged sword, allowing for seeds of delusion to blossom and consume the creative, analytical genius.

Of course, these "findings" are just conjecture, based on the diagnostic workups of hundreds of patients I have evaluated who fit Hemingway's profile. Though any clinician may argue with these hypothetical scan predictions, there is no doubt of his diagnosis based on a retroactive comprehensive review of the forensic evidence.

We would next discuss the results in detail, meeting with Ernest and Mary, to report exactly what illnesses we had found and to outline a full plan of treatment. I would explain that he suffered from a form of dementia, from multiple causes. And I would explain that his psychosis, the fears of excessive surveillance, the conviction that he had somehow broken the law, and so on, might be part of this overall illness. His delusions might have also been driven by his depression to some extent, as patients with severe depression can become psychotic, but his were more characteristic of those seen in dementia. It would be important to express that he likely did have an FBI file, as did many others who were involved in the Spanish Civil War or who had an extensive background on Cuban soil, but it would be important to distinguish between realistic insights and excessive and unrealistic worry. Also, depression had come and gone throughout his life; now it was severe and best categorized as a chronic, underlying illness, exacerbated by the dementia. Both diseases would require treatment. I would propose exactly what I do with every patient who has dementia, no matter how mild or severe: treat aggressively.

First we would have to approach his drinking. All of the strategies planned would be defeated by continued alcoholism.

Hemingway's doctors allowed him wine while hospitalized and drank with him at dinner parties, but alcohol had taken too much of a toll to be allowed to continue to flow freely. Though Hemingway found life almost intolerable when not drinking, he would be reassured that at least we would not risk a withdrawal syndrome once he entered into treatment. For such cases, a detoxification regimen would be advised, but there is a subset of patients, albeit this is extremely rare, for whom we prescribe a daily amount of medication simply to keep them from abusing alcohol. Benzodiazepines, such as diazepam (Valium), are cross-tolerant with alcohol; that is, Valium provides the same (or a similar) level of anxiety relief as patients felt when drinking, prevents withdrawal syndromes (in 90 percent of alcoholics) who make it their substitute, and does not further damage the liver and brain.

Again, this approach is recommended only rarely, and it can be rightly criticized as substituting one addiction for another, but it would be one that would likely keep Hemingway engaged in treatment. His history was that of the patient who, when ordered into abstinence, eventually defies any such order or alcohol limit and continues to decline with further alcohol overuse.

Psychotherapy would be critical, and though there would be no talking him out of his delusions at this point, we would encourage him to focus on his health, remind himself he is safe, and buy some time until other treatments could take hold. Until the medications begin to work, we simply deemphasize the paranoia until it can be confronted with success. Again, the "reality-based therapy" would be essential—he *did* have an FBI file, and he should have been the least surprised by that fact. The "crimes" for which he worried about being punished (sexual liberties with a minor, taxes on gambling winnings, Valerie's immigration status—he even worried that a state trooper might arrest him for driving home with bottles of wine in his car) were nowhere in the file.

There are many antidepressant options available now, with far fewer risks than their 1961 predecessors. Ketamine, a newer strategy, may rapidly resolve suicidal tendencies. Short-term studies have shown response rates far beyond those of traditional antidepressants, but critics claim its effect is not sustained and that any psychoactive compound will alter mood states temporarily. Transcranial magnetic stimulation (TMS) is another new therapy, which uses magnetic fields to stimulate nerve cells in the brain. It is also very effective after repeated sessions (usually over twenty). In Hemingway's case, with demonstrated suicidal intent, ketamine could be administered in the hospital. Ongoing antidepressant therapy would include a discussion of TMS with antidepressants. The agent used often in more senior patients is vortioxetine (Trintellix). It has been shown to not only improve depression but also improve cognitive abilities in studies.

But the platform of his depression and dementia therapy would be a daily pill containing B vitamins and micronutrients. New data indicate that the root cause of depression is linked to low levels of B vitamins across the blood-brain barrier. B vitamins, particularly B9 (folate), B12 (cobalamin), and also B6 (pyridoxine), are necessary co-enzymes in the synthesis of serotonin and norepinephrine.[2] For decades we were told that low levels of serotonin and norepinephrine (chemical messengers in the brain, or neurotransmitters) were the *cause* of depression, but it seems now they are just symptoms of depression. The root cause is an *inability to synthesize enough of these messengers*, particularly in the presence of stress. When B vitamins are low, then neurotransmitter production is low.

Though their dietary and supplement intake is often fine, the majority of depressed individuals have less than optimal levels of B vitamins for use in the brain's chemical pathways. The reason for this is that there are multiple variances in our abilities to metabolize B vitamins to the forms needed by the brain. We can now prescribe these metabolized or reduced forms and circumvent the pathways that caused the deficiencies.

The current product that provides the full array of vitamins and micronutrients essential for the synthesis of the neurotransmitters deficient in depression is Enlyte. It may be stand-alone therapy for depression or combined with antidepressants. In a case as severe as Hemingway's it would be used in combination with other agents and has proven to be very safe.[3]

Next we turn to the underlying illness, the dementia itself. All of our current dementia therapies are indicated for the Alzheimer's type, but when patients present with other types or with a mixed dementia like Hemingway's, we often treat them the same as Alzheimer's patients. They may actually have a component of Alzheimer's dementia as well, and many do, but, even if they don't, they may still benefit from the medications, lifestyle changes, and natural remedies, despite the exact category of illness.

The nonpharmaceutical options are welcomed by virtually all patients, and Hemingway was already used to the exercise regimen of walking the roads of Ketchum each day. Exercise does improve brain functioning, even in dementia cases. The mechanism is not fully understood, but improving blood flow while busying mind and body seem intuitively beneficial. Also, soft music should play while the patient sleeps to keep the brain "active" through the night—another drugless strategy for preserving cognitive ability.

The cornerstone of preventing and treating dementia is addressing the various contributors to premature cell death. Two naturally occurring toxins are the principal culprits: homocysteine and free radicals. Homocysteine is an amino acid that our cells create from metabolizing a naturally occurring one (methionine). It is damaging to our cells, and high levels are associated with apoptosis, the process of pre-programming a cell for premature death. Homocysteine-lowering agents are wise for everyone to take, and fortunately, they are the same pre-metabolized B vitamins used for depression, so there would be overlap in therapeutic value in Hemingway's case. Free radicals are the result of the chemical reactions occurring in every cell, which release particles that are impelled by sheer electrical charge to attach to some other molecule. They are damaging to our cells, and the brain generates antioxidants to protect itself. "Oxidative stress" describes the state of imbalance between free radicals and the antioxidants needed to clear them.

However the brain's natural antioxidant chemicals can be easily overwhelmed, and taking a chemical precursor for the brain's natural "garbage collector" drastically boosts the system. That precursor is an amino acid, n-acetyl-cysteine (NAC); the brain converts it to glutathione, which eliminates free radicals. Thus, NAC is our best defense against oxidative stress. Fortunately, it is safe and natural (a protein building block, that is, an amino acid). It can be ingested and crosses the blood-brain barrier. It is the most potent antioxidant we can take.[4]

New evidence suggests that taking omega-three fatty acids or "fish oil" may also be of benefit in dementia. For brain health, we usually prescribe the docosahexaenoic acid type (or DHA). The mechanism of the benefit is unknown, but DHA constitutes approximately 50 percent of brain cell membranes. Since the loss of membrane integrity is thought to be critical in the cascade of events that results in cell death, it makes sense to provide the body with this raw material.[5]

Yet with regards to Hemingway's principal cause of dementia, that from traumatic brain injury, there is now a natural pill designed specifically to address the vulnerability of progressive cognitive decline in CTE patients. This agent combines the antioxidant NAC, with the folate, B12, and B6 vitamins mentioned, but also two more ingredients: lithium orotate and theracurmin. The lithium is delivered as a "micro-dose," much lower than needed for bipolar therapy but still allowing for reduced inflammation and protection from brain cell death. Theracurmin is a form of curcumin more easily used by the body, used for TBI patients for its antioxidant and anti-inflammatory properties. For cases such as his, already symptomatic, two Luma tablets per day is recommended.

Another component in the mechanism of brain cell death is the influx of calcium ions from outside the cell's membrane into the cell itself.

And this calcium accumulation may be accelerated in damaged brain cells, such as those found in people who have suffered strokes or concussions. A prescription medication, memantine (Namenda), is thought to help prevent this mechanism of cell death and improve cognitive functioning in some patients with dementia.[6] Even when patients report no noticeable improvement in memory, it is best to continue this medication because it may help prevent a further decline.

Other prescription medications include donepezil (Aricept) and rivastigmine (Exelon), which may improve memory in some patients. Because the brain uses acetylcholine to store and retrieve memories, medications that block the metabolism of acetylcholine may be of benefit (these medications are inhibitors of the enzyme that breaks down acetylcholine, acetylcholinesterase, and for rivastigmine, butyrylcholinesterase as well). The cholinesterase inhibitors are not wonder drugs, but about a third of patients see some modest benefit. They also seem to work better when combined with memantine rather than when administered alone.

For his delusional beliefs, an antipsychotic would be indicated given the severity and torment of these delusions. The few agents available during Hemingway's stay at Mayo would have most likely caused many side effects, such as cognitive dulling, movement issues from drug-induced Parkinsonism (temporary), and sluggishness. The risks would likely outweigh the benefits. Today we have a newer generation of medications for delusions that do not affect dopamine receptors directly (the cause of most side effects); rather, they affect muscarinic receptors. The current agent (more on the way) is xanomeline-trospium, and though not indicated for Hemingway's dementia-related delusions (only schizophrenia) it would be the safest place to start with little risk involved.

Though this seems like a great many things to recommend all at once, three of his prescriptions would have been for vitamins, omega three fatty acids (fish oil), and amino acid formulations. Further, I stress to patients that it is not the *number* of drugs you are taking but the *number of receptors* they affect in the body that matters. I would rather prescribe five separate agents that target five separate receptors in the brain than one medication that targets ten receptors. And when it comes to preserving the brain's microanatomy and functioning, any and all strategies should be considered.

Thus, Hemingway's modern medical chart would read as follows:

Assessment
Dementia, mixed etiology: principally CTE, with vascular and
   alcohol-associated components.

Depression and delusions secondary to the above.

Medical issues of note: history of multiple bodily traumas, hepatitis A while in Italy, hypertension, fatty liver disease, and consider pre-diabetes vs. diabetes.

Treatment Plan

1. Discontinue alcohol, monitor for withdrawal and treat as needed, consider low dose diazepam to prevent relapse.
2. Enlyte once daily, for depression therapy and lowering HCY.
3. Luma TC twice daily for treatment of CTE, dementia, and ongoing protection of the central nervous system.
4. Consider additional omega threes and NAC, clinician's choice.
5. TMS daily vs. Ketamine three times a week for depression and suicidality.
6. Vortioxetine for ongoing antidepressant therapy with and after ketamine or TMS treatments.
7. Recommended also: memantine capsule + rivastigmine patches for memory enhancement and to slow decline.
8. Optional: xanomeline-trospium, a safe option for delusions.
9. Address hypertension and as needed, and address high glucose levels.
10. Exercise the body and the brain, and keep writing!

And one final recommendation: remove all guns from the home. It is now standard to ensure that the patients at risk have no access to firearms. In Hemingway's case, simply locking them up would not stop a man who famously elaborated that death is the easiest thing to find, as findable as a razor, or a bottle of Seconal.

Results with this type of aggressive therapy have been generally positive. If such a plan had been fully implemented, Hemingway's future would have been vastly different—but for his time, his diagnosis, and the options available, his outcome was inevitable.

Enlyte = metabolized B vitamins and micronutrients (zinc, magnesium, iron, CoQ-10, PS omega-3s)

Exelon = rivastigmine

Luma = metabolized folate, B6, and B12, lithium orotate, NAC, theracurmin

Namenda = memantine

Trintellix = vortioxetine

Valium = diazepam

Epilogue

He thought of the ruins of the Grecian worship, and it seemed, a temple
was never perfectly a temple, till it was ruined and mixed up with the
winds and the sky and the herbs.

D. H. Lawrence, *The Rainbow*

Because grace under pressure is more than just suffering; it is an active
achievement, a positive triumph and the figure of St Sebastian is its best
symbol, if perhaps not in art generally, but certainly in the art of writing.

Thomas Mann, *Death in Venice*

Hemingway's ending appeared to set the tone for the decade. Marilyn
Monroe overdosed thirteen months later on Nembutal and chloral hy-
drate, and JFK was murdered in November 1963. The *Louisville Courier-
Journal* understood perfectly what Hemingway and the legend of Hemingway meant: "It is almost as though the Twentieth Century itself has
come to a sudden, violent, and premature end."

As Montale observed, Hemingway "died twice." The false alarm after
the African plane crashes only added to the myth. The banner headline
that he clipped from the front page of the *New York Daily Mirror* read:
"HEMINGWAY, WIFE KILLED IN AIR CRASH."[1] And he kept two scrapbooks of
the obituaries that followed, referring to them for entertainment at various times for the rest of his life. Though he was fairly well battered at this
point, the evidence still indicates that the only thing that could bring him
down was himself.

Suicide, in modern Western society, is virtually always considered the
product of a deranged mind. By definition, suicidality *is* mental illness,
and attempting or just threatening suicide constitutes legal grounds for
forcing an individual into psychiatric treatment. But it is not a diagnosis

itself; rather, it is a symptom of a larger ailment that requires medication and psychotherapy until the patient is deemed (to a "reasonable degree of medical certainty") no longer in a state of acute danger of self-harm. In the United States, a completed suicide by a patient who is receiving mental health care is the number one reason psychiatrists are sued. Suicide is the tenth leading cause of death among adults and the second among teens. Each year, nearly a million people worldwide take their own lives. Unlike Hemingway, the majority of patients who are successful in their suicide attempts never come to the attention of a psychiatrist or therapist before their deaths—fewer than half do.

Mike in *The Sun Also Rises* explains that he went bankrupt in two ways, "Gradually and then suddenly."[2] The last years of Hemingway's life testify that a man can also decline in physical and mental health with the same trajectory. Health matters are certainly the responsibility of the biographer, yet one is entitled to ask what they matter to the student of the work. Yet because so much Hemingway scholarship involves exactly what he resisted—his fiction *as* autobiography—a clear understanding of his mental state at the time of his writing is critical. It seems the works can never stand apart from his large shadow; such is the price of legend. But what scholars have generally missed is that when Hemingway identified his therapist as his typewriter, he was identifying the fact of his *working*, not the content he produced, as doing the work of therapy (of course, it would have been of no use to tell him that both were in fact therapeutic).

His Nobel Prize acceptance speech, which was written in 1954, contained the lines "There is no lonelier man than the writer when he is writing except the suicide. Nor is there any happier, nor more exhausted man when he has written well. If he has written well everything that is him has gone into the writing and he faces another morning when he must do it again. There is always another morning and another morning."[3] He deleted the passage, but, in contemplating the honor and magnitude of the Nobel Prize, few would bring suicide into the discussion and, oddly, place it on par with the writing life. And, yes, when he wrote well, he did pour all of himself into the work, but the fatalistic passage applies more accurately to Sisyphus than to the majority of professional writers.

Suicide was an unusually common theme in his work, his letters, and his conversations. He insisted that his mother send the pistol that his father had used to kill himself; he had plans to exorcise the demons. Though Leicester had also requested the handgun, their mother deferred to Ernest's request. In her classic passive-aggressive manner, Grace mailed it in a box that contained a chocolate cake (a book for "Bumby," cookies, and two of her paintings—desert scenes). Of course, the gun arrived covered in chocolate. Despite her irreverence, Hemingway still gave it what most conclude was a "ritualistic burial" in a mountain lake.[4]

In 1936, he told Archie MacLeish that he would never kill himself because of what the trauma might do to his sons, which is indeed why many patients seek help rather than commit the act: they don't want to leave their children with the trauma and legacy of suicide. During the Spanish Civil War, he expressed to the Stalin operative Joris Ivens that the best way was not like his father's method, with a bullet through the temple, but "with a shotgun in the mouth."[5] He actually asked his friend Clara Spiegel to make a suicide pact with him and proposed they warn each other if either of them ever planned to carry it through. She rejected the idea. When Hemingway arrived home in Ketchum after his last hospital admission, she invited him to dinner, but he asked her to come to his home instead, specifically on July 2; after that date, he warned, "he would have no social life." Clara didn't take him seriously, as she believed he was crying wolf yet again.[6]

There were numerous suicidal threats and discussions, as well as an unusually high number of other suicides that touched his life: Dr. Hemingway, Hadley's father, Helen Breaker, Harry Crosby, Jules Pascin, and Charles Fenton. And there was no shortage of suicide attempts by others: his Grandfather Hall, Scott Fitzgerald, and Jane Mason. Even Hemingway's love interest (or infatuation) from his early teens, Prudence Boulton, who appears as the Indian girl Prudence Mitchell in the story "Ten Indians," committed suicide at age sixteen. She was rumored to be pregnant by the older man she lived with at the time. They both swallowed strychnine.[7]

And though his feelings toward his third wife, Martha, were less than generous after they parted ways, he still admired her 1944 novel, *Liana,* a complex work that has been called essentially an allegory of the end of her marriage with Ernest. The book ends with Liana's suicide. And Martha *also* committed suicide. She was just shy of ninety years of age when she overdosed, suffering from cancer and near total blindness.

As a young man in 1926, the year he filed his first set of divorce papers, Hemingway agonized over loving two women and expressed his suicidality to both of them. He described perfectly how the depressed mind wanders into thoughts of self-destruction: "When I feel low, I like to think about death and the various ways of dying. And I think about probably the best way, unless you could arrange to die some way while asleep, would be to go off a liner at night. That way there could be no doubt about the thing going through and it does not seem a nasty death. There would be only the moment of taking the jump and it is very easy for me to take almost any sort of jump. Also it would never be definitely known what had happened and there would be no post mortems and no expenses left for any one to pay and there would always be the chance that you might be given credit for an accident."[8] In a passage he wrote for *To Have and Have Not,* his 1937 Depression-era book of complicated morality, and then deleted, he described this exact death. And he eerily predicted the very method of death for the poet Hart Crane, with all the attendant ambiguities he had described.

Hemingway and Crane shared the exact same birthday, July 21, 1899, and Crane, like Ernest, also drank heavily, but, more like Scott Fitzgerald, he held his liquor less well. He was suffering from writer's block, something he hoped a trip to Mexico on a Guggenheim Fellowship would cure. On the liner home, he was beaten after making homosexual advances to the wrong crew member (biographers report that this was not the first time; he seemed to have a knack for choosing the least receptive and most violent individuals). Thus, beaten up, depressed, drinking, and probably intoxicated while en route to New York in 1932, he jumped off the USS *Orizaba* in the Gulf of Mexico; reports are conflicting regarding his last words and whether he reached for a life preserver or sank, ignoring it.[9]

All of these examples and thoughts served to erase the taboo; suicide was certainly not an unknown exit, and it was justified if the suffering was great enough. And Hemingway had been daring himself for decades. He was playing a dangerous one-sided game of chicken in his head for most of his life. But he didn't blink; he was too ill to play the game anymore. He just reached the point where he "couldn't stand things."

He had written in September 1936: "Me I like life very much. So much it will be a big disgust when have to shoot myself. Maybe pretty soon I guess although will arrange to be shot in order not have bad effect on kids."[10] Notice the choice of "when I *have to* shoot myself," as if the act would be a duty, not a choice. And during this year he was writing beautifully and was financially secure, and Martha Gellhorn was still three months away from strolling into Sloppy Joe's intent on destroying his second marriage. And his second wife was wealthy, attractive, and devoted. She catered to him, was of great assistance to his professional writing, allowed him plenty of freedom to pursue the sporting life and Jane Mason, and missed his intimacy when he was away. Perhaps it was because of his bitter break with Jane in April that he wrote about "blowing my lousy head off." But still this happened during one of his most successful years, even according to the hated critics.

One of the more intriguing theories of his suicide relates to his very literary style. We turn to art, as Picasso said, to wash away the dust of everyday life. But when the art itself gives no comfort and serves instead as a close-up mirror in the harshest of light, the escape hatch is closed.

The story *Soldier's Home* begins "Krebs went to war from a Methodist college in Kansas. . . . There is a picture which shows him on the Rhine with two German girls and another corporal. Krebs and the corporal look too big for their uniforms. The German girls are not beautiful. The Rhine does not show in the picture."[11] If one dedicates a lifetime to the art of deconstruction, of raining on every parade, it is little consolation in the end that the rain's description was clean and pure and true. Suicide seems almost inevitable when one couples this mindset with the sensitivity displayed in "Ten Indians," in which a boy is teased by friends about a love interest, only to be told by his father she had been "threshing around" in the woods with another boy. The story ends with the line "In the morning there was a big wind blowing and the waves were running high up on the beach and he was awake a long time before he remembered that his heart was broken."[12]

Another valid consideration is the destructive aspect of fame. The reason Hemingway inspires so many biographies is not only that his writing is compelling to so many but that his life actually reads like a novel—a Midwestern boy selected from obscurity becomes the first American to survive a wounding in Italy during World War I, moves to Paris, and, as a press man, interviews Mussolini in Milan in 1922. When he next encountered Mussolini, at the Conference of Lausanne, he spotted the dictator reading a book, ignoring the proceedings and posing as an aloof intellectual. It was Hemingway who walked up and discovered Il Duce holding a French-English dictionary upside down. He met Clemenceau, dined with Franklin and Eleanor Roosevelt, hiked the Alps, became a definer of the Lost Generation, socialized with the literary giants of the twentieth century, supported the antifascists in Spain (and thereby personified the historical oversimplification of the conflict), reported on and saw combat in World War II, hunted big game, claimed to hunt Nazi subs, bought an early painting by Miró, published masterpieces, and won the Nobel Prize. He seems to have been at every right place, at every right time. And as celebrity overtook him, his very presence *became* the right place and the right time. Even J. D. Salinger (during his pre-recluse, World War II soldier days) came to call and pay homage to Ernest at the Ritz in Paris.[13]

It is common for a celebrity or one who has lived an accomplished life to become a cliché. Numerous figures achieve such status in the popular psyche. Among our writers, Kerouac will always be the beatnik, Fitzgerald the Jazz Age golden child, Whitman forever the wise old man and national poet laureate. What is astonishing about Hemingway is how many different clichés he contains. His very suicide is a cliché—that of a man who saw a painful and disabled future and wanted no part of it. His final act has even been described as "courageous" and "the right thing to do" by some of those who loved him.

But the paradox of his fame was that, though he fostered it, he was never comfortable in the public eye. There were surprisingly few public appearances. In Paris, in 1937, he spoke to the Anglo-American Press Club and again at the meeting of The Friends of Shakespeare and Company at Sylvia Beach's bookshop. At both, he "stuttered and stammered" and overall gave the impression that he'd "rather be somewhere else."[14] When he spoke before 3,500 people at Carnegie Hall (another thousand had to be turned away because the hall was at maximum capacity), as part of the introduction to the film *The Spanish Earth,* he came on stage drunk, sweating, and extremely nervous. He spoke for only seven minutes, but no matter—his very presence carried the day and the antifascist sentiment, or whatever sentiment. He was like the Beatles—people came to *see them,* not *hear* them. He exited the stage to thunderous applause and was off to Bimini.

Despite the extremely thorough and generally excellent biographical scholarship, one must understand each retelling with this subtext: "this is the life of a functional alcoholic, and the last ten years of this life involved a decline into dementia caused by multiple factors, insidious at first, and rapidly in the last two years." Thus, the abusiveness, the paranoia, the inability to write, the personality changes, and the frailty all make sense, at least from a neuropsychiatric perspective. From a psychoanalytic standpoint, one of Faulkner's biographers summed up Hemingway's life in just four words: Hemingway "confused person and persona."[15] Yet he was incapable, biologically, of escaping it. His CTE and dementia had solidified the very worst aspects of that persona.

Yet the person forged ahead, seemingly without fear of anything, the sole exception being the inability to produce, that one day the creative well would run dry for good. However lonely the writing trade, it was life sustaining. When it was destroyed, so was the life. Hemingway wrote early in his career that he was so far ahead of us that he could eat regularly, but the problem with being so far ahead was that no one could really understand him, much the same problem his friends Pound and Joyce encountered. In his book *Concerning the Spiritual in Art,* Wassily Kandinsky wrote:

> The life of the spirit may be fairly represented . . . as a large
> triangle . . . the whole triangle is moving slowly, almost invisibly

forwards . . . what today can be understood only by the apex and to the rest of the triangle is an incomprehensible gibberish, forms tomorrow the true thought and feeling of the second segment. At the apex of the top segment stands often one man, and only one. His joyful vision cloaks a vast sorrow. Even those who are nearest to him in sympathy do not understand him . . . they abuse him as charlatan or madman.[16]

As time pulls us forward, we are gaining on the lonely man at the apex.

Notes

Introduction

1. *In Our Time*, 16–19. Hemingway's father did indeed provide free medical care to the Chippewa who lived near the family's vacation cottage, Windemere, in Michigan. Grace had named the cottage after England's Lake Windermere as a nod toward her British heritage.

2. *In Our Time*, 61. Even as a young writer, Hemingway understood that psychosis robs one of the insight that one may indeed be ill ("When you got it you don't know about it."). This was an issue he would face years later when he became paranoid and unable to be reassured. Ad Francis was a composite of Ad Wolgast, "the Michigan Wildcat" (lightweight champion in 1910), and Oscar "Battling" Nelson (who was described as having an almost inhumane capacity for taking punishment). A more severe case of dementia pugilistica has perhaps never been documented as in the sad life of Ad Wolgast (Paul Smith, *A Reader's Guide*, 116–17).

3. Baker, *Selected Letters*, 697.

4. *Complete Short Stories*, 517, 531.

5. Lynn, *Hemingway*, 582.

6. Hotchner, *Papa Hemingway*, 9.

7. Cohen-Solal, *Sartre*, 323. Much to the disappointment of Mary Hemingway, who had hoped the great existentialist would leave her with profound enlightenment, Sartre and Hemingway, both solidly in middle age, spoke mainly about the business of publishing and royalties rather than sharing philosophical insights. Sartre was also accompanied by his mistress, a young, attractive New York–based actress named Dolorés. This likely served to embolden and justify Hemingway's infatuation with his Venetian muse, Adriana Ivancich.

8. Hotchner, *Papa Hemingway*, 285.

Chapter 1 | Inheritance

1. General discussion of the Battle of Vicksburg derived from *American Experience—Ulysses S. Grant, Warrior President*, PBS, 2002.

2. Sanford, *At the Hemingways* (quotation repeated in Burwell, *Hemingway*).

3. Bassoe, *Nervous and Mental Diseases*, 1919. Now the paradigm has come full circle: modern psychiatry is more biological and neurological (that is, neurochemical) in theory and practice than ever.

4. Spanier and Trogdon, eds., *The Letters of Ernest Hemingway*, 1: 119.

5. Burwell, *Hemingway*, 195.

6. Sanford, *At the Hemingways*, 229.

7. Burwell, *Hemingway*, 195.

8. Mellow, *Hemingway*, 362–63.

9. Reynolds, *Young Hemingway*, 84.

10. Mellow, *Hemingway*, 372–73.

11. Lynn, *Hemingway*, 592.

12. Mellow, *Hemingway*, 368.

13. Bondy et al., "Genetics of Suicide," 344–51.

14. Reynolds, *Hemingway: The 1930s through the Final Years*, 232.

15. Fitch, *Sylvia Beach*, 190.

16. Lynn, *Hemingway*, 114.

17. Meyers, *Hemingway*, 2.

18. Baker, *Hemingway: A Life Story*, 1–3.

19. Burwell, *Hemingway*, 190–91.

20. Burwell, *Hemingway*, 191.

21. Discussion of Mariel and Margaux Hemingway from "The Hemingways Revisited," *Town and Country*, September 2011, and various Internet searches of archived news items.

22. John Hemingway, *Strange Tribe*, 208.

23. John Hemingway, *Strange Tribe*, 136.

24. Lynn, *Hemingway*, 225. Stein's assessment that "Up in Michigan" is "inaccrochable" is derived from the French word "accrocher" or "to hang." If a painting is distasteful, it is unhangable.

25. Letter of Dr. Hemingway to Ernest Hemingway, October 22, 1926, JFK Library.

26. Letter of Grace Hall Hemingway to Ernest Hemingway, January 2, 1927, JFK Library. Robert Bridges, the editor at Scribner's, would excise eight particularly unpleasant profanities and one blasphemy from *A Farewell to Arms* (four were reinserted by Maxwell Perkins).

27. Letter of Grace Hall Hemingway to Ernest Hemingway, July 24, 1920 (hand delivered), Humanities Research Center, Texas University (also reproduced in Reynolds, *Young Hemingway*, 136).

28. Baker, *Hemingway: A Life Story*, 72.

29. Reynolds, *Young Hemingway*, 136.

30. Lynn, *Hemingway*, 29.

31. Baker, *Selected Letters*, 670.

32. Meyers, *Hemingway*, 148.

33. Mellow, *Hemingway*, 372.

34. Burwell, *Hemingway*, 25. Rumors of Grace Hemingway's lesbianism have not been substantiated.

Chapter 2 | Trauma Artist

1. Baker, *Selected Letters*, 751. Another biographer whose work tormented Hemingway during the same period was Charles Fenton, who jumped to his death from a hotel window in Durham, North Carolina, a year before Hemingway's suicide. Hemingway was aware of Fenton's death, even referencing it in

a letter to Carlos Baker while he was hospitalized: "Hope that won't set a bad example to my other biographers." Hemingway wrote to Fenton several times, at one point asking him to "cease and desist" when it came to talking to family and invading his privacy. But at the conclusion of one letter, Hemingway added, "And I hope you will work on someone else, scholarly and decent as your approach is."

2. Lynn, *Hemingway*, 78.

3. Lynn, *Hemingway*, 59. Some of the professional boxers Hemingway claimed to spar with included Harry Greb (American Light Heavyweight Champion from 1922 to 1923 and World Middleweight Champ from 1923 to 1926), Tommy Gibbons (who won 96 of his 106 fights and lost by decision to Jack Dempsey after fifteen rounds), Jack Blackburn (who later trained Joe Louis), and Sam Langford (a Canadian who won the World Colored Heavyweight Championship five times).

4. Edward Michael McKey of the ARC Rolling Canteen Service was also a victim of an Austrian shell, which killed him on June 18, 1918, near Fossalta.

5. Meyers, *Hemingway*, 30. (Meyers references *Report of the Department of Military Affairs: January to July 1918* [Rome: Department of Information, American Red Cross, 1919], p. 14.) Morris indicates Hemingway likely never drove an ambulance, rather used a bicycle most of the time to reach the trenches. James M. Morris, *The Ambulance Drivers: Hemingway, Dos Passos, and a Friendship Made and Lost in War* (Boston: Da Capo Press, 2017).

6. Meyers, *Hemingway*, 31. (Ted Brumback reported that Hemingway did not carry another wounded man.)

7. Meyers, *Hemingway*, 32.

8. Baker, *Hemingway: A Life Story*, 45.

9. Meyers, *Hemingway*, 33–34.

10. Meyers, *Hemingway*, 203.

11. Baker, *Selected Letters*, 274. The photos depicting the famous scar were by Helen Breaker, a bridesmaid at Hemingway's first wedding. She was hoping to make a name for herself as a photographer when she took these highly competent shots. Scribner's had asked for some new photos for publicity purposes, and Breaker's fit the bill. Despite her success and the establishment of her own studio in Paris, she committed suicide after her eyesight began to deteriorate. Many years later, Hemingway claimed (to Hotchner) one of the most unusual connections in his life, involving Dr. Carl Weiss, the doctor who stitched his wound that night at the Neuilly hospital. In 1935, this very doctor confronted and punched Senator Huey Long, and, though the events of those moments are still controversial, he is believed to have then shot and thus assassinated Long (though one theory holds that Long was shot by his bodyguards in the confusion). Weiss was the son-in-law of Judge Pavy, who was a political opponent of Long's, and that day Pavy was being ousted from power by Long's gerrymandering. Yet though this has been repeated in many Hemingway studies as fact, it is yet another seductive Hemingway fabrication: Dr. Weiss did practice at the American hospital at Neuilly-sur-Seine, but he did not arrive in Paris until June 1929, sixteen months after Hemingway pulled the skylight onto his forehead.

12. Letter (via telegram) of Ezra Pound to Ernest Hemingway, March 11, 1928,

JFK Library: full text (stationery heading, left to right): "Ezra Pound res publica, the public conventence RAPALLO/VIA MARSALA, 12 INT. 5/11 Marzo -28/My Dear Mr Hemingway :/ I am deeply distressed ,/sympathetic or compassionate as the case may be. And/relieved to hear that you are resuming yr. usual/or un-ditto life ,/BUY Haow the hellsufferin tomcats/did you git drunk enough to fall upwards thru/the blithering skylight !!!!!!!!"

This is one of numerous unusual letters he would send to Hemingway and scores of others. Since his college days, Pound was in the habit of creating his own phonetic spellings of words, making them quite idiosyncratic but still decipherable. Over time, his letters would become more difficult to decode because of his use of multiple languages, neologisms, and idiosyncratic abbreviations. As his psychotic illness evolved, the line between eccentricity of language and frank psychosis would become ever blurrier.

13. Reynolds, *Hemingway: The 1930s through the Final Years,* 194.

14. Baker, *Hemingway: A Life Story,* 390–91.

15. Capa, *Slightly Out of Focus,* 129–31. Though Hemingway and Capa were friends, there was great tension between them at times. When Capa was visiting in Idaho after the Spanish Civil war and doing a photo shoot on Hemingway for *Life,* Ernest became angry at Capa's repeatedly shooting him with a glass to his lips. He even caught a hot flashbulb as it ejected from Capa's camera and threw it back at him, hitting Capa between the eyes. He demanded that he not be portrayed as just a "rummy" and asked Capa if he was his friend or just a "son of a bitching target" to him. Capa flew into a rage, but the situation cooled, and he eventually took the film out of his Leica and handed it to Hemingway. Capa's famous photo "Falling Soldier" is the main photographic symbol of the Spanish Civil War, yet recent research indicates that in all likelihood it was staged. The mountains in the background are not the site where Capa claimed the photo was taken (the landscape indicates it was photographed near Espejo, thirty-five miles southeast of Cerro Muriano, the site Capa reported). Also, the individual Capa identified in his photo as Federico Borrell Garcia actually died while taking shelter behind a tree at Cerro Muriano. Further, Capa's negatives indicate this was one in a series of photos that were staged, and, though Capa reported that the Loyalist's death was from machine-gun fire, not a sniper's bullet, there is no evidence of any fighting at the location where the photo was taken. Though "falling," the portion of the soldier's body visible has no discernible trauma, and if he was indeed in hostile territory, he was very obviously and unwisely exposed to his enemies. Curiously, the "staging" of the photo has led some to conclude that Capa was responsible for the man's death; they speculate that he was shot by a sniper while posing for a staged photo, but, again, no evidence supports that there was such action in this area.

16. Baker, *Selected Letters,* 723. During his World War II "correspondent" experiences, Hemingway was documented as using his celebrity and stature to coax military men into defying their duty and the normal chain of command, placing himself and others in dangerous situations.

17. Reynolds, *Hemingway: Final Years,* 103 (quotations and narrative also confirmed in Capa, *Slightly Out of Focus*).

18. Baker, *Selected Letters,* 723.

19. Lynn, *Hemingway*, 527–28.
20. Baker, *Hemingway: A Life Story*, 485.
21. Meyers, *Hemingway*, 504.
22. Reynolds, *Hemingway: Final Years*, 273.
23. Baker, *Hemingway: A Life Story*, 520.
24. Reynolds, *Hemingway: Final Years*, 273.
25. Baker, *Hemingway: A Life Story*, 521.
26. Meyers, *Hemingway*, 504. Some biographies list further injuries from the second crash, such as ruptures of his liver, right kidney, and spleen, but these could be fatal, and such conditions, even if so minor as to be survivable, were undiagnosable in the bush.
27. Baker, *Hemingway: A Life Story*, 229.
28. Baker, *Selected Letters*, 361.
29. Baker, *Selected Letters*, 828.
30. Mellow, *Hemingway*, 122.
31. Hemingway, *The Sun Also Rises*, 192.

Chapter 3 | Giant Killer

1. Hotchner, *Papa Hemingway*, 5.
2. Trimble, *The Soul in the Brain*, 217.
3. Gooch, *Flannery O'Connor*, 2464–70 (digital).
4. Donaldson, *Hemingway vs. Fitzgerald*, 241.
5. Baker, *Selected Letters*, 20.
6. Baker, *Selected Letters*, 25.
7. Baker, *Selected Letters*, 690.
8. Donaldson, *Hemingway vs. Fitzgerald*, 243.
9. Lynn, *Hemingway*, 122.
10. Baker, *Selected Letters*, 20.
11. Baker, *Selected Letters*, 302.
12. Donaldson, *Hemingway vs. Fitzgerald*, 245.
13. Lynn, *Hemingway*, 553
14. Baker, *Selected Letters*, 661. A collection of Lord Byron's letters sold at auction for just over $459,000 in October 2009.
15. Baker, *Letters*, 667. Hemingway did reference other young Italian ladies in a 1950 letter: "Adriana and I talk English and sometimes Spanish; also French. With Contessa Valeria de Lisca I talk French. With Giovanna Tofani I talk English. She talks it much better than I do." According to the Hemingway researcher Jobst C. Knigge, "Before Hemingway left Italy for Cuba in 1950, he invited Adriana and her friend Giovanna Tofani to see him at the Finca Vigía. Gio, as Hemingway called her, had already the permission of her mother to leave for Cuba. But in summer 1950, while holidaying in Capri together with Adriana she met her future husband, industrialist Giuseppe Fiorentini. He talked her out [of going] to Cuba and pushed for an immediate marriage, that took place in September."
16. Lynn, *Hemingway*, 534.
17. Letter of Mary Hemingway to Ernest Hemingway, May 6, 1950, JFK Library; also in Burwell, *Hemingway*, 49.

18. Knigge, "Hemingway's Venetian Muse," 56.

19. Reynolds, *Hemingway: Final Years*, 309.

20. Reynolds, *Hemingway: Final Years*, 350. In a 1952 letter to Harvey Breit, he discussed his use of vitamins, particularly B1, and further observed: "Then if you are really run down and fatigued and gloomy there is no reason why you shouldn't take Methyltestosterone. You don't have to take it as a shot in the ass. And it is not to make you fornicate more. Paul explained to me that it was good for the head and for the whole general system. . . . I explained to him that I had no need for any sexual stimulation and didn't want to take anything that would get me into any more trouble than I got into already. But he explained that this was something that kept your head in good shape and counter-acted the gloominess everybody gets."

21. Arnold, *The Idaho Hemingway*, 232–38.

22. Karl, *William Faulkner*, 1026. While Hemingway was busy boxing, getting blown up, dodging bullets, or climbing into doomed aircraft, Faulkner's preferred method of trauma seemed to be falling off his horse. He even suffered from discrete episodes of amnesia, which seemed independent of alcoholic blackouts. Such micro-episodes of profound amnesia are harbingers of Alzheimer's—yet he did not live long enough for this form of dementia to fully manifest.

23. *The New Yorker*, November 20, 1926, p. 38. Iris March was a character in the 1924 novel *The Green Hat*, which in 1925was made into a Broadway play starring Katherine Cornell. It also played in London's West End with Tallulah Bankhead taking the lead, and Greta Garbo was the star of the 1928 silent movie version.

Chapter 4 | Dementia, Disinhibition, and Delusion

1. Arnold, *The Idaho Hemingway*, 211–12.

2. Baker, *Hemingway: A Life Story*, 469–70; Mellow, *Hemingway*, 553.

3. Baker, *Hemingway: A Life Story*, 469.

4. Baker, *Selected Letters*, 699–700.

5. Kert, *The Hemingway Women*, 477.

6. Baker, *Hemingway: A Life Story*, 476–77. Hemingway described Cantwell in a letter of October 1949 to Buck Lanham as a conflation of three individuals: "the hero is a combination of Charlie Sweeny, who used to command a regiment in the Foreign Legion, me, who never could command my way out of a wet bunch of willows, and you."

7. Baker, *Hemingway: A Life Story*, 472.

8. Meyers, *Hemingway*, 442. The information on Gianfranco is largely taken from Meyers's biography (pp. 442–43), as his book details the most information on Adriana's brother. He also indicated that Gianfranco married a Cuban girl, "Cristina Sandoval, whom Hemingway disliked. But after they returned to Italy, she fell in love with the more glamorous Nanyuki Franchetti and left Gianfranco."

9. Burwell, *Hemingway*, 221.

10. Burwell, *Hemingway*, 221.

11. Baker, *Hemingway: A Life Story*, 492.

12. Meyers, *Hemingway*, 445.

13. Kert, *The Hemingway Women*, 477

14. Kert, *The Hemingway Women*, 478–79.

15. Meyers, *Hemingway*, 618, note 32.

16. Baker, *Hemingway: A Life Story*, 517.

17. Baker, *Hemingway: A Life Story*, 518.

18. *True at First Light*, 281,

19. Baker, *Hemingway: A Life Story*, 519,

20. Hotchner, *Papa Hemingway*, xv. Hemingway expressed frustration in his "Africa Journal" when her vigilant mother prevented them from sleeping together: "on the day in my life which offered the most chances of happiness." Jeffrey Meyers, "Review of True at First Light," September 18, 1999.

21. JFK Library, "Africa Journal."

22. *True at First Light*, 31–32.

23. Burwell, *Hemingway*, 143.

24. Meyers, *Hemingway*, 502.

25. Burwell, *Hemingway*, 143. In a 1957 letter to Harvey Breit, he curiously wrote of Debba in a literary context. It is not clear how much Breit knew about the Debba situation, but Hemingway anticipated the possibility that Debba would one day be discussed in criticism: " . . . Carlos Baker really baffles me. Do you suppose he can con himself into thinking I would put a symbol into anything on purpose? It's hard enough to just make a paragraph. What sort of symbol is Debba, my Wakamba fiancée? She must be a dark symbol."

26. Burwell, *Hemingway*, 48.

27. *Under Kilimanjaro*, 174.

28. *True at First Light*, 35.

29. Meyers, *Hemingway*, 508.

30. Lynn, *Hemingway*, 570.

31. Reynolds, *Hemingway: Final Years*, 298.

32. Lynn, *Hemingway*, 449. Hemingway was listed as a member of the board of directors of the League of American Writers during the summer of 1939 (FBI file, "Subject: Ernest Hemingway").

33. FBI file, "Subject: Ernest Hemingway."

34. Meyers, *Hemingway*, 518–19.

35. Leicester Hemingway, *My Brother Ernest Hemingway*, 136.

36. Montale, *Satura*, 183 (poem translated by the author).

Chapter 5 | Free Fall

1. Baker, *Hemingway: A Life Story*, 535.

2. Meyers, *Hemingway*, 513–15. The Baroja works he owned in Spanish were: *La busca, La decadence de la cortesia y otros ensayos, Locuros de Carnaval, Memorias,* and *El pais vasco. He also owned,* in English translation, *The Lord of Labraz* and *Red Dawn.* See also Baker, *Hemingway: A Life Story*, 535.

3. Baker, *Selected Letters*, 873–74.

4. Baker, *Hemingway: A Life Story*, 536.

5. Davis, "A Very Moveable Meal," 5.

6. Baker, *Selected Letters*, 396.

7. Reynolds, *Hemingway: Final Years*, 300.

8. Baker, *Hemingway: A Life Story*, 537.

9. Voss, *Picturing Hemingway*, 42.

10. Voss, *Picturing Hemingway*, 45.

11. Reynolds, *Hemingway: Final Years*, 310.

12. Baker, *Hemingway: A Life Story*, 541.

13. Voss, *Picturing Hemingway*, 47.

14. Baker, *Hemingway: A Life Story*, 545.

15. Baker, *Hemingway: A Life Story*, 545.

16. Baker, *Hemingway: A Life Story*, 549.

17. Baker, *Hemingway: A Life Story*, 550. Turnbull also earned a Ph.D. in European history in 1954. He taught humanities at MIT, then American literature at Brown. In addition to writing about Scott Fitzgerald, he edited two collections of Fitzgerald's letters and in 1967 published a well-received biography of Thomas Wolfe. Like Fitzgerald and Hemingway before him, he suffered from depression, and in 1970 he committed suicide.

18. Meyers, *Hemingway*, 420–21.

19. Meyers, *Hemingway*, 541.

20. Baker, *Hemingway: A Life Story*, 553.

21. Mellow, *Hemingway*, 600.

22. Burwell, *Hemingway*, 183.

23. Meyers, *Hemingway*, 542; Valerie Hemingway, *Running with the Bulls*, 142.

24. Mellow, *Hemingway*, 600–601.

25. Swann Auction Galleries, sale 2211, lot 198. http://catalogue.swanngalleries .com/asp/fullCatalogue.asp?salelot=2211+++++198+&refno=++631102&saletype.

26. Lynn, *Hemingway*, 583.

Chapter 6 | Stigma

1. *Complete Short Stories*, 310.

2. Baker, *Selected Letters*, 628.

3. Baker, *Selected Letters*, 314.

4. Donaldson, *Archibald MacLeish*, 198.

5. Turnbull, *Letters of F. Scott Fitzgerald*, 312.

6. Meyers, *Hemingway*, 545.

7. Mellow, *Hemingway*, 549.

8. Lynn, *Hemingway*, 161

9. Baker, *Selected Letters*, 789.

10. Ellmann, *James Joyce*, 676–78.

11. Lynn, *Hemingway*, 136–37.

12. Baker, *Selected Letters*, 206.

13. Baker, *Selected Letters*, 240.

14. Baker, *Selected Letters*, 802, 862.

15. Reynolds, *Young Hemingway*, 69.

16. *A Moveable Feast*, 207.

17. Hahn, *Masson*, 6–7. Masson would paint his delirious vision of the "torso of light" in 1925 and titled it *Armor*. It shows an abstracted and beautiful feminine torso. In his sketch of a harsh landscape, meant as a reference to the

Spanish Civil War, land morphs into skeletal claw and skull—and just to the right of the exact center of the drawing, one fist rises from the earth defiant.

18. Item #186 at the JFK Library.

19. Mellow, *Hemingway,* 443.

20. Meyers, *Hemingway,* 244.

21. Hilary Hemingway, *Hemingway in Cuba,* 19.

22. Mellow, *Hemingway,* 425.

23. Meyers, *Hemingway,* 246. A Cuban newspaper reported that Jane was "shot by revolutionaries" and thus fell from her balcony. There has also been speculation that she was under the influence of painkillers prescribed after her car wreck, and the authors of *Hemingway in Cuba* claim that Jane was actually sneaking out of her art studio for another date with Ernest when she slipped and fell. Yet, her husband certainly didn't express this theory and felt it necessary for her to receive psychiatric treatment.

24. Kert, *The Hemingway Women,* 250.

25. Meyers, *Hemingway,* 249–50.

26. Mellow, *Hemingway,* 459.

27. Baker, *Selected Letters,* 550.

28. Tryphonopoulos and Adams, *Ezra Pound Encyclopedia,* 144.

29. Carpenter, *Ezra Pound,* 654

30. Baker, *Hemingway: A Life Story,* 537.

31. Cornell, *The Trial of Ezra Pound,* 161. Ezra Pound's lawyer has been criticized for not realizing the possibility that his client's insanity defense would lead to his indefinite incarceration. However, Cornell did file a petition for a writ of habeas corpus in 1948 seeking Pound's release, and he planned an appeal when the petition was refused. Yet it was Dorothy Pound who wrote to Cornell: "Please withdraw the appeal at once. My husband is not fit to appear in court and must still be kept as quiet as possible; the least thing shakes his nerves up terribly." For reasons that remain obscure, Pound's wife sealed his fate.

32. Baker, *Selected Letters,* 544–45.

33. Baker, *Selected Letters,* 548–49.

34. Turnbull, *F. Scott Fitzgerald,* 193.

35. Baker, *Selected Letters,* 553–54

36. Spanier and Trogdon, *The Letters of Ernest Hemingway,* 364.

37. Lynn, *Hemingway,* 428.

38. Donaldson, *Hemingway vs. Fitzgerald,* 230.

39. Donaldson, *Hemingway vs. Fitzgerald,* 231.

40. Turnbull, *F. Scott Fitzgerald,* 323

41. Cline, *Her Voice in Paradise,* 359. About 20 percent of psychotic patients treated with insulin comas had seizures (depending on how quickly the blood glucose dropped), which may have conveyed some benefit for that small percentage. But the efficacy of coma therapy was being questioned by the early 1950s. In 1953 a British psychiatrist published "The Insulin Myth" in *Lancet,* and in 1957 the results of a study in which patients were given either insulin coma treatment or identical treatment but with sedation produced by infusing a barbiturate showed that there was no difference in outcome between the two groups. When Dr. Max Fink published a study in the *Journal of the American*

Medical Association in 1958 in which he showed that chlorpromazine (Thorazine) was just as effective as insulin coma in treating psychosis but had far fewer side effects, he helped end the era of insulin coma and ushered in the age of pharmacotherapy.

42. Burwell, *Hemingway*, 232.

43. *Brideshead Revisited* quotation from film version, Granada Television, episode 2, "Home and Abroad."

44. Burwell, *Hemingway*, 232.

45. Baker, *Selected Letters*, 437–38.

46. Burwell, *Hemingway*, 151, 225.

47. Turnbull, *F. Scott Fitzgerald*, 279–80.

48. Turnbull, *Letters of F. Scott Fitzgerald*, 544–45.

49. Turnbull, *Letters of F. Scott Fitzgerald*, 545.

50. Turnbull, *Letters of F. Scott Fitzgerald*, 426–27. Scott repeatedly incorporated private matters into his fiction. He violated Zelda's fragile trust terribly with the publication of *Tender is the Night* in 1934, in which he excerpted sections of her most troubled letters and assigned them to the equally troubled Nicole Diver. The year following his forced supervision by an RN, Fitzgerald wrote "An Alcoholic Case," a story involving a nurse who feels duty-bound to stay with her patient, an alcoholic cartoonist. Such thinly veiled self-pity or "public whining" was not what Hemingway was encouraging, particularly since the story also appeared in *Esquire*.

Chapter 7 | Mayo

1. Meyers, *Hemingway*, 545.

2. Hotchner, *Papa Hemingway*, 275.

3. Reynolds, *Hemingway: Final Years*, 349.

4. Baker, *Selected Letters*, 909.

5. Wagner-Martin, ed., *Hemingway, Seven Decades of Criticism*, 375.

6. Cecil, *Textbook of Medicine*, 657.

7. Cecil, *Textbook of Medicine*, 1659–60.

8. Norman, *Ezra Pound*, 257.

9. *A Moveable Feast*, 11.

10. Baker, *Selected Letters*, 916–18.

11. Reynolds, *Hemingway: Final Years*, 354.

12. Meyers, *Hemingway*, 559.

13. Arnold, *The Idaho Hemingway*, 227.

14. Baker, *Selected Letters*, 921.

Chapter 8 | The Body Electric

1. *A Farewell to Arms*, 54–56.

2. Hotchner, *Papa Hemingway*, 280.

3. Kert, *The Hemingway Women*, 461–62.

4. Baker, *Selected Letters*, 910.

5. FBI file, Subject: Ernest Hemingway.

6. Kert, *The Hemingway Women*, 503.

7. Reynolds, *Hemingway: Final Years*, 351.

8. Baker, *Hemingway: A Life Story*, 563.

9. Arnold, *The Idaho Hemingway*, 228

10. Thomas Bevilacqua and Robert K. Elder, *Mythbusting Hemingway: Debunking Hemingway Myths and Celebrating the Extraordinary Stories of His Life* (Lanham, MD: Lyons Press, 2023), 168.

11. Howard Rome to Mary Hemingway, November 1, 1961.

Chapter 9 | Working Man

1. Stevens and Swan, *De Kooning*, 209.

2. Stevens and Swann, *De Kooning*, 567.

3. Stevens and Swann, *De Kooning*, 593.

4. Stevens and Swann, *De Kooning*, 599.

5. Stevens and Swann, *De Kooning*, 602.

6. *A Moveable Feast*, 23.

7. Lynn, *Hemingway*, 68.

8. Donaldson, *Cambridge Companion to Hemingway*, 130.

9. Reynolds, *Young Hemingway*, 49.

10. Parker, "The Artist's Reward," 28.

11. Baker, *Selected Letters*, 200.

12. Kert, *The Hemingway Women*, 432.

13. Kert, *The Hemingway Women*, 456–57. One need only frame the opposite of her assessment to see her true desires: "I am *not* boring, do *not* overdrink and lay in hotel rooms, i.e., am *not* promiscuous, and you love me, don't you?"

14. Donaldson, *Cambridge Companion to Hemingway*, 129. An unlikely champion of *Across the River* was Evelyn Waugh, who believed the critics so harsh because Hemingway displayed "something they find quite unforgivable—Decent Feeling" (Lynn, *Hemingway*, 558.)

15. Burwell, *Hemingway*, 48.

16. Burwell, *Hemingway*, 95–97.

17. Kert, *The Hemingway Women*, 374.

18. Wagner-Martin (ed.), *Hemingway: Seven Decades of Criticism*, 365.

19. Kert, *The Hemingway Women,*198.

20. Baker, *Hemingway: A Life Story*, 461

21. Burwell, *Hemingway*, 211.

22. Burwell, *Hemingway*, 211.

23. Burwell, *Hemingway*, 145.

24. Valerie Hemingway, *Running with the Bulls*, 213.

25. Lynn, *Hemingway*, 477.

26. Mellow, *Hemingway*, 590.

27. Hotchner, *Papa Hemingway*, 242.

28. *A Moveable Feast*, 230.

Chapter 10 | *A Moveable Feast*

1. Hotchner, *Papa Hemingway*, 57. Hemingway was having no luck with his title search. He chose "The Eye and the Ear," an imitation of his former work.

Like the title *The Sun Also Rises,* it was derived from Ecclesiastes: "All things are full of labour; man cannot utter it: the eye is not satisfied with seeing, nor the ear filled with hearing."

2. *A Moveable Feast,* xiii.

3. Burwell, *Hemingway,* 234–35.

4. Tavernier-Courbin, *Hemingway's A Moveable Feast,* 37.

5. Tavernier-Courbin, *Hemingway's A Moveable Feast,* 26.

6. *A Moveable Feast,* xiv.

7. Baker, *Hemingway: A Life Story,* 540.

8. Tavernier-Courbin, *Hemingway's A Moveable Feast,* 105.

9. Singh, *Montale: Selected Essays,* 137. I have translated Montale's quotation slightly differently than Singh, substituting "costly" for "precious."

10. *A Moveable Feast,* 4.

11. *A Moveable Feast,* 125–26.

12. Lynn, *Hemingway,* 280.

13. Lynn, *Hemingway,* 282. Ernest had hoped to learn from a "successful writer" on the trip, but the disaster that ensued left no room for tutoring. And after reading Scott's suggestions on his manuscript of *A Farewell to Arms* in 1929, Hemingway wrote "Kiss my a—." on Fitzgerald's nine page holograph memo about the novel, but there *is* evidence that he took some of Scott's suggestions when he revised the novel in proof.

14. *A Moveable Feast,* 138.

15. Lynn, *Hemingway,* 282.

16. *A Moveable Feast,* 141. Attacking Scott Fitzgerald was almost a hobby. The first printing of "The Snows of Kilimanjaro" (in 1936) included the lines "He remembered poor Scott Fitzgerald and his romantic awe of them and how he had started a story once that began, 'The very rich are different from you and me.' And how someone had said to Scott, Yes, they have more money. But that was not humorous to Scott. He thought they were a special glamorous race and when he found they weren't it wrecked him just as much as any other thing that wrecked him." In subsequent printings, Scott becomes "Julian," as Fitzgerald asked Hemingway to remove his name, but the damage was done. Some months later Hemingway would explain he was trying to give Fitzgerald a "jolt" that would be good for him, a warning shot across the bow to help a friend. This is a pretty weak excuse for the lines that were published in *Esquire* and considering that the "other things that wrecked" Scott could mean only alcohol and Zelda. Perhaps he believed what Oscar Wilde had said, that a "true friend will stab you in the front." Furthermore, there is evidence that Hemingway, not Fitzgerald, was the one informed that the rich "have more money" by the Irish literary critic Mary Colum (Lynn, *Hemingway,* 438).

17. *A Moveable Feast,* 8, 75.

18. *A Moveable Feast,* 88.

19. Fitch, *Sylvia Beach and the Lost Generation,* 343–44. Hemingway likely took comfort in the fact that Lewis was a terrible judge of character; in 1931 he actually wrote a book, *Hitler,* in which he praised his subject as a peacemaker.

20. Lynn, *Hemingway,* 375.

21. Koch, *The Breaking Point,* 216.

22. Lynn, *Hemingway*, 270.

23. Lynn, *Hemingway*, 251.

24. Tavernier-Courbin, *Hemingway's A Moveable Feast*, 95–96

25. Tavernier-Courbin, *Hemingway's A Moveable Feast*, 96.

26. *A Moveable Feast*, 86.

27. Baker, *Hemingway: A Life Story*, 416–17.

28. Baker, *Selected Letters*, 577.

29. Burwell, *Hemingway*, 225.

30. Burwell, *Hemingway*, 225.

31. Tavernier-Courbin, *Hemingway's A Moveable Feast*, 15–17.

32. Tavernier-Courbin, *Hemingway's A Moveable Feast*, 211.

33. Burwell, *Hemingway*, 152.

34. Burwell, *Hemingway*, 151.

35. Mary Hemingway, *How It Was*, 126.

36. John Hemingway, *Strange Tribe*, 113.

37. Kert, *The Hemingway Women*, 463.

38. Kert, *The Hemingway Women*, 464–65.

39. Mellow, *Hemingway*, 209.

40. Smith, *A Reader's Guide to the Short Stories*, xv.

41. *A Moveable Feast*, 70.

42. *A Moveable Feast*, 185.

43. *A Moveable Feast*, 230.

44. Burwell, *Hemingway*, 145.

45. Burwell, *Hemingway*, 149.

Chapter 11 | Alone

1. Arnold, *The Idaho Hemingway*, 2–4.

2. Arnold, *The Idaho Hemingway*, 4.

3. Hotchner, *Papa Hemingway*, xviii.

4. Meyers, *Hemingway*, 561.

5. Arnold, *The Idaho Hemingway*, 230.

6. Burwell, *Hemingway*, 200, 205.

7. Meyers, *Hemingway*, 560.

8. Burwell, *Hemingway*, 230.

9. Meyers, *Hemingway*, 562.

10. Meyers, *Hemingway*, 563.

11. Hotchner, *Papa Hemingway*, viii.

12. Mary Hemingway to the director of the National Gallery of Art, May 30, 1976.

13. Reynolds, *Hemingway: Paris Years*, 295.

14. Soby, *Joan Miró*, 32.

15. O'Rourke, *Grace under Pressure*, 16–18.

16. Meyers, *Hemingway*, 166.

17. Kert, *The Hemingway Women*, 190–91.

18. Meyers, *Hemingway*, 563.

19. Fallaci, "My Husband Ernest Hemingway," 62–68. Mary had attempted to give President Kennedy advice on how to deal with Castro at the dinner for

Nobel laureates that she attended in Ernest's place. Kennedy's response to her foreign policy lesson has been described by witnesses as "irritated" and "amused and exasperated."

20. Meyers, *Hemingway*, 566, 621.

21. Burwell, *Hemingway*, 10.

22. Lynn, *Hemingway*, 517–18.

23. Lynn, *Hemingway*, 521–22.

24. Arnold, *The Idaho Hemingway*, 228.

25. *Look*, September 6, 1966, 18, 62–68.

Chapter 12 | Modern Times

1. Small et al., "PET and NFL," 142–44.

2. Bolander-Gouaille and Bottiglieri, *Homocysteine*, 21–28.

3. Refsum, "The Hordaland Homocysteine Study,"1731–40; Enlyte: prescribing information/package insert.

4. Adair et al., "Controlled Trial of N-acetylcysteine,"1515–17; Arakawa and Yoshihisa, "N-acetylcysteine and Neurodegenerative Diseases," 308–14.

5. Sinn, "Effects of n-3 Fatty Acids, EPA v. DHA, on Depressive Symptoms," 1682–93.

6. Namenda (memantine): full prescribing information. Actavis.com, 2013.

Epilogue

1. Donaldson, *Cambridge Companion to Hemingway*, 1.

2. *The Sun Also Rises*, 136.

3. Burwell, *Hemingway*, 25.

4. Meyers, *Hemingway*, 556.

5. Meyers, *Hemingway*, 557.

6. Meyers, *Hemingway*, 558.

7. Lynn, *Hemingway*, 113.

8. Baker, *Hemingway: A Life Story*, 167.

9. Mariani, *The Broken Tower*, 421.

10. Baker, *Selected Letters*, 453.

11. *Complete Short Stories*, 111.

12. *Complete Short Stories*, 257.

13. Lynn, *Hemingway*, 514.

14. Baker, *Hemingway: A Life Story*, 312–14.

15. Karl, *William Faulkner*, 1012.

16. Kandinsky, *Concerning the Spiritual in Art*, 10–11.

Bibliography

Archival Material

Hemingway, Ernest, and others, Collected letters, manuscripts, and documents. The Hemingway Archives at the John Fitzgerald Kennedy Presidential Library and Museum, Boston, Massachusetts (hereafter JFK Library).

National Gallery of Art, Provenance file for *The Farm*, courtesy of Ann Helpburn.

U.S. Federal Bureau of Invention. File, Subject Ernest Hemingway. www.FBI.gov.

Books

Arnold, Tillie. *The Idaho Hemingway.* Buhl: Beacon, 1999.

Baker, Carlos. *Ernest Hemingway: A Life Story.* New York: Collier, 1969.

Baker, Carlos. *Ernest Hemingway: Selected Letters 1917–1961.* New York: Scribner's, 1981.

Bassoe, Peter, ed. *Nervous and Mental Diseases.* Practical Medicine Series, vol. 8. Chicago: Year Book Publishers, 1919.

Bolander-Gouaille, Christina, and Teodoro Bottiglieri. *Homocysteine: Related Vitamins and Neuropsychiatric Disorders.* Paris: Springer, 2007.

Bowker, Gordon. *Pursued by Furies: A Life of Malcolm Lowry.* New York: St. Martin's Press, 1997.

Brodsky, Louis D. *William Faulkner: Life Glimpses.* Austin: University of Texas Press, 1990.

Brodzky, Horace. *Pascin.* London: Nicholson and Watson, 1946.

Burwell, Rose M. *Hemingway: The Postwar Years and the Posthumous Novels.* New York: Cambridge University Press, 1996.

Capa, Robert. *Slightly Out of Focus.* New York: Modern Library, 2001.

Carpenter, Humphrey. *A Serious Character: The Life of Ezra Pound.* New York: Delta, 1988.

Cecil, Russell L., ed. *A Textbook of Medicine.* Philadelphia: Saunders, 1931.

Cecil, Russell L., and Robert F. Loeb, ed. *A Textbook of Medicine.* 10th ed. Philadelphia: Saunders, 1959.

Cline, Sally. *Zelda Fitzgerald: Her Voice in Paradise.* New York: Harper and Row, 1970.

Cohen-Solal, Annie. *Sartre: A Life.* New York: Pantheon, 1987.

Conover, Anne. *Olga Rudge and Ezra Pound: "What Thou Lovest Well . . ."* New Haven: Yale University Press, 2001.

Cornell, Julien. *The Trial of Ezra Pound*. New York: John Day, 1966.Donaldson, Scott. *Hemingway vs. Fitzgerald: The Rise and Fall of a Literary Friendship*. New York: Overlook, 1999.

Donaldson, Scott. *Archibald MacLeish: An American Life*. Houghton Mifflin: New York, 1992.

Donaldson, Scott, ed. *The Cambridge Companion to Ernest Hemingway*. Cambridge: Cambridge University Press, 1996.

Ellmann, Richard. *James Joyce*. New York: Oxford University Press, 1983.

Fitch, Noel R. *Sylvia Beach and the Lost Generation*. New York: Norton, 1983.

Flory, Wendy S. *The American Ezra Pound*. New Haven: Yale University Press, 1989.

Gajdusek, Robert E. *Hemingway and Joyce: A Study in Debt and Payment*. Corte Madera: Square Circle Press, 1984.

Gajdusek, Robert E. *Hemingway's Paris*. New York: Scribner's, 1978.

Gooch, Brad. *Flannery: A Life of Flannery O'Connor*. New York: Little, Brown, 2009.

Hahn, Otto. *Mason*. New York: Abrams, 1965.

Hemingway, Ernest. *Under Kilimanjaro*. Edited by Robert W. Lewis and Robert E. Fleming. Kent: Kent State University Press, 2005.

Hemingway, Ernest. *In Our Time*. New York: Scribner's, 1925.

Hemingway, Ernest. *The Sun Also Rises*. New York: Scribner's, 1926.

Hemingway, Ernest. *Across the River and into the Trees*. New York: Scribner's, 1950.

Hemingway, Ernest. *Islands in the Stream*. New York: Scribner's, 1970.

Hemingway, Ernest. *The Garden of Eden*. New York: Scribner's, 1986.

Hemingway, Ernest. *The Complete Short Stories of Ernest Hemingway*. New York: Scribner's, 1987.

Hemingway, Ernest. *True at First Light*. New York: Scribner's, 1999.

Hemingway, Ernest. *A Moveable Feast: The Restored Edition*. New York: Scribner's, 2009.Hemingway, Hilary. *Hemingway in Cuba*. New York: Rugged Land, 2003.

Hemingway, John. *Strange Tribe*. Guilford: Lyons Press, 2007.

Hemingway, Leicester. *My Brother Ernest Hemingway*. Sarasota: Pineapple Press, 1996.

Hemingway, Mary. *How It Was*. New York: Knopf, 1976.

Hemingway, Valerie. *Running with the Bulls: My Years with the Hemingways*. New York: Ballantine, 2004.

Hotchner, A. E. *Papa Hemingway*. New York: Carroll and Graff, 1999.

Kandinsky, Wassily. *Concerning the Spiritual in Art* [Über das Geistige in der Kunst]. New York: Dover, 1977.

Kaplan, Harold I., and Benjamin J. Sadock. *Comprehensive Textbook of Psychiatry*. Vol. 6. Baltimore: Williams and Wilkins, 1995.

Karl, Frederick R. *William Faulkner: American Writer*. New York: Weidenfeld and Nicolson, 1989.

Kert, Bernice. *The Hemingway Women*. New York: Norton, 1983.

Koch, Stephen. *The Breaking Point: Hemingway, Dos Passos, and the Murder of Jose Robles*. New York: Counterpoint, 2005.

Lynn, Kenneth. *Hemingway.* Cambridge, Mass.: Harvard University Press, 1987.

Mariani, Paul. *The Broken Tower: The Life of Hart Crane.* New York: Norton, 2000.

Mellow, James R. *Hemingway, A Life without Consequences.* Reading: Perseus, 1993.

Meyers, Jeffrey. *Hemingway: A Biography.* New York: Da Capo, 1999.

Montale, Eugenio. *Satura.* New York: Norton, 1971.

Naifeh, S., and G. Smith. *Jackson Pollock.* New York: Potter, 1989.

Norman, Charles. *Ezra Pound.* New York: Macmillan, 1960.

Oliver, Charles M. *Ernest Hemingway A to Z.* New York: Checkmark Books, 1999.

Ondaatje, Christopher. *Hemingway in Africa: The Last Safari.* New York: Overlook Press, 2004.

O'Rourke, Sean. *Grace under Pressure: The Life of Evan Shipman.* Lexington, Ken.: Harvardwood, 2010.

Preston, Paul. *The Spanish Holocaust.* New York: Norton, 2012.

Reynolds, Michael. *The Young Hemingway.* New York: Norton, 1986.

Reynolds, Michael. *Hemingway: The Paris Years.* New York: Norton, 1989.

Reynolds, Michael. *Hemingway: The Homecoming.* New York: Norton, 1992.

Reynolds, Michael. *Hemingway: The Final Years.* New York: Norton, 1999.

Reynolds, Michael. *Hemingway: The 1930s through the Final Years.* New York: Norton, 2012.

Sanford, Marcelline Hemingway. *At the Hemingways.* Moscow: University of Idaho Press, 1999.

Silver, Jonathan M., Thomas W. McAllister, et al., eds. *Textbook of Traumatic Brain Injury.* Washington, D.C.: American Psychiatric Association, 2011.

Singh, G., trans. *Montale: Selected Essays.* Manchester, UK: Carcanet, 1978.

Smith, Denis M. *Mussolini: A Biography.* New York: Vintage, 1983.

Smith, Paul. *A Reader's Guide to the Short Stories of Ernest Hemingway.* Boston: Hall, 1989.

Soby, James T. *Joan Miró.* New York: Doubleday, 1959.

Spanier, Sandra, Albert DeFazio, et al., eds. *The Letters of Ernest Hemingway 1923–1925.* Cambridge: Cambridge University Press, 2013.

Spanier, Sandra, and Robert W. Trogdon, eds. *The Letters of Ernest Hemingway 1907–1922.* Cambridge: Cambridge University Press, 2011.

Stevens, M., and A. Swan. *De Kooning: An American Master.* New York: Knopf, 2006.

Tavernier-Courbin, Jacqueline. *Ernest Hemingway's A Moveable Feast: The Making of a Myth.* Boston: Northeastern University Press, 1991.

Trimble, Michael. *The Soul in the Brain.* Baltimore: Johns Hopkins University Press, 2007.

Tryphonopoulos, Demetres P., and Stephen J. Adams, eds. *The Ezra Pound Encyclopedia.* Westport, Conn.: Greenwood, 2005.

Turnbull, Andrew. *Scott Fitzgerald.* New York: Grove Press, 1962.

Turnbull, Andrew. *The Letters of Scott Fitzgerald.* New York: Delta, 1965.

Voss, Frederick, *Picturing Hemingway.* New Haven: Yale University Press, 1999.

Wagner-Martin, L., ed. *Hemingway: Seven Decades of Criticism.* East Lansing: Michigan State University Press, 1998.

Zasler, Nathan D., Katz, Douglas I, et al., eds. *Brain Injury Medicine: Principles and Practice.* 2nd ed. New York: Demos, 2012.

Articles

Adair, John C., et al. "Controlled Trial of N-acetylcysteine for Patients with Probable Alzheimer's Disease." *Neurology* 57 (2001): 1515–17.

Arakawa, Motoki, and Yoshihisa, Ito. "N-Acetylcysteine and Neurodegenerative Diseases: Basic and Clinical Pharmacology." *The Cerebellum* 6 (2007): 308–14.

Bjelland, Ingvar, et al. "Folate, Vitamin B-12, Homocysteine, and MTHFR 677C-T Polymorphism in Anxiety and Depression." *Archives of General Psychiatry* 60 (2003): 618–26.

Bondy, B., et al. "Genetics of Suicide." *Molecular Psychiatry* 11 (2006): 336–51.

Davis, Alexander. "A Very Mobile Meal: The Evolution of Ernest Hemingway's A Moveable Feast." M.A. thesis, University of Otago, Dunedin, New Zealand, 2013.

Dounce, Harry Esty. Review of *The Sun Also Rises. New Yorker.* November 20, 1926, 88, 90.

Fallaci, Oriana. "My Husband, Ernest Hemingway." *Look,* September 6, 1966, 62–68.

Farah, Andrew. "Atypicality of Atypical Antipsychotics Revisited." *Current Psychiatry Reviews* 9 (2013): 216–24.

Flora, Joseph M. "Ernest Hemingway and T. S. Eliot: A Tangled Relationship." *Hemingway Review* 32 (2012): 72–87.

Folstein, Marshal, et al. "The Homocysteine Theory of Depression." *American Journal of Psychiatry* 163 (2007): 861–67.

Hahn, Otto. *Masson.* New York: Abrams, 1965.

Hinterberger, M., et al. "Conversion from Mild Cognitive Impairment to Dementia: Influence of Folic Acid and Vitamin B12 Use in Vita Cohort." *Journal of Nutrition, Health and Aging.* 16 (2012): 687–94.

Knigge, Jobst C. "Hemingway's Venetian Muse Adriana Ivancich." Humboldt University, Berlin, 2001.

Parker, Dorothy. "The Artist's Reward." *New Yorker,* November 30, 1929, 28–31.

Refsum, Helga. "The Hordaland Homocysteine Study: A Community-Based Study of Homocysteine, Its Determinants, and Associations with Disease." *Journal of Nutrition* 136 (2006): 1731–40.

Sinn, N., et al. "Effects of N-3 Fatty Acids, EPA v. DHA, on Depressive Symptoms, Quality of Life, Memory and Executive Function in Older Adults with Mild Cognitive Impairment: A 6-Month Randomised Controlled Trial." *British Journal of Nutrition* 107 (2012): 1682–93.

Small, Gary W., et al. "PET Scanning of Brain Tau in Retired National Football League Players: Preliminary Findings." *American Journal of Geriatric Psychiatry* 21 (2013): 138–44.

Vakhapova, V., et al. "Phosphatidylserine Containing ω-3 Fatty Acids May Improve Memory Abilities in Non-Demented Elderly with Memory Complaints: A Double-Blind Placebo-Controlled Trial." Dementia and Geriatric Cognitive Disorders 29 (2010): 467–74.

Index